ERIC DICKERSON'S SECRETS OF PRO POWER

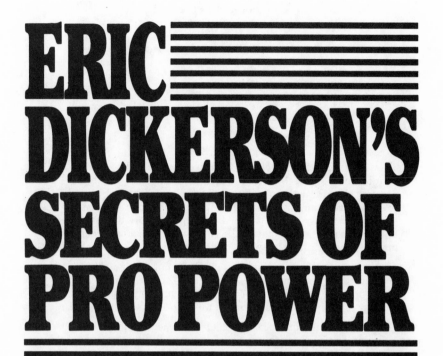

ERIC DICKERSON
with Richard Graham Walsh

Foreword by Ron Meyer

Amistad

New York, New York

This book is dedicated
to those football players
who want it as badly as I do.

This book presents a serious exercise regimen. The reader
should understand that not all drills contained in this book
are suitable for everyone, and this (or any other physical
exercise program) can result in injury. To reduce the risks,
you should always consult a medical expert before beginning
an exercise program, particularly if you have any special
medical condition or are taking medication.

The material presented in this book is not intended as a
substitute for medical advice, and the authors and publisher
disclaim all responsibility for any injury that may result from
attempting any of the drills contained in this book.

First published in October 1989 by Warner Books as an
Amistad book. First issued as an Amistad Press, Inc., trade
paperback in March 1993.

Amistad Press, Inc.
1271 Avenue of the Americas
New York, NY 10020

Distributed by:
Penguin USA
375 Hudson Street
New York, NY 10014

Designed by H. Roberts

1 2 3 4 5 6 7 8 9 10

Library of Congress Cataloging-in-Publication Data
Dickerson, Eric, 1960–
    [Secrets of pro power]
    Eric Dickerson's secrets of pro power / Eric Dickerson with
Richard Graham Walsh : foreword by Ron Meyer.
        p. cm.
    Originally published: New York, NY : Warner Books, © 1989.
    ISBN 1-56743-018-X : $9.95
    1. Football—Training. 2. Physical education and training.
I. Walsh, Richard Graham. II. Title. III. Title: Secrets of pro power.
[GV953.5.D53 1993]
796.332'07—dc20   93-100
                                                                CIP

Contents

Foreword

Before I tell you about this book, let me first talk about its author, a guy who began rewriting the National Football League record book soon after he first put on an NFL uniform. Eric Dickerson joined the Los Angeles Rams out of Southern Methodist University in 1983 and has gone on to become the most productive ball carrier of his time. In addition to setting virtually every Ram club record, Dickerson holds NFL season records for the most 100-yard games rushing, with 12; the most yards from scrimmage, with 2,244; and—in one of the most coveted records of all—the most yards rushing in a single season, with 2,105. All were accomplished in the storybook year of 1984, only his second in professional football. In 1985, he went on to set the record for rushing yardage in a playoff game, shattering the Dallas Cowboys defense for 248 yards.

Traded to the Colts several games into the 1987 season, Dickerson's torrid pace didn't miss a beat. He rushed for 1,288 yards in 11 games, 9 of them with his new Indianapolis team. His average of 117 yards a game easily led the league, and he probably would have led the NFL in yards gained rushing for the fourth time in his 5-year career had he played the entire season. In 1988 Dickerson did pick up his fourth rushing title as he led the league with 1,659 yards in a full season of play.

Perhaps even more impressive is that Dickerson has averaged more than 14 touchdowns a year and more than 113 yards rushing per game since he's been in the league, both NFL records, and has averaged more than 100 yards rushing per game in playoff competition. Even though he missed 2 games in 1985 and 5 in 1987 because of contract problems, his average rushing yardage per season is a mind-boggling 1,652.5, by far the highest in NFL history. He has rushed for just under 10,000 yards in only 6 years. In short, Eric Dickerson is well on his way to becoming the greatest running back of all time.

Dickerson's running style is unique. He has the power to run right over would-be tacklers, the moves to leave them flatfooted, and the speed to run away from them. He's like a lion on the prowl with a football, hunting for the end zone, or like a thoroughbred in shoulder pads, sprinting down the home stretch. Give him a step and he'll take 6 points.

Yet there have been other running backs in the league with great physical gifts. Why is it that none of them have come close to matching his success?

A good part of the answer is that Dickerson is considered one of the hardest workers in the game. Through his year-round training programs he has fine-tuned his excellent natural skills, staying head and shoulders above his competitors. He has developed his speed and quickness to their limits with his systematic sprinting program. He has maximized his ball-carrying power with his taxing strength workouts. He has remained limber and resilient to football contact with his smart, modern stretching routine.

Yet it is Dickerson's work on stamina development that stands out. He's known as Mr. Fourth Quarter, the guy who's just getting warmed up when everyone else has run out of gas. The football field can be littered with players sucking for air like fish out of water, and Eric Dickerson will sprint right by them and not even be breathing hard. His stamina is legendary.

The biggest advantage to Dickerson's Spartan program is that it has helped him avoid serious injury while playing the most dangerous position in the game. Here is a guy who has started in 73 consecutive games since he has been in the league, and he has not missed a game because of injury in his professional career. Such incredible durability has resulted from Dickerson's view that hard training is more than simply part of his job. With Eric Dickerson, hard training is a way of life.

Now let me tell you about the book itself, starting out by saying that I wish there had been a book like this available when I first began coaching football. If there had been, and if I had read it and applied its contents, my teams would have been that much better. It's that simple. The same principle holds true today. Any football player who reads this work and applies its contents will be a better player. To understand why, let's talk about football training for a bit.

Football training methods have improved dramatically over the years. We've come a long way from the time when weight training was thought to slow you down by making you muscle-bound. Or from when health foods and vitamins were for faddists, if not eccentrics (and certainly not for rough-and-tumble football players). From when sprinting speed was considered to be unalterable through training. From when stretching was for ballet dancers, not for burly guys in helmets and shoulder pads. And from when it was thought that nothing could be done about the fact that some football players were bigger and stronger than others.

Although there is vastly improved knowledge available about how to train for football, too many young players continue to train the wrong way. While any number of them are dedicated to improving themselves physically, they lack the latest state-of-the-art knowledge for maximum results. They know little, if anything, about diet, especially the latest discoveries. They have only an elementary knowledge of flexibility and stretching, and if they work on their agility at all, it is probably in a way that is not very "football specific." They want to improve their sprinting speed, but all they know is to get out and sprint (and there is a lot more to it than that). They misuse weights and other strength-training equipment, neglecting many muscle groups that are important for football. They condition themselves the wrong way, fail to organize their workout time for maximum efficiency, and—very importantly—might not be motivated to train as hard as they can since they probably don't realize the outstanding results that are possible with the correct methods.

The result of all of this is a misdirected, inefficient, and incomplete football workout program. While undoubtedly better than no program at all, it does not even come close to developing their physical capacity to the maximum.

This book corrects all of that. It guides the football player through the latest and most effective training methods available. It tells him everything he needs to know—and then some—about diet, stretching, running, lifting weights, and otherwise preparing his body for football. It is not only invaluable for the young football player, but is must reading for dedicated football players at all levels.

In short, I strongly recommend that you read the contents of this book thoroughly and apply them diligently. If you are serious about playing up to your potential, you can ill afford not to.

Ron Meyer
Former Head Football Coach,
Indianapolis Colts

Preface

This is a book about physical training for the individual football player. It emphasizes getting the body ready to play football rather than the actual playing itself. It contains workout methods, techniques, and schedules gathered from both substantial research and years of practical experience.

Why put all this effort into a manual on training for football? Why not simply play the game? It must be kept in mind that football is a tough, demanding sport, and participation in it requires careful preparation. Lack of this preparation will keep the football participant from reaching his maximum playing potential. It will also increase his chance of serious injury.

The game of football requires specialized skills in blocking, tackling, throwing, catching, running, kicking, and the like. These skills can be improved with sound coaching on techniques and fundamentals, and with actual game experience. Yet with other things being equal, the ability to block, tackle, throw, catch, run, and kick is limited by the level of flexibility, quickness, agility, speed, strength, and stamina of the individual football player. This book will aid in developing these traits.

The risk of injury is always present for the football player. Not only is injury damaging to the body, but the injured player is of no use to his team. An injured All-American sits on the bench the same as an injured third stringer.

The athlete who is better prepared physically minimizes this risk of injury. He will be hurt less frequently, and his injuries will be less serious. This book aids the football player in physically preparing himself to both prevent and minimize injury.

Every physical trait that is important to the football player is covered in great detail. After an initial chapter on diet and other health factors, there are complete chapters on the development of flexibility, quickness/agility, sprinting speed, strength, and stamina. Each chapter defines the appropriate physical trait, discusses its importance to football, describes the various ways it is measured, mentions (if applicable) given standards at various levels of competition, and outlines a thorough, scientifically valid workout program to develop it. There is also a chapter on coordinating a complete workout schedule so that each of the physical traits is included in the total program.

The final chapter, in many ways the most important of the book, deals with motivation. It includes the training success stories of a number of football players as examples of what hard work can accomplish.

The methods of this book must be consistently applied in order for physical improvement to occur. While not every subscriber to such methods will become a star football player, all should realize varying degrees of improvement. Indeed, no book or workout program can take an athlete beyond his potential. Yet it is the purpose of this work to guide the athlete in reaching that potential. Those who apply intense effort toward the offered methods, month after month and year after year, might realize improvement that they never thought possible.

It is suggested that the entire book be read before beginning a workout program. It is also strongly suggested that the safety procedures described be strictly adhered to, and that anyone following the workout methods offered receive and pass a complete physical examination beforehand.

It is hoped that this work will be of aid to the many football players across the country.

Eric Dickerson, Los Angeles Raiders

Introduction:
Common Training
Principles

Certain principles are common to all football training. Regardless of what physical trait you are working on, you should adhere to these principles for maximum results. Note that many of these principles will be referred to repeatedly throughout the book in order to reinforce their importance.

WARM UP THOROUGHLY

Proper warm-up is needed before any vigorous training activity. It basically consists of performing the activity you are going to do, starting very slowly and very gradually increasing the intensity as you get loose. It also includes stretching, especially the muscles you will use in the activity; you increase the degree of stretch that you utilize as you get warm.

Warm-up is a very important concept and will be described in more detail throughout the book.

WARM DOWN ADEQUATELY

Warming down after exercise is important, especially if the exercise has been vigorous. It not only helps to eliminate some of the muscle soreness that can follow a heavy workout, but in the extreme it can help prevent strain on your heart.

Warming down is simple, amounting to a gradual decrease in exercise intensity. This means jogging and then walking following sprinting, or some types of lighter exercise following heavy weight work. You should also include stretching as part of your warm-down, especially after weight work.

Warm-down does not have to be completely exercise specific. The main thing is that you want to keep from shocking your system by a sudden ceasing of vigorous exercise.

INCREASE EXERCISE INTENSITY GRADUALLY

You should increase your workout level very gradually, not only when warming up but from session to session as well. This will aid in preventing injury and in keeping you from overtraining and going stale. Remember that it takes time for your body to adjust to exercise; you must work with it by giving it that time.

ALTERNATE HARD AND EASY WORKOUTS

This is particularly important when you do the same exercises each workout. Thus, you ordinarily don't want to do two tough, pure speed workouts or two tough conditioning workouts on consecutive days, at least for extended periods. With strength workouts, you should exercise entirely different muscle groups when you work out two days in a row.

This axiom is perhaps not quite as applicable for flexibility and quickness/agility work since these workouts are not as taxing. Yet, if you should have an unusually long workout with either of these, you can lighten up if working on them the next day.

EMPHASIZE PEAK-OUTPUT EXERCISE

Since the game of football is played with relatively short bursts of all-out effort, you should train for it with relatively short bursts of all-out effort. This type of effort is called peak-output, or anaerobic, exercise, and it is anything done with the full power of your body behind it, whether sprinting up a hill or pressing a pair of dumbbells overhead. Any other type of exercise is not specific to building football fitness and should be used as a warm-up, warm-down, or as a supplement on a light day. The exercises contained within this text are therefore primarily peak-output exercises.

TRAIN WITH CONSISTENCY

Consistency is one of the most important principles of sound football training. It is far more effective to train consistently for months on end, with gradually increased intensity, than it is to train extremely hard for just a few weeks. With consistent training, today's tough workout can be next month's moderate workout and next year's light workout.

AVOID OVERTRAINING

Overtraining can result from training too hard and/or too long, particularly when your body is not ready for it. Certain studies have shown that up to 60 percent of athletic injuries are caused by it. Some of the symptoms of overtraining are: soreness, stiffness, nervousness, weight loss, loss of appetite, headache, and, especially, a drop in performance, chronic fatigue, and a generally lethargic feeling about your workouts both physically and mentally.

You can minimize the possibility of overtraining by increasing your training load gradually, training with consistency, utilizing a balanced workout schedule, and alternating hard and easy workouts. You can also minimize overtraining—or at least combat the overtraining syndrome, if you experience the earlier mentioned symptoms—by taking some time off. You might avoid any kind of football-related workout for several days, instead enjoying some easy hiking, swimming, or bicycle riding. When you do resume your football training, make your first workout back a relatively easy one so that you give your body a chance to readjust.

KEEP ACCURATE RECORDS

Record-keeping is an important part of any training program. You need records of your workouts to chart your progress. You also need them to plan your workouts, as you want to know what you did last time.

A good workout record system should name the exercise, the intensity (distance sprinted, weight lifted, etc.), the number of repetitions, the recovery interval (jogging, walking around, etc.), and any other important factors (such as the grip on the bar, the condition of the ground, etc.). It should also contain a short space for any comments.

Since record-keeping is so important, and since each chapter featuring training will involve slightly different record-keeping methods, this topic will be covered in each individual chapter.

1

You Are What You Eat: Diet and Other Health Factors

"What you put into yourself is very important."

The late Fred Hofmeister,
former gym owner,
Indianapolis, Indiana

AN OVERVIEW OF DIET

DIET DEFINED

Diet is what you ingest into your body, including all foods, water, and even drugs. While the latter are not nutrients in the strict sense, they nonetheless not only influence bodily functions but can also affect how nutrients react in your system. Thus you must give drugs every bit of the consideration that you give foods for purposes of athletic performance and, more importantly, health.

IMPORTANCE OF DIET

Any training program must begin with a good diet. It makes no sense to dive gung ho into your workouts without having a solid nutritional base with which to back up your efforts. No matter how hard you train, you will never reach your maximum in developing strength, speed, and stamina if your diet is lacking.

5

Actually, there is little, if any, argument on the importance of diet to athletes. Where the controversy lies is in comparing their dietary needs to those not involved in sports or other strenuous activity. Do athletes need a special diet? My answer is both yes and no. In one sense, there is really no such thing as a special diet since we all need basically the same nutrients to sustain life and health, whether we are active or not. In another sense, athletes, as well as others under stress, do have special dietary needs since they use up these nutrients at a somewhat greater rate. Finally, diet is of special importance to the athlete since without a good one he pays a greater price in performance than the less active individual. A sedentary office worker might get by on a breakfast of coffee and doughnuts and a lunch of soda and french fries. Yet any football player who consistently relied on such "foods" would ultimately pay the price of decreased performance.

DIET FUNDAMENTALS

FOOD GROUPS

The standard and most basic method of classifying foods is to list them in 4 distinct groups. These are:

Group 1: Dairy Products. Included are milk and its derivatives such as cheese, cottage cheese, yogurt, butter, buttermilk, skim milk, and the like.

Group 2: Meat Group. This category is also termed the high-protein group, and it includes all meats, eggs, poultry, fish, and, by some classifications, other high-protein foods such as nuts, peas, and beans.

Group 3: Fruit and Vegetable Group. This group covers the many different fruits and vegetables.

Group 4: Cereal and Grain Group. Various breads, pastas, and cereals make up this group. These foods come from such grains as wheat, rye, oats, barley, and rice.

The importance of consistently eating adequate amounts from each of these 4 groups cannot be overemphasized. In fact, if the topic of diet was to be summed up with one bit of advice, it would be to eat as wide a variety as possible from each of these 4 groups on a daily basis. This practice will assure dietary soundness more than anything else you can do.

CALORIES

All food contains calories. A calorie is a measurement of the amount of heat a substance gives off when burned. So when you metabolize, or "burn," food within your body, you are utilizing energy measured in the form of this caloric heat. Foods high in calories are high in this heat energy, and those low in calories are low in heat energy.

Calories come from any of the 3 basic components that make up all foods: protein, carbohydrates, and fats. Ordinarily, carbohydrates are first used for fuel, and a diet low in carbohydrates will force the body to burn fats. If both carbohydrates and fats are low, the body must use valuable protein for its caloric needs.

How important are calories? The calorie is the basic unit of fuel by which your body functions; without calories, your body could not sustain life, let alone run the 40-yard dash. Yet the caloric value of a food says nothing about its nutritional value. As you will see, you have to know more about a food than the number of calories it has if you want to practice good nutrition.

PROTEIN

Protein is the building block for all of your body's tissues, including muscle tissue. Next to water, it is the most plentiful substance in your body. It is present in every living cell.

All animal flesh and dairy products are high in protein, and foods from these groups are known as "complete" proteins. This means that they are proteins that contain adequate amounts of the 8 essential amino acids that must be included in your diet for proper protein synthesis. Other high-protein foods, such as various peas, beans, and nuts, are termed "incomplete" proteins, because they are low in one or more of the 8 essential amino acids. Yet these incomplete proteins can be efficiently utilized by your body if you supply the needed amino acids by eating complete proteins with them.

The recommended amount of protein for adults is 1 gram for every 2.2 pounds of body weight. Yet the recommended dosages get increasingly larger as age decreases, all the way to 1 gram of protein per pound of body weight for infants up to 6 months. The obvious reason for the greater protein needs of infants is their greater rate of growth. By contrast, adults, who are not growing, need less protein to maintain the growth they have already achieved.

As an athlete in heavy strength training, you are in effect trying to stimulate muscular growth, even if you are not trying to gain body weight. If this growth is to occur, your body must have adequate amounts of protein available to build body tissues faster than the rate at which they are destroyed. Whether adequate protein is received can be determined by measuring your body's nitrogen intake and excretion, since nearly all protein is 16 percent nitrogen. When nitrogen intake exceeds excretion, your body is in the positive nitrogen balance condition it needs in order to build muscle tissue.

According to some sources, positive nitrogen balance can best be achieved by consuming 25 to 35 grams of protein every 3 to 3½ hours, such amount varying with individual protein synthesis ability. These sources point to a study in which more than half of a group of Olympic weightlifters were in negative nitrogen balance when tested at several points despite averaging 140 grams of protein a day. Researchers also claim that protein needs increase greatly in cold weather and that the amounts of protein available in like quantities of the same foods vary greatly. Unfortunately there is a lack of documented research on the protein requirements of people in heavy strength training.

Other authorities believe muscular growth can occur with less protein than this. They feel that such amounts are not only unnecessary but can lead to long-term health problems, particularly in view of the high fat and cholesterol content of many high-protein foods.

Actually, your protein needs should be met as long as your meals are balanced and your caloric intake is adequate. You will automatically receive more protein by consuming the extra calories needed to fuel your heavy workouts. You can include a little protein in your between-meals snacks to keep your nitrogen balance consistently positive.

CARBOHYDRATES

Carbohydrates are the major energy source for all of your body's activities, including muscular exertion. They also aid in protein and fat metabolism. Good quality carbohydrates contain important vitamins and minerals and often come packaged with proteins.

It can be said that carbohydrates are your body's most preferred nutrient. Not only are they its best energy source—better than fats and proteins—they are also the easiest food for your body to digest. This works out quite well, for next to water they are the largest single component of most diets.

Your body eventually converts most carbohydrates into a simple sugar called glucose, commonly referred to as blood sugar. This glucose is then transported to tissues of your body for energy producing purposes. It is especially important that your brain and muscles receive a constant supply of glucose to maintain the mental alertness and quick reflexes that you need for athletic competition.

The glucose that you do not use is either turned into fat and stored, or converted into a substance called glycogen. This glycogen is then stored in your liver or directly in your muscles; it is available for any all-out exercise of more than several seconds time (sounds like football-playing exercise). Since your body's ability to store glycogen is limited, you need a constant supply of carbohydrates to keep your reserves up.

With regard to your carbohydrate intake, I think you should simply let your body "seek its own level." Concentrate on a variety of good foods, work out hard, and don't even worry about your carbohydrate intake. If you're a bit overweight, you might want to reduce your overall calories some, but it is not a good idea to go to extremes regarding reduction of your carbohydrates. Also, always get your carbs from good sources. Skip the candy, cake, pie, doughnuts, and white bread, concentrating instead on fresh fruits, fresh vegetables, and whole grains. The latter are better utilized as energy sources and superior in their overall nutritional makeup.

FATS

Fats have received somewhat of a bad image in our society, perhaps because so many people associate them with being overweight. Yet fats are an essential part of your diet, serving as the most concentrated form of food energy. According to some nutritionists, they are also necessary for the absorption of the fat-soluble vitamins (A, D, E, and K) and are required to keep the body from losing needed heat. (Ever wonder why Eskimos are on the chubby side?) Fats also offer physical protection to a number of internal organs, serving as a sort of shock absorber.

Fats also act as taste and appetite appeasers, slowing down your stomach's digestive juices and allowing food to stay in your stomach longer for a greater sensation of fullness. (Thus, as shall be seen, your pre-exercise meal should be low in fat.)

Ordinarily, there is no reason to be concerned about getting enough fat in your diet. The chances are next to impossible that you are not receiving an adequate amount, and unless you are substantially over-weight you don't have to be overly concerned about an excess. Yet you might want to keep in mind that once your football days are over and you are exercising less, you should probably reduce your overall fat and caloric intake.

WATER

Water is indispensable to the human body. It is contained in every cell and is necessary for virtually every bodily process. Whereas you can survive for weeks without food, you can go only days without water. A loss of as little as 10 percent of your body's water supply can be fatal.

Your water supply takes on a particular importance when you are in hard training. While the average guy loses about 2.5 quarts of water a day, as an athlete you can easily lose more than this in just one hot-weather workout. A study of football players in Florida one September showed an average of nearly 4 quarts of water loss per person in a 2-hour practice.

When you are working out, you should take a little more water than is indicated by your thirst. A good rule of thumb is to drink 10 or 12 ounces every 20 or 30 minutes, whether you are thirsty or not. You may need even more water than this in extreme weather and/or exercise conditions, and by all means take more if you are thirsty. It is probably better to take this extra water through more frequent breaks rather than in larger amounts per break, if you are able to.

VITAMINS

Vitamins are substances that perform many specific and vital functions within your body. They are basically catalytic in nature, meaning that they assist and regulate various activities regarding your body's metabolism. In a sense, they act as a sort of "spark" for your food assimilation, getting the reactions going.

With a few exceptions, your body cannot manufacture the vitamins it needs. Thus you have to get your vitamins from your food or from vitamin supplements. As for obtaining them from food, keep in mind that no single food contains all of the vitamins you need. This is one reason you should always eat a wide variety of foods. Any additional, or supplemental, vitamins can be obtained with vitamin pills, as science can isolate any vitamin into pill form.

Vitamins are classified into 2 general groups: water-soluble and fat-soluble. The water-soluble vitamins include the B-complex vitamins and vitamin C. These are measured in milligrams (mgs) and require water for absorption into your body. They are also lost from your body through a water base (your urine) and in essence are not really stored to any extent. You have to continuously replace these water-soluble vitamins; some nutritionists suggest that they be taken several times a day.

The fat-soluble vitamins are A, D, E, and K. These are measured in International Units (I.U., or units) and require fat for absorption. These vitamins are not lost through urination. Instead, they are stored in the liver and other fatty tissues of your body. Because of this storage, you can get by for longer periods of time with a lessened intake of the fat-soluble vitamins, and excessive amounts of them can actually be damaging. Yet this is certainly no reason to neglect these important nutrients.

MINERALS

Minerals are inorganic substances present in your body; by weight, you are about 4 or 5 percent mineral matter. Like vitamins, minerals are an absolute necessity, as your tissues and fluids need them for many functions. They are also similar to vitamins in that they are obtained from the food you eat and are available in supplemental pill or capsule form.

Minerals are used in complex ways that are interrelated. For example, the presence of one mineral within your body might not be effective unless another mineral is also supplied in adequate amount. In fact, no one mineral can function without affecting others.

Your body needs 17 different minerals, which can be divided into 2 groups: macrominerals, which are needed in relatively large amounts and are measured in milligrams (mg.), and "trace" minerals, needed in smaller amounts and measured in micrograms (mcg.).

APPLICATION TO THE DIET

FOOD SUPPLEMENTS

There is considerable controversy on whether supplementary vitamins and minerals are needed. Some claim that the typical American diet contains ample amounts of nutrients to meet the vitamin and mineral needs, or Recommended Daily Allowances (RDAs), set by the National Research Council. Others feel not only that the RDAs are often not met, but that they are set far too low to begin with. Although the debate is still going on, there are probably more nutritionists and physicians recommending nutritional supplements now than ever before.

The RDAs were arrived at by determining what was in the typical American diet and then adding a margin of safety. Those advocating supplements criticize this method. They say it is hardly a process based on clinical studies of the effects of various nutrients on different people. Their viewpoint is that nutritional needs vary with age, sex, environmental conditions, body size, growth rate, and activity level, among other factors. Other losses result from common drugs such as caffeine, nicotine, alcohol, aspirin, and various antibiotics, as well as sugar and sugar substitutes and any kind of mental or physical stress, including intensive training.

The most recent evidence indicates that nutritional supplements probably do some good, and yet this statement must be taken the correct way. Supplements will not aid you directly in lowering your 40-yard dash time or increasing your bench press. Yet some nutritionists claim that supplements will indirectly improve your overall energy level and possibly result in your being able to train harder, longer, and more frequently.

Supplementary vitamins and minerals can also help you to maintain your health. Research indicates that the period of your most rapid muscular growth corresponds with the period of your lowest immunity to various infectious diseases. This is due not only to the strain of your growth-promoting workout, but also to the period of protein synthesis that follows. Thus if you want to ensure good health, you might benefit from some supplementation both to safely recover from heavy training and for the period of regrowth.

Yet the bottom line is that you should not depend on vitamin and mineral supplements as a means of football fitness. They cannot take the place of intensive, football-related exercise. Nor do supplements —or anything else, for that matter—take the place of a wholesome, balanced diet. While your performance could suffer slightly without supplemental nutrients, you might not be able to perform at all without a sound diet. This is why I rely mainly on a sound diet for my training and playing endeavors.

The following table contains the names of the various vitamins and minerals, their RDAs, suggested megadoses, and comments on their usage. The jury is still out as to the amounts needed, and the answers might well lie somewhere between the two extremes, varying, of course, with the individual. If you do go for higher amounts, do so conservatively, increasing (and decreasing) your quantities gradually and taking your vitamins and minerals with meals unless otherwise indicated.

OTHER FOOD SUPPLEMENTS

There are a number of other "high tech" nutritive substances for which strong claims are made. Many of these are fairly recently marketed, and there has been some interesting research on their effects, particularly with regard to building muscle mass. There is no guarantee that they will work for you, however, as some athletes swear by them and others have been disappointed in the results. Personally, I think that these products can be of some benefit when combined with hard training and a good natural diet.

I cannot tell you which of these products you should use. Your best bet is to check the muscle magazines for advertisements (as well

VITAMINS AND MINERALS

Item	RDA	Megadose	Comments
Vitamin A	5,000 I.U.	15,000–20,000 I.U. (some call 30,000 optimal)	More effective with C, E, selenium, and 50 mg. chelated zinc.
Vitamin B-1, or riboflavin	1.5 mg.	25–100 mg. (200–1,000 mg. under stress)	Take with other B vitamins, especially if using large dosages.
Vitamin B-2, or thiamine	1.7 mg.	50–100 mg. (up to 500 mg. under stress)	Keep dosage fairly equal to that of B-6.
Vitamin B-3, or niacin	1.8 mg.	200–500 mg. (up to 3,000 mg. under stress)	Always take with meals. Since amounts needed vary considerably, may have to adjust.
Vitamin B-5, or pantothenic acid	7.0 mg.	100–200 mg. (600–1,200 mg. under stress)	Take 1 mg. folic acid and 100 mg. biotin for every 300 mg.
Vitamin B-6, or pyridoxine	2.0 mg.	50–100 mg. (up to 500 mg. under stress)	Increase dosage with high protein. Keep B-2 dosage on about same level.
Vitamin B-12, or cobalamin	3.0 mcg.	25 mcg.	Injections of 500 to 3,000 mcg. every 3 to 7 days used by some.
Biotin	200 mcg.	100 mg. per every 300 mg. B-5	Maintain this 1-to-3 ratio with B-5.
Choline		1,000–3,000 mg.	Important with high fat intake. Take with equal amounts of inositol, and with B-6 and E.

Folic acid	400 mcg.	5–15 mg. (some physicians say more)	Take at least 1 mg. for every 300 mg. B-5. Get good supply of B-12 with folic acid.
Inositol		1,000–3,000 mg.	Take with equal amounts choline.
PABA		Controversial: some recommend none and others up to 1,000 mg.	Watch for side effects if trying high dosages.
Vitamin C	60 mg.	2,000–5,000 mg. (15,000 or more under severe stress)	Take with 100 mg. each of rutin and hesperidin. Take some C between meals, dissolved in liquids.
Vitamin D	400 I.U.	400–800 I.U.	Less if big milk drinker or sun lover. Check multiple vitamin for D amount. Do not overdose. Take 10 parts A to 1 part D.
Vitamin E	30 I.U.	800–1,200 I.U.	Take with at least 50 mcg. selenium, 250 to 500 mg. cysteine.
Vitamin F		None recommended.	
Vitamin K	140 mcg.	None recommended.	
Vitamin P, or bioflavonoids		300–600 mg.	Take 100 mg. each of rutin and hesperidin with vitamin C.

Item	RDA	Megadose	Comments
Calcium	800–1,200 mg.	Up to 1,600 mg.	Take with magnesium, A, C, and, if applicable, D. Take in divided dosages with acidic fruit or juice.
Chlorine		None recommended.	Take plenty of E if your water supply is chlorinated.
Chromium	50–200 mcg.	250–1,000 mcg.	No supplement needed if 2 tablespoons brewer's yeast is taken daily.
Cobalt		None recommended.	
Copper		None recommended.	
Fluoride		None recommended.	
Iodine	150 mcg.	150 mcg.	Take kelp if you do not use iodinized salt.
Iron	18 mg.	18 mg.	Check multiple vitamin/mineral tablet for iron content. Take liver if low.
Magnesium	400 mg.	500–800 mg.	Take about twice as much calcium as magnesium. Take same way as calcium.

Manganese	2.5–5 mg.	15–25 mg.	Take with meals. Might need less if whole grains, eggs, green vegetables, and nuts are consumed.
Molybdenum		None recommended.	
Phosphorous		None recommended.	
Potassium	1,875–5,625 mg.	Generally none recommended.	Can take 500 mg. tablets under certain stressful conditions.
Selenium	50–200 mg.	200–1,000 mcg.	Take with food, vitamin E.
Sodium	1,100–3,300 mg.	None recommended.	Use Lite salt on food to aid in sodium/potassium balance.
Sulfur		None recommended.	
Zinc	15 mg.	40–70 mg.	Take with C and its accessories.

as articles) on them, and then write and/or call the manufacturers and distributors for literature, especially for research results. You might also inquire about them at your local health food store as well as at the gym where you work out. Yet remember that what works for one person may not necessarily work for another, and you may have to try a number of them to find out what works for you. Since many of these products are not cheap, your pocketbook might dictate to what extent you can experiment.

HEALTH FOODS

Health foods can be defined as foods or food supplements that have significant nutritive value. Strictly speaking, any true food that you eat is a health food. Yet some advocates claim that certain health foods actually contain special properties or benefits that are unique to the food itself. Although these claims have not been scientifically proven, the fact remains that most of the so-called health foods are highly nutritious.

It would be impossible to list all of the health foods and their possible benefits here. If you desire more information about them, you might try a visit to your local health food store.

GAINING WEIGHT

As a football player, you want to be as heavy as possible while retaining your quickness/agility, speed, and stamina. The extra weight will help you to generate more force upon contact and will also help in absorbing the shock of contact. It will make you tougher to move around, aid you in resisting injury, and probably help you psychologically. Yet these positive benefits of weight gain will take place only if the gain is in solid muscle.

You should not try to gain weight too quickly. A goal of 1 pound every 2 weeks is a good rule of thumb. This standard will better assure that your gain is in muscle, for most people cannot grow new muscle faster than this. A gradual weight gain will also give your body time to adjust to the new weight, helping you to retain your quickness/agility, speed, and stamina. My gains in body weight have always been gradual, even when I first started playing organized football as a skinny grade school kid.

To better assure a gradual weight gain, follow the practice of eating 5 moderately sized meals a day instead of 3 bigger ones. Also, refrain from trying to gain by eating junk food. You're going to have to consume more calories, but do so with nutritious, lightly processed foods from many different sources.

A good weight-gaining program goes hand-in-hand with a good strength-training program. You might be able to gain some solid body weight without strength work if you're real skinny to begin with. Yet eventually you'll have to pump some iron to get any heavier, at least if you want your gain to be muscle instead of fat. (Chapter 5 gives complete details on strength training.)

LOSING WEIGHT

Losing weight amounts to making more withdrawals (calorie burning) than deposits (calorie eating). As with gaining weight, it should be done gradually, mainly to help your body conserve strength. A weight loss of 1 pound every week or 2 is a realistic rate.

A very important consideration in any weight loss program is assuring that your nutritional needs are met. This is accomplished by substituting good lower-calorie nutrition for higher-calorie nutrition. In other words, you want to make sure you are getting plenty of vitamins, minerals, protein, and water, and cut down a little bit on carbohydrates and fats. It is here that nutritional supplements can be very beneficial. Not only do supplementary vitamins and minerals help, but many health foods pack a lot of nutrition per calorie.

A major problem with losing weight is that people get too hung up on it. They're overly worried about body weight itself and tend to ignore the fact that body fat can be lost while overall body weight is maintained through an increase in muscle mass. Thus the term "overweight" is often thrown around when "overfat" might be more accurate.

Even more important than your percentage of body fat is the actual state of football fitness you are in. Factors such as 40-yard dash time, various agility test times, flexibility test results, stamina tests, various strength tests of large muscle groups, etc., are much more correlated to football performance than the percentage of fat your body carries. Remember, you're a football player, not a Greek Adonis entering a body beautiful contest.

PRE-EXERCISE MEAL

If you are in a situation where you are eating a meal specifically as a prelude to heavy exercise (including, of course, your actual games), you should follow certain guidelines. You want to make your meal modest in size, low in fats and protein, and high in carbohydrates. The meal will provide some fuel for muscular work but is consumed mainly to prevent gastric disturbances. It can be taken in liquid form a good hour or more before exercise. The closer to exercise time that you take it, the smaller it should be.

A good recipe for a pre-exercise meal is to take about six ounces of your favorite fruit juice and add a ripe, mashed up banana to it, blending the two together. Then add a pinch of honey and/or blackstrap molasses and a couple of tablespoons of yogurt, if you can handle it. You might blend in a tablespoon of pure malt as a flavoring touch.

JUNK FOODS

I like to define junk foods as foods that are not really foods. This is not true in the literal sense, for these "foods"—from potato chips to "fortified" chocolate cupcakes—do have some food value. They possess calories, if not much else, and while the body needs calories, there are undoubtedly much better sources. Common sense tells you that an apple is better food than a candy bar or that whole grain bread is better than a doughnut.

A major disadvantage of junk foods is that they are sometimes eaten in place of good wholesome food. Naturally, this practice has potentially devastating effects if you are in hard training, for nothing can take the place of good wholesome food. Many junk foods are also fried in grease, heavily salted, possess little fiber, and are excessively high in sugar. It is therefore advised that you avoid junk foods, or at least eat them only moderately. I like the taste of some junk foods myself, but I eat them only in moderate amounts.

OTHER HEALTH FACTORS

DRUGS

Having served as the National Football League's spokesperson for the "Just Say No" anti-drug campaign, I feel very strongly that no chapter on diet and health factors can be complete without reference to drugs. Consequently, I have included a chart that lists the physical, psychological, and legal consequences of today's most abused substances. It outlines quite clearly the prices you pay for using these dangerous items.

One widely used drug is nicotine, the substance found in cigarettes. Nicotine is the most addictive substance known to man, with 73 percent of those who use it eventually hooked. In its pure form, it is a deadly poison to the body, and of course the cigarettes that contain it are extremely damaging to both athletic performance and general health.

Smoking will rob you of your endurance as an athlete. Cigarette smoke contains carbon monoxide, which combines with the hemoglobin in your red blood cells to prevent them from carrying oxygen. The result is a decrease in the amount of oxygen that gets to your muscles for energy.

It would be difficult to find a person, athlete or otherwise, who was glad they took up smoking. It would be equally difficult to find a person who was not glad they quit. It is common knowledge that smoking is a killer habit with no place in athletics. Thus if you smoke, the advice is simple and obvious: Quit immediately!

Another commonly abused drug is alcohol, found in liquor, wine, and beer. Alcohol is a depressant to the central nervous system and impairs motor performance even at low levels of consumption. This results in diminished hand-eye coordination, complex coordination, balance, and visual tracking, as well as seriously slowed reflexes. It also adversely affects the liver's lactic acid processing, resulting in greater lactic acid levels in your muscles and reduced muscular endurance.

Another distinct disadvantage of alcohol is that it is illegal for certain age groups, mainly for all people under 21 in most states. Thus you should refrain from alcohol use completely if you are not of drinking age, and it's a good idea to use it only very moderately in any event.

SUMMARY OF DRUG EFFECTS

Drugs	Legal status, manufacture, and sale	Legal status, possession, and usage	Withdrawal symptoms	Physical dependence	Death by overdose	Accident proneness during use	Suicide tendencies
LSD	Felony	Misdemeanor, various state laws	No	No	No	Yes	Yes
Marijuana	Felony	Violation, misdemeanor, or felony	No	No	No	Yes	Very rare
Heroin	Felony	Felony	Vomiting, diarrhea, tremors, aches, gooseflesh, sweats, etc.	Yes	Coma, respiratory failure, shock	Yes	Yes
Barbiturates	Legal medically, felony for illegal sale	Misdemeanor, various state laws	Delirium, tremors, convulsions	Yes	Coma, respiratory failure, shock	Yes	Yes

Amphetamines	Felony for illegal sale	Misdemeanor, various state laws	Depression, apathy, muscle aches	Yes	Convulsions, coma, cerebral hemorrhage	Yes	Yes
Cocaine	Felony	Felony	No	No	Convulsions, respiratory failure	Yes	Yes
Airplane glue	No restrictions	None, or misdemeanor by city or state law	Mild	Rare	Asphyxiation, heart stoppage	Yes	Unknown
Alcohol	Various state laws for illegal stills	Sales to minors a misdemeanor; various state laws on driving, disorderly conduct	Delirium, other symptoms, tremors, convulsions	Yes	Coma, respiratory failure	Yes	Yes

Drugs	Physical complications	Chromosomal changes	Mental complications during use	Mental complications after use	Tolerance	Manner used	Abuse trend
LSD	Rare	Questionable	Panic, paranoid states, anxiety	Amotivation?, flashbacks, psychoses, paranoia, anxiety reactions, brain damage	Extremely rapid	Orally, injection	Decreasing
Marijuana	Bronchitis, conjunctivitis	Questionable	Rare panic or paranoid states	Amotivation?, rare psychoses, rare flashbacks	Yes	Orally, smoking	Increasing
Heroin	Infections, hepatitis	Reported	Coma	Asocial and antisocial reactions	Yes	Injection, snorting, least effective orally	Decreasing
Barbiturates	Overdose	Unknown	Intoxication, acting-out behavior	Psychoses	Yes	Orally, injection	Increasing

YOU ARE WHAT YOU EAT: DIET AND OTHER HEALTH FACTORS

Amphetamines	Malnutrition, needle contamination	Unknown	Paranoid, assaultive	Paranoid psychoses, asocial reactions	Yes	Orally, injection, nasal and other membranes	Decreasing
Cocaine	Malnutrition, perforated nose septum from sniffing	Unknown	Excited state, intoxication	Probable brain damage, paranoid psychoses	Yes	Injection, nasal and other membranes	Increasing
Airplane glue	Bone marrow depression, liver and kidney damage	Unknown	Excited state, intoxication	Brain damage?	Slight	Inhalation and sniffing	Stable
Alcohol	Gastritis, pancreatis, cirrhosis, neuritis	Unknown	Intoxication, acting-out behavior	Brain damage, psychotic reactions	Partial	Orally	Increasing

From Brent Q. Hafen and Brenda Peterson, *Medicine and Drugs: Problems and Risks, Use and Abuse*. Philadelphia: Lea & Febiger, 2nd Edition, 1978. Used by permission.

Another commonly used drug is caffeine, which is technically a member of the amphetamine group. It is contained in coffee, tea, and soft drinks, and these also contain the related drugs theophylline and theobromine. All are nervous system stimulants that adversely affect the kidneys, blood pressure, digestion, heart rate, and general metabolism. Caffeine has also been linked to cancer.

It might be well to avoid coffee, tea, and soft drinks. They have no food value, are habit forming, and are possibly somewhat damaging.

ANABOLIC STEROIDS

Other drugs of concern in football training come under the general heading of anabolic steroids. These drugs are synthetic derivatives of testosterone, a male hormone, and have anabolic (building) effects. They were originally developed to treat people who had experienced severe problems in body weight and/or muscle tissue loss (victims of illness, burns, surgery, etc.) or who had hormonal difficulties. Yet over the past few decades, athletes desiring greater strength and weight gains have been combining them with intensive heavy weightlifting.

It is not recommended that you take anabolic steroids. There is a list of damaging side effects associated with their use, including, but not limited to, high blood pressure, kidney damage, liver damage, nausea, acne, stomach bleeding, growth stunting, loss of sex drive, interference with sexual development, sterility, masculinizing effects, excessive water retention, and cancer. They are particularly dangerous to young athletes still in their formative growth years.

SLEEP

Sleep is extremely important to the hard-training football player. Heavy exercise is very stressful, and proper rest is necessary to give your body time to recuperate. The best workout program in the world will be rendered less effective without adequate rest.

Individuals have varying sleep requirements, ordinarily ranging from 7 to 9 hours. Yet the amount of sleep itself is not as important as the quality of sleep. A calm, relaxed 7 hours is of more value than a restless 8 or 9 hours.

A good night's sleep begins with a good sleeping environment. Generally a dark, quiet room is best, although you might like a little light and softly played music. Your bed should be as comfortable as possible, and to effect this you can experiment with pillows, sheets, covers, and bed location.

Since sleep slows down your mental and physical systems, if possible you should avoid doing anything that stimulates your mind or body just before bedtime. This would include heavy exercise, arguing, reading that hard-to-put-down book, and the like.

Warm milk can help you sleep, for it contains both calcium and the amino acid tryptophan. You can also take tryptophan in isolated form, going with about 2,000 mg., along with 1,000 mg. of vitamin C and 100 mg. of vitamin B-6. Other safe sleeping aids are niacinamide (a form of niacin) and the B vitamin inositol taken together, and the herbs lady slipper, passiflora, and valerian. You can also try a product called Sleepytime Tea.

You might go with a leisurely 15-minute walk before retiring. A hot bath can help you sleep by relaxing you, and a hot shower is good if you don't have a bathtub. You can soak your feet in a hot tub or bucket, especially if you've been up and on them for any length of time.

It is okay to eat moderately before going to bed, especially if you are hungry. Yet you should avoid fried foods, sugar, and large amounts of fruit. Your pre-bedtime meal can be moderate in protein, and complex carbohydrates are also good. I hate to go to bed on an empty stomach and like a snack before retiring. I simply cannot sleep if I am hungry.

One key to sleeping well is to go to bed at the same time every night, a practice that I try to adhere to. If you consistently go to bed at 10 o'clock, your body will prepare itself for sleep at that time. Your pulse, breathing rate, body temperature, and blood pressure will all fall in anticipation of sleep.

If you follow all of the mentioned practices for good sleeping and still have trouble falling asleep, you might try setting your alarm and then getting up when it goes off, regardless of how you slept. For example, if you retire at 10 and consistently get up at 6, your body will eventually go to sleep when it needs to in order to rise at 6.

INJURIES

Injuries are an unfortunate part of both playing football and training for football. Although good hard training will lower your chances of getting hurt in the long run, there is always the chance of being hurt when you train. To minimize this chance, follow the common training principles covered in the Introduction.

A lack of flexibility can lead to injury. As your muscles become stronger, they can become shorter and less flexible if you do not stretch them. To guard against this, a systematic stretching program should be emphasized. Such a program is covered completely in the next chapter.

Muscular imbalance goes hand in hand with poor flexibility as a major cause of injury. It can readily occur when one group of muscles is developed and its opposing group is relatively neglected, often causing muscle pulls in the weaker group. Exercising in a manner that strengthens and stretches opposing muscle groups can help prevent this particular problem.

If injury occurs, remember the word RICE. These letters stand for rest, ice, compression, and elevation. Rest is of obvious necessity as it keeps you from aggravating your injury further. Ice will limit swelling and speed healing, as will a gentle compress and an elevation of the injured part. You can leave the ice on for up to 3 hours, removing it every half hour or so to minimize numbing and cramping, then reapplying it again in 15 minutes.

Speaking of ice, I use it on my muscles after taxing strength workouts, rubbing it against them to expedite the removal of waste products, especially lactic acid. In essence, you have broken down or "injured" your muscles after heavy strength work, and the application of ice expedites the "healing" process. I always make sure that I am cooled off some before applying ice to my muscles, and you should do the same.

Ordinarily heat should not be applied to an injury during the first 48 hours since it will cause blood to rush to the injured area and cause swelling. After 48 hours, heat applied to the injured area can be useful in increasing circulation, which carries away wastes and delivers nutrients.

If your injury causes severe pain or occurs in a joint, check with your doctor or trainer and follow their advice. If they tell you to cut down or eliminate your training for a while, by all means do it. There are times when complete rest is necessary to recover from injury, and it's better to lose a little sharpness than to aggravate your injury and retard the healing process.

A FINAL WORD

In closing, let it once again be said that what you put into your body is every bit as important as how you exercise it, and so is how you take care of it off the field and out of the gym. And if you think you can skimp on your diet, cheat on your sleep, and occasionally dabble in drugs without having your performance affected, you're lying to yourself. Because to reach the top of your game you need it all: solid diet, common sense health habits, and sound training procedures. Hopefully, this initial chapter has given you the foundation for the first two, so let's move to the chapters that cover the techniques and methods of the training itself.

2

You Must Be Limber: Exercises for Flexibility

"He touched his head to the floor from a sitting position.
I tried . . . but couldn't do it. My father at the age of
fifty was more flexible after a couple weeks of yoga
lessons than I, a professional athlete at the age of
twenty-six."

Rocky Bleier,
Fighting Back

AN OVERVIEW OF FLEXIBILITY

FLEXIBILITY DEFINED

Flexibility can be defined as the ability to bend, turn, or twist without
breaking. It is easy to see how this definition applies to your body: If
you can bend, turn, and twist without "breaking," you are flexible.
The degree to which you are flexible is the range of motion through
which you can do these things, or the extent to which your muscles
and tendons can stretch before being damaged.

Flexibility is specific to the joints and muscles involved. This is
to say that a person can be extremely flexible in one muscle group and
not at all flexible in another. For example, you might be very flexible
in your shoulders and very tight in your hamstrings. Accordingly, there
is no one flexibility exercise that will increase your overall range of
motion.

It is important to remember that flexibility is not a trait that can
be developed overnight. It takes months, or even years, of consistent
stretching to develop a good level of flexibility.

IMPORTANCE OF FLEXIBILITY

Flexibility offers the football player a greater resistance to muscle injury and a greater range, as well as a greater economy, of muscle movement. It can also relieve muscle tension and muscle soreness, relaxing your muscles and stimulating blood circulation through them. This can aid in faster and more effective recovery from your tough workouts and ball games.

Another important advantage of increased flexibility is psychological. When you're flexible and properly warmed up, you're going to be less likely to hold back, even if subconsciously, when sprinting all out. This is particularly true if you've ever suffered the pain and disability of a pulled muscle from a lack of flexibility.

I know that I have to be completely warmed up and stretched out before any all-out activity, be it a game, a practice, or an off-season training session. I just can't go if I don't feel loose and ready to shift into high gear without fear of muscle pulls due to my muscles not being warm and flexible.

FLEXIBILITY STANDARDS

The majority of flexibility standards are from a physical education perspective rather than a football perspective. In other words, most tests and measurements for flexibility have been done in gym classes rather than on the football field. So there are not really any flexibility measurements to gauge how you stack up against other players. Additionally, the idea behind flexibility training is to improve your range of motion for better performance rather than to meet a particular standard.

DEGREE OF FLEXIBILITY IMPROVEMENT

It is difficult to measure flexibility improvement in comparative terms. This is due not only to the problems with flexibility standards, but also because there is no readily measurable starting point in assessing a degree of improvement. If you went from 160 to 200 pounds in weight-lifting, you would have improved by 25 percent. Yet if you went from being able to touch your fingertips to the floor (from a standing position with your knees straight and your feet together) to being able to place your palms flat on the floor, it would be difficult to state the percentage of improvement. Rather, you would be limited to stating that your flexibility improved so many inches for a particular movement.

Yet it is still probably safe to say that most individuals can improve their flexibility to the point that a lack of flexibility is not detrimental to their athletic performance, including injury resistance. It might take a little longer for some people to attain optimal flexibility (and some people have greater flexibility potential than others), but for practical purposes nearly all healthy people can become flexible enough for their sport, including football.

FLEXIBILITY EMPHASIS

Flexibility training has been increasingly emphasized in football circles over recent years. In the NFL, for example, some teams employ flexibility coaches, specialists whose sole task is to develop and maintain flexibility among all of the squad members. On the Colts, our strength and conditioning coach, Tom Zupancic, sees to it that we are well stretched out before any heavy practice activity and of course before every game. Additionally, there has been considerably more emphasis on flexibility at the college, high school, and youth levels of football.

FLEXIBILITY STRENGTH

Flexibility is extremely important if you are on a heavy strength-training program. When you work out for size and strength, your muscle fibers not only become denser due to an increase in circumference, they can also shorten. This shortening can adversely affect your range of muscle motion if you do not simultaneously lengthen, or stretch, your muscles when strengthening them, and this is why I stretch after every strength training session. In fact, the term "muscle-bound," commonly applied to muscular people who lack mobility and/ or coordination, actually means a lack of muscle flexibility. You want to avoid this at all costs by putting in a little overtime on your stretching when you are on any weightlifting program. Remember, strengthening muscles shortens them, and stretching lengthens them.

LIMITS ON FLEXIBILITY

There are limits on just how flexible each individual can become. These limits are apparently the result of heredity, as some people seem to be very loose-jointed naturally and thus have greater flexibility potential. I have always been fairly flexible, for example, able to stretch myself pretty well on most flexibility drills the first time I tried them. Size seems to have something to do with this, as big, heavy guys are usually not as naturally limber as smaller, lighter guys. Yet there are many exceptions, and a big, relatively inflexible guy who consistently stretches can become more flexible than a smaller, naturally flexible guy who does not stretch.

EXCESSIVE FLEXIBILITY

Is there such a thing as too much flexibility? Probably. There are some people who have so much flexibility around certain joints that the affected joint lacks in strength and stability. In the extreme, there are certain medical conditions that cause this hyperflexibility. Although you won't develop one of these conditions through excessive stretching, you can cause yourself some trouble if you stretch your muscles too much in relation to strengthening them. If you do not have enough strength to keep from bending your joints beyond your ability to control them with your muscles, you are more susceptible to injury through your joints popping out of place. So just as you should stretch your muscles as you strengthen them, you should strengthen them as you stretch them. Once again, stretching lengthens your muscles and strength training shortens them. Do both for best results.

FLEXIBILITY EQUIPMENT

Certain gadgets are available that can help your stretching; and you might have seen them advertised in the various martial arts magazines. Some of them are expensive and elaborate, running several hundred dollars or so and coming with cranks to aid you in extending your stretch and gauges to measure your progress. The simpler ones basically amount to a device that you grip while you brace its padded ends against your feet as you sit on the ground with your legs spread wide.

As you bend at the waist and pull yourself toward the ground as you grip it, this gadget will aid you in getting your legs even farther apart. It is priced in the $30 to $35 range as of this writing. You might want to page through some martial arts magazines and check out the various brands.

Other items that are used for stretching drills include benches, bleacher seats, stairs, cyclone fences, and other generally readily accessible things, including a training partner. For practical purposes, these devices are as effective as the commercially available stretching gadgets.

FLEXIBILITY WORKOUT PRINCIPLES

DRESS PROPERLY

As with all of your workout activity, you must dress properly for your flexibility drills. This means wearing loose-fitting workout clothing that is appropriate for the weather.

WARM UP BEFORE STRETCHING

Although flexibility work is considered part of your warm-up routine, you should actually warm up some before you stretch. Your muscles should be warm before you stretch them in any serious manner. If you attempt to stretch when cold, your muscles, ligaments, and tendons are not as pliable, and this can cause slight internal injury even if you stretch slowly. Cold muscles are also harder to stretch, and thus you will not be able to stretch them as far.

You can warm up by light jogging, rope skipping, calisthenics, or any activity that uses the muscles you are going to stretch. You will need to warm up a little more in cold weather, making sure you wear the appropriate clothing to retain your body heat.

If you want a really good flexibility workout, jog for 10 minutes or so in sweats to raise your overall body temperature, and then go through a very thorough stretching routine. While performing such a workout depends upon your time schedule, it's good to do something like this about once a week. I like this kind of a workout the day after a game, feeling that it helps me to get over the soreness.

FOLLOW PROPER STRETCHING MECHANICS

You should observe the following mechanics when you stretch:

Move into and out of the stretched-out position very slowly.
Do not bounce or jerk at any time during the movement.
Do not stretch to the point of intense pain.
Hold the fully stretched-out position for about 10 seconds.
Try to find a reference point to monitor your progress.
Try to stretch just a little farther each session.

STRETCH BEFORE AND AFTER VIGOROUS ACTIVITY

An important consideration for your flexibility program is knowing when to stretch. It is obvious that you should stretch before any vigorous physical activity, such as sprinting. In fact, except in an emergency you should never sprint without being thoroughly warmed up and stretched out. To do otherwise is to invite severe muscle pull, among other injury possibilities.

You should also stretch after any vigorous physical activity, such as running or sprinting, agility drills, weightlifting, or any supplementary sport such as tennis, handball, or basketball. While many people follow a good stretching routine prior to such activities, they neglect to stretch after them as part of a warm-down procedure.

You can stretch after football practice. A good time to do this is following the sprints that often end practice. Be sure to warm down a bit by jogging and walking a few minutes before you stretch after heavy sprinting. This is a practice that I adhere to faithfully.

USE A STRETCHING PARTNER

Some of the upcoming stretching exercises suggest a partner, but you probably won't need one when you begin. Whenever you do use a partner, be sure that you have him apply and release any pressure very slowly, and always do the same when you are helping him. You might practice commands on each other, using terms such as "more," "less," "slower," "stop." Getting your communication down pat will prevent "too much, too soon." I use a stretching partner when I can find one, and we communicate in this fashion.

KEEP RECORDS OF STRETCHING WORKOUTS

You can keep records of your flexibility work to insure that you are doing a good variety of exercises and perhaps to gauge progress. Your record sheet can be set up using the following headings:

Date	Exercise	Apparatus	Approximate time	Comments

FLEXIBILITY EXERCISES

FLEXIBILITY ZONES

By dividing your body into various flexibility zones, you can cover all of your major muscle groups. Here is an example of such a zone classification followed by static flexibility drills for each zone. (Note that certain of the upcoming drills work muscle groups from more than one zone.)

Zone 1: Feet, ankles, calves, Achilles tendon
Zone 2: Quadriceps (front of thigh)
Zone 3: Hamstrings (rear of thigh), buttocks
Zone 4: Groin (inner thigh), hips
Zone 5: Lower back
Zone 6: Abdominals, obliques
Zone 7: Arms, chest, shoulders, lats
Zone 8: Wrists, hands
Zone 9: Neck

ZONE 1 EXERCISES

Pointed Toe Ankle Stretch
Group: Ankles, Achilles tendon
Equipment: Chair or bench
Procedure:

(1) Sit in a chair or on a bench and hold one leg straight out with the knee locked.
(2) Keeping your knee locked, point your toes and move your foot as far as you can to the right and hold.
(3) Next move your foot as far as you can to the left and hold.
(4) Move your foot straight back as far as you can and hold.
(5) Switch legs and repeat.

Comments: This is a simple but effective exercise that also works on your Achilles tendon. I do it on a regular basis.

Standing Ankle Inversion
Group: Ankles, feet
Equipment: Simple support
Procedure:

(1) Stand and support yourself with your hand on a wall or other firm support.
(2) Slowly rotate the instep of one foot up until you are standing on the other edge of your foot and feeling the pressure on the outer portion of your ankles. Hold this position carefully.
(3) Repeat with the other foot.

Comments: If done faithfully, this simple exercise can save you from injury. You should adjust the amount of body weight you place on the exercised ankle until the stretch feels "just right."

Shin and Ankle Stretch
Group: Shin, ankle
Equipment: Chair or bench
Procedure:

(1) Sit in a chair and curl the toes of one foot back underneath so that the "knuckles" of your foot are against the floor.

(2) Keeping this foot on the floor, move your knee forward as you lean back, stretching your shin muscles and your ankles.

(3) Repeat with the other foot.

Comments: This simple exercise hits another neglected muscle group, and consistent practice of it could save you from a sprained ankle. Additionally, the more flexibility you develop with this exercise, the better you'll be able to perform any quadricep stretching exercise and the more flexibility you will realize in that group.

Reverse Calf Stretch

Group: Ankles, calves, Achilles tendon
Equipment: Wall
Procedure:

(1) Stand next to the corner of a wall. Keeping your heels on the ground, place the ball of one foot high against the wall.

(2) Without moving the position of your feet, slowly lean past the wall at its corner, stretching your calves even farther.

(3) Repeat with the other foot.

Comments: This exercise should be done immediately after running, since it stretches out the Achilles tendon and calves, which are shortened by running. It is for this reason that I perform this stretch after each time that I run. A good place to do this stretch is against a curb, and you can also do it off a 4-by-4 board. There are even some boards specially put together at a 90-degree angle for this stretch.

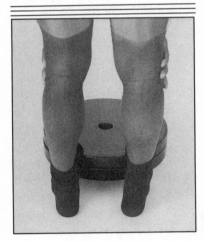

The reverse calf stretch gets your Achilles tendons as well as your calves. This stretch is a must after running.

ZONE 2 EXERCISES

Lying Quad Stretch
Group: Quadriceps
Equipment: None
Procedure:

(1) Sit down on the ground with one foot tucked up under your buttocks and your other leg extended out in front of you.
(2) Keeping both legs stable, slowly lean back until you are lying on your back, concentrating on stretching the muscles in the front of the thigh of the leg that is tucked under.
(3) You may push down on this leg to increase the stretch.
(4) Switch legs and repeat.

The lying quad stretch works your all important quadriceps muscle group. This stretch may also be performed while seated.

Comments: With so much emphasis on stretching the hamstrings, quadriceps flexibility can be neglected. Yet it is very important to stretch this muscle group, because it gets so much work and develops so much strength.

You should do this stretching exercise and its derivatives on a regular basis, particularly after any intense leg workout (sprinting, load sprinting, leg presses, squats, etc.). Since I do a lot of leg work involving my quads, I must do it on a regular basis. You might have to jockey for position some as you do this movement, always trying to gain maximum quadriceps stretch as you lie back. Let the stretch sensations that your quadricep gives you be your guide here.

Seated Quad Stretch
Group: Quadriceps
Equipment: Bench or table
Procedure:

(1) Sit on the edge of the bench or table with your legs draped down toward the floor.
(2) Maintaining this position, bring one foot up and tuck it under your buttocks so that the sole of your foot is against your buttocks.
(3) Lean backward and push down on the leg that is tucked under, stretching your quadriceps muscles (front of thigh). As you advance, have a partner aid you in stretching the leg down even more.
(4) Switch legs and repeat.

Comments: This exercise works the same muscle groups as the lying quad stretch. It has the advantage of your being able to push your quadriceps down as you lean back, making for a greater stretching range. Although with a partner you will be able to stretch even farther, you should advance to this stage gradually.

ZONE 3 EXERCISES

The Straight Stretch
Group: Hamstrings, lower back
Equipment: None
Procedure:

(1) Stand with feet together and knees locked.
(2) Keeping the knees locked, slowly bend at the waist and move your hands toward the ground.

Comments: There are some loose standards for this popular, simple movement, for if you can place your palms directly on the ground, you have good flexibility here. Once you can achieve this, give yourself an additional challenge by trying to do the same thing while standing on a 2-by-4, and then even progress to a 4-by-4.

The straight stretch is simple and effective. Keep your knees locked when doing this movement.

I do this stretching movement regularly, including it in every flexibility workout. I make it a point to always be loose enough to readily place my palms flatly on the ground in this straight stretch movement before I even think about sprinting.

Sit and Reach
Group: Hamstrings, lower back
Equipment: None

Here is the sit and reach stretch done with one leg tucked under. You can also do this movement with both legs out in front of you.

Procedure:

    (1) Sit on the ground with your legs straight out in front of you.
    (2) Bending at the waist, reach your hands as far down between your legs as you can, moving your head toward the ground.
    (3) Try to keep your legs straight at the knee as you do this.

Comments: This flexibility exercise is popular in physical education circles, serving as a major test for flexibility in the areas indicated. This exercise stretches the same basic muscle groups as the straight stretch.

Knee Lock Stretch

Group: Lower hamstrings, upper calves, lower back
Equipment: None
Procedure:

    (1) From a standing position, cross one leg in front of the other.
    (2) Using the front leg to help immobilize the rear leg at the kneecap, and also concentrating on locking the knee of the rear leg, bend at the waist and move the hands as close to the ground as possible.
    (3) Switch legs and repeat.

Comments: This stretch gets the important and neglected area just behind the knee, and it even works on the upper calf muscles a bit. Try to eventually place both palms flat on the ground when in this knee-lock position. Be sure to do this exercise for both sides equally.

The knee lock stretch forces you to do things strictly. It stretches your calves as well as your hamstrings and lower back.

Kneeling Upper Hamstring Stretch

Group: Upper hamstrings, buttocks, hips, lower back
Equipment: None
Procedure:

    (1) Place one knee on the ground adjacent to your opposite foot with about 12 inches of space between them.

    (2) Keeping this knee and your opposite foot stable, bend at the waist and lower your head toward the ground.

    (3) Switch knees and repeat.

Comments: This is a top-notch stretching exercise for your upper hamstring group. When you do it, concentrate on stretching the area where your hamstrings meet your buttocks. Eventually try to place your head on the ground next to your foot.

Standing Upper Hamstring Stretch

Group: Upper hamstrings, buttocks, hips, lower back
Equipment: Fairly high table, bench, or step
Procedure:

    (1) Raise the bottom of one foot up onto the table or bench, and secure it, making sure your leg is bent at the knee.

The standing upper hamstring stretch works your hamstring/ buttocks tie in. This stretch may also be done while kneeling.

(2) Holding on to the device for support, bend at the waist and slowly move your head down toward your raised foot.

(3) Switch legs and repeat.

Comments: This is a variation of the kneeling upper hamstring stretch, and it works your muscles at a little different angle. For variety, you can do this standing upper hamstring stretch utilizing objects of varying heights. I like to place one foot flat up on some bleacher seats, using seats of different heights for variety.

Anchor Stretch

Group: Hamstrings, lower back
Equipment: Very low stationary object
Procedure:

(1) From a standing position, bend forward both at the waist and the knees, and secure the back of your head against a low, stationary object.

(2) Keeping your head against this object, gradually attempt to straighten your knees.

(3) When you reach the position where you can't straighten your knees any more, hold this position.

Comments: You can use a table, bed, bleacher seat, cyclone fence, low bench, or similar object to anchor yourself. The key is to get your head as low as you can, securing it well as you straighten your knees. You will actually be able to see your muscles quiver as you do this drill. It is rather intense, so work into it gradually.

I do this stretching drill regularly, but only after warming up with some other hamstring stretches. I move into it gradually, straightening my knees slowly as I feel the pressure on my hamstrings.

Front Splits

Group: Hamstrings, quadriceps, hips, lower back
Equipment: Wall (optional)
Procedure:

(1) Slide one foot straight forward and the other foot straight backward, lowering your crotch as near to the ground as possible.

(2) Then grab your front foot and push it forward even farther, keeping your rear foot steady.

(3) Once your position has stabilized, bend at the waist and lower your head toward the ground, trying to get it past your knee.

(4) Switch legs and repeat this exercise.

Comments: This is one of the top lower-body stretching exercises there is. If you're doing it on a bench, grab around the bench and slowly pull your trunk down once your legs are completely stretched out. You can also prop your rear leg against a wall and then see how far out you can get your lead leg, gauging your progress.

The front splits is a stretching exercise that I must do on a regular basis. I keep track of my range of motion by stabilizing my rear leg and referencing the distance that I am able to extend my front leg.

Side Splits, or Angle Stretch

Group: Hamstrings, groin, hips, lower back
Equipment: Sturdy bench or bleacher seats helpful
Procedure:

(1) From a standing position, spread your legs as far apart as you can (stand on the bench or bleacher seats, if you're using either one).

(2) Holding this position, bend at the waist and lower your trunk as far down as possible. (Grab on to the bench or bleacher seats and pull yourself down, if you're using either one.)

(3) Constantly work at getting your legs farther apart and your head lower.

Comments: This is a stretching exercise in which equipment can help you. The use of a bench or bleacher seat, as described, will help you in getting your legs farther apart since your feet will more readily slide along its surface than along the ground (especially if you remove your shoes). This same equipment will also aid you in pulling your trunk down since it gives you something to grip on to.

Lying Hamstring Stretch

Group: Hamstrings, hips, lower back
Equipment: None
Procedure:

(1) Lie on your back with your hands at your sides.

(2) Keep one leg on the ground. Raise the other leg up and back as far as you can, keeping it straight and not grabbing it.

(3) Stretch to your maximum for about 10 seconds without touching your leg. Then grab it and pull it back farther for another 10-second stretch. You might anchor your other foot with something at this time.

Comments: This exercise is a favorite out on the football field when done with a partner who pushes your leg back, and we do it with partners on the Colts.

The lying hamstring stretch also works the groin when done as shown. This is another stretch where a partner can help you.

The reason to first do this drill without touching the leg you are stretching is that it works on your own motor control for moving and stretching your muscles. Be sure to take the precautions mentioned earlier if you use a partner.

Vertical Support Hamstring Stretch
Group: Hamstrings, hips, lower back
Equipment: Cyclone fence, bleacher seats, very high rung
Procedure:

(1) From a standing position, place one foot straight out in front of you and then up onto a secured object.
(2) Keeping your foot on this object, jockey for a position of greatest flexibility, if you are able to, by moving back on your other foot and/or bending at the knee.

Comments: You might have to swing your foot to "catch" the support object, so be sure you are particularly warmed up for this exercise. A cyclone fence or a flight of stairs that you can approach from the side are both good objects to use. I like to do this drill when I am working out on my own and have no stretching partner.

Head-to-knee Stretch

Group: Hamstrings (especially lower part), hips, lower back
Equipment: Bench or table
Procedure:

(1) Sit with one leg on the edge of the bench (or table) and straight out in front of you, draping the other leg over the side to the floor.

(2) Keeping your knee locked and the back of your leg flush to the bench, grip the bench and bend at the waist to pull your head down toward an area just inside your locked knee.

Comments: The key to this stretch is to keep your knee locked and completely flush to the bench. This will work the area right behind your knee, where it's easy to lose flexibility. Try to eventually get your head down past your knee, or below the surface of the bench. It is always best to do this drill on some type of bench or table that you can grab in order to pull yourself down, a procedure that makes for a maximum stretch. This is a tough drill and I do it often.

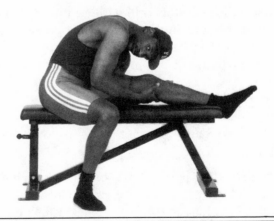

The head-to-knee stretch is done on a bench, and you can grab the bench and slowly pull your upper body down farther.

ZONE 4 EXERCISES

Crucifix Stretch

Group: Groin, hamstrings, hips, lower back
Equipment: Two foot supports and a pulling object or partner
Procedure:

    (1) Sit on your buttocks, spread your legs as far apart as you can, and prop your feet against something to support this position.
    (2) Bend at the waist and grab on to something to pull yourself toward the ground, and/or have your partner push you down.

The crucifix stretch is tough since it works your groin and hamstrings simultaneously. You can have someone slowly push you down from behind or else grab on to something and pull yourself down.

Comments: This is one of the toughest and most effective lower-body flexibility exercises. It works 2 major joints that complement each other. Remember that this is an intense exercise and should be done slowly.

    While it can be hard to find 2 solid objects just the right distance apart for your feet, you can readily improvise your own apparatus. Take a couple of good-sized spikes and pound them into the ground at the desired distance, and then pound in a third spike to form the apex of a triangle, using it to grip with. This is the means by which I first did this drill, and I found that it worked very well for me.

Seated Groin Stretch

Group: Groin, hips
Equipment: Wall, partner
Procedure:

(1) Sit with your back against a wall and your knees out to the side with the soles of your feet together.
(2) Keeping your feet together, place a hand on the inside of each leg and press down.
(3) For best results, have a partner help you push your legs down.

The seated groin stretch hits an important muscle group. For best results, have a partner gently press just inside your knees.

Comments: Not only are many people fairly tight in the groin muscle area, but you really can't get much leverage pushing on your legs from the above-mentioned position. For these reasons, this stretch works best with a partner. If you are really tight in this area, you can have your partner very gently step on the inside of your legs to stretch your groin. It is probably best to have him gradually lower his weight onto you from a position above you, all the while able to grab something and stop his movement should his weight become too much

Standing Hip Stretch
Group: Groin, hips
Equipment: None
Procedure:

(1) Stand with feet somewhat greater than shoulder width apart.
(2) Bending your knees and keeping your back straight, lower your buttocks straight down toward the ground.
(3) Concentrate on stretching your hips and your groin.

Comments: You can conceivably have a partner push you down with this exercise, although this would be a bit awkward to implement. You can do this drill with your feet placed varying distances apart for variety. I like this drill because it is simple and effective.

ZONE 5 EXERCISES

Bridge Up
Group: Lower back, abdomen, chest, shoulders, neck
Equipment: Wall
Procedure:

(1) Lie on your back with your head away from the wall and, with your feet kept firmly on the ground, place your toes up against the wall.
(2) Place your hands just over your shoulders so that your palms are on the floor and your thumbs are inside.
(3) Tilt your head back, arch and raise your hips, and walk your hands in toward the wall.

As you can see, the bridge up stretches more than your lower back muscles. It may take a little time and effort to do this stretch correctly, but the results make it worthwhile.

Comments: This fine all-around stretching exercise should be a regular part of your program. Ultimately, you should chart your progress by measuring how close to the wall you can get. A partner could help you here. I personally find this movement somewhat of a chore to do, but I still do it a couple of days a week.

The Arch Stretch
Group: Abdominals, chest, shoulders, neck
Equipment: High bench, anchor for feet
Procedure:

(1) Sit on a high bench and, with your feet draped down near the floor, anchor them.
(2) Lean backward until your head and arms are hanging down on the side of the bench opposite your feet.
(3) Relax and let your arms hang down toward the floor as loosely as possible.

Comments: This stretch is very similar to the bridge up; the major difference is that it allows your arms and shoulders to hang loosely. (With the bridge up, you must use them to support yourself.) A good place to do this stretch is on bleachers since you can use them to anchor your feet. This is an effective and relaxing stretch.

Trunk Extension
Group: Abdominals, lower back
Equipment: Partner

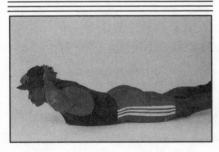

The trunk extension stretches the muscles of your lower back, an often neglected muscle group.

Procedure:

    (1) Lie face down on the floor with your partner sitting on your legs and pressing down on the area just below your buttocks.

    (2) Place your hands behind you at the small of your back, and raise your trunk up off the ground as far as possible.

Comments: This simple but effective exercise works yet another neglected muscle group and should be done at least a few times a week. I make sure to do it this often.

ZONE 6 EXERCISES

Side Bend Stretch
Group: Obliques
Equipment: None

The side bend stretch works your obliques, a neglected muscle group regarding flexibility (and strength) development. Note the rubber cable which adds resistance, enabling you to stretch farther.

Procedure:

(1) Stand with your feet about shoulder width apart and your arms at your sides.
(2) Bend to the side, keeping your knees locked and lowering your arm straight down along your leg and toward the ground.
(3) Repeat to the other side.

Comments: I like to perform this stretch movement with dumbbells, a variation which will be covered in the chapter on strength. Another effective way of doing the side bend stretch is with a rubber cable; simply step on one end of the cable with your foot, grab the other end with your hand, and stretch the cable as you do the movement. The side bend stretch is a simple exercise, and yet it requires concentration. Try to emphasize the stretch of the muscles just below your ribs as you do this movement.

Abdominal Arch
Group: Abdominals, lower back
Equipment: None
Procedure:

(1) Stand with your feet about shoulder width apart.
(2) Arch your back and stretch your abdominals, bringing your elbows behind you.

Comments: This is a simple, effective stretch that primarily works your abdominals. I do it as a matter of course each time I stretch out.

ZONE 7 EXERCISES

Reach Stretch
Group: Major upper body muscles
Equipment: Wall
Procedure:

(1) Stand with the front of your body against a wall.
(2) Rise up on the toes of one foot and reach your opposite arm up as high as possible along the wall.
(3) Switch sides and repeat.

Comments: This drill stretches a number of major muscle groups and is also good for your calves. The way to do it is to find some reference point and try to reach beyond it as you progress. For variety, you can do this stretch with both arms, as well as off of both feet, using one or both arms. You might want to stretch your calf muscles afterward, as this drill contracts them quite strenuously. I like to perform this stretch both before and after strength training sessions.

Hang Stretch

Group: Major upper body muscles
Equipment: Chinning bar
Procedure:

(1) Grab a chinning bar with your palms facing away from you.
(2) Hang your entire body from the chinning bar, striving for maximum stretch.

Comments: This simple yet effective stretching exercise is good for any number of your body's large muscle groups. A good time to do this stretch is right after a weightlifting session.

Shoulder Elevation

Group: Shoulders
Equipment: Yardstick
Procedure:

(1) Lie face down on the ground with your arms straight out in front of you.
(2) Gripping the yardstick and keeping your chin on the floor and your wrists and elbows straight, raise the yardstick as high as you can.

Comments: This is not a very common or impressive stretch movement, but it does stretch your shoulders, which are an often neglected muscle group. You can eventually use a partner in this exercise, having him grip the yardstick and pull it higher than you normally could get it, the result being an increased stretch. Have him go slowly. I do this stretch periodically to be sure that I am maintaining adequate flexibility in my shoulders.

Shoulder Cable Stretch
Group: Shoulders, chest
Equipment: Towel or rubber cord
Procedure:

(1) Grip a towel or rubber cord with your hands somewhat wider than shoulder width. (You might have to experiment to get the correct gripping distance.)

(2) Locking your elbows and keeping your arms absolutely straight, raise the device over your head and behind you.

(3) At the point where you feel tightest, pause and let the stretch take effect.

(4) You may also pause at any other points within the movement.

Comments: This drill is particularly effective if you are doing a lot of upper-body strength work. It can help you to smooth out your throwing motion if you throw the football at all. You can gradually grip the device with your hands closer together for extra resistance, something that I try to do. I also like to do this exercise with a rubber cord.

The shoulder cable stretch can be done with a bicycle inner tube. Be sure to keep your arms straight when doing this movement.

Shoulder Pullover Stretch

Group: Shoulders
Equipment: None
Procedure:

(1) Place your hand under one of your elbows.
(2) Exerting pressure on the elbow, rotate this arm up and straight back in a circular plane.
(3) Finish in a position with your elbow somewhere near the back of your head, and hold this position with your hand still exerting pressure at the elbow.
(4) Repeat with the other arm.

Comments: This stretching exercise gets its name from its simulation of the bent arm pullover motion done with barbells. Like all shoulder stretching exercises, it is a must if you are working your shoulders with weights. This exercise may easily be done in a sloppy and less effective fashion if you do not concentrate on it. I do it regularly, concentrating on good positioning and slow, steady stretching.

Hand Clasp Shoulder Stretch

Group: Shoulders, chest, lats
Equipment: None
Procedure:

(1) Place one arm behind you with your hand in the small of your back.
(2) Bring your other arm straight back over your shoulder and move your hand down toward the area of the small of your back where your first hand is.
(3) Grasp the fingers of your two hands firmly together, and pull, emphasizing a stretch in the shoulder region of the arm that is over your shoulder.
(4) Repeat this drill with the position of your arms switched.

Comments: This is a fine stretching drill for your chest and shoulders, and you can use it both before and after weightlifting. If at first you can't bring your hands close enough together to grasp them, use a towel for the connection. Be sure to emphasize a pull in that shoulder region of the arm that is back over your shoulder.

ZONE 8 EXERCISES

Lateral Fingers Stretch

Group: Hands
Equipment: Flat surface
Procedure:

(1) Lay one hand on a flat surface.
(2) Spread your forefinger and index finger apart and hold, using the fingers of your other hand.
(3) Resist with the fingers of your other hand as you move the forefinger and index finger back together.
(4) Repeat this procedure with your index finger/ring finger and ring finger/little finger.
(5) Switch hands and repeat the process.

Comments: If done faithfully, this little exercise could conceivably save you a dislocated finger. Although it takes only a few minutes a day, it requires intense concentration for maximum benefit. I do this exercise before every practice or training session where I handle the ball.

Fingers Joint Stretch

Group: Hands
Equipment: Flat surface
Procedure:

(1) Lay one hand on a flat surface.
(2) Keeping the hand flush to the surface, separately grab each finger and pull up and back slightly.
(3) As you return each finger back to the table after stretching it, resist it with the hand that originally stretched it.
(4) Repeat with the other hand.

Comments: This is another off-beat exercise that doesn't exactly ring a bell when you say flexibility. Yet doing it just a few minutes a day can help your flexibility and the stretch in your fingers, aiding you particularly if you handle the ball a lot. Thus this is another exercise that I do for ball handling.

Hand Fan Stretch
Group: Hands
Equipment: Flat surface
Procedure:

(1) Lay one hand on a flat surface.
(2) "Fan" the hand as wide as possible, creating maximum distance between all of the fingers and thumb.
(3) Repeat with the other hand.

Comments: The hands are often overlooked as far as flexibility goes, and this simple drill works them well. Yet you have to really concentrate on spreading everything as far as possible if you want to benefit from this exercise. You can use your free hand to help get the maximum spread. I do this exercise whenever I stretch out my hands.

Finger/Wrist Stretch
Group: Hands, wrists
Equipment: Flat surface
Procedure:

(1) Place one hand on a flat surface with the edge of the surface roughly even with the area where your fingers meet your palm.
(2) Keeping pressure on your fingers and hand, bend your wrist so that your forearm moves up and forward.
(3) Repeat with the other hand.

Comments: This exercise stretches your fingers quite well, and it also stretches your wrist to some extent. If you wish to place more stretching pressure on your wrist and less on your fingers, move your hand up so that your wrist is roughly even with the edge of the surface and perform the same motion. I do this exercise 2 or 3 times weekly.

ZONE 9 EXERCISES

Neck Stretch
Group: Neck
Equipment: None (towel optional)

Procedure:

(1) Standing or sitting erect, tilt your head back as far as you can.
(2) Tilt your head straight forward as far as you can.
(3) Turn your head to the right as far as you can.
(4) Turn your head to the left as far as you can.
(5) Move your head straight down toward your right shoulder as far as you can.
(6) Move your head straight down toward your left shoulder as far as you can.

Comments: This series of neck stretches should take about a minute, or about 10 seconds for each one. You can force the issue a little bit with your hands if you're unusually inflexible in your neck, and you can use a towel in step 1.

A strong, flexible neck is a must for football. Chapter 5 presents exercises for building strength in this region.

BALLISTIC STRETCHING

The emphasis so far has been on static stretching, or stretching in which motion is not the main point of the stretch. The idea has been to slowly ease into a position where the muscles are stretched to the maximum desired distance, and then to hold this position. In contrast to this is a method called ballistic stretching, a type in which motion is emphasized throughout the stretch. Ballistic stretching involves moving quickly through the range of stretching motion, and no attempt is made to hold the position of greatest stretch. An example of a ballistic stretch is to swing your leg up into the air as if you were trying to punt a football. A static stretch employing the same muscle group would move the leg up slowly and hold it there in the stretched-out position.

Ballistic stretching can be more dangerous than static stretching. As you approach your "injury point" when stretching, your stretch receptors warn you by giving preliminary pain signals. During a ballistic stretch, you are usually moving your muscles too quickly to stop in response to any pain.

Some advocates of static stretching discourage ballistic stretching altogether. Yet this is impractical, for athletic movements in general consist of ballistic stretching motions. When you throw or kick a ball, or when you run and jump, you are stretching your muscles ballistically. Also, you are giving them an extreme ballistic stretch when you sprint. Thus to refrain from all ballistic stretching would be to refrain from many athletic movements.

Keep the following very important points in mind regarding ballistic stretching:

Always do your ballistic stretching after your static stretching, and only when you are thoroughly warmed up.

Increase the speed and range of motion of your ballistic stretches very gradually. Begin with slow, rhythmical swinging motions and ever so gradually move a little farther and faster.

Do not overdo your ballistic stretching motions in terms of the number of repetitions, for this could cause injury. Remember, they are for the purpose of developing flexibility rather than stamina.

Following are some ballistic stretching movements.

Front-back Leg Swing
Group: Hamstrings, quadriceps, hips
Equipment: Support object (fence, goal post, wall)
Procedure:

(1) Holding on to the support piece for balance, stand on one leg.
(2) Swing the opposite leg straight back, allowing your knee to bend and your foot to go up and touch your buttocks, if comfortable.
(3) Then swing your leg straight forward and up as if punting a football.
(4) Repeat this back-forward cycle in a continuous motion.

Comments: This is an outstanding exercise to do before heavy sprinting, and I like it for this purpose. And yet you must be absolutely sure you are thoroughly warmed up and that you have completed a static stretching sequence before undertaking it. This exercise is very stressful for your quadriceps and hamstrings, so always, always stretch these groups statically beforehand. Also, if you do not feel totally loose or otherwise ready for it, postpone or avoid this exercise.

Once you have started this front-back leg swing drill, you can increase both your speed and your range of motion. You eventually want to do this maneuver as quickly and through as large a range of motion as possible, but it should be months before you attempt such an all-out approach. To begin, perform only 10 or so repetitions with each leg, working up to 15 or 20 as you improve. For variety, you can rise up on your toes as you do the forward swing, eventually even swinging your leg with such force that it carries the opposite foot right off the ground. Again, it takes time to work up to this, so you must be patient.

Straight Side Leg Swing

Group: Groin, hips
Equipment: Support object
Procedure:

(1) Hold on to the support object for balance and stand on one leg.
(2) Swing the opposite leg straight out sideways away from your body, keeping the knee locked.
(3) Bring the leg back in and repeat the cycle.
(4) Switch legs and do the exercise to the opposite side.

Comments: You have to be very careful with this exercise since it works your groin area, a place where many people lack strength and flexibility. Be sure you have done some static stretching exercises for your groin area before performing this particular ballistic exercise technique. Increase your speed and range of motion very slowly with this drill. I do this exercise only after a very thorough warm-up, increasing my speed very, very gradually.

Cross-over Leg Swing

Group: Groin
Equipment: Support object
Procedure:

(1) Hold on to the support object for balance and stand on one leg.
(2) Swing the other leg laterally, in front of the leg you are standing on.
(3) Next swing this leg out sideways away from your body, keeping your knee locked.
(4) Swing the leg back in to the position in front of the leg you are standing on and repeat the cycle.
(5) Switch legs and do the exercise to the opposite side.

Comments: This exercise also works your groin, and the extra maneuver of swinging your leg in front of the one you are standing on gives you a little different angle. When doing this exercise, be sure to increase your speed and motion range very gradually. Also be sure you have done some static stretching for your groin beforehand.

Wood Chopping

Group: Hamstrings, lower back, shoulders, neck
Equipment: None
Procedure:

(1) Stand erect with your feet spread a little wider than your shoulders and with your knees slightly bent.
(2) Bend at the waist, and go down moving your hands toward the ground in a chopping motion.
(3) Raise up by straightening your back when your arms are on the upstroke.
(4) Continue this up-and-down chopping motion cycle.

Comments: This is a multiple joint stretching exercise, good for coordinating flexibility among various muscle groups. Be sure you are warmed up and statically stretched before trying this exercise. As a general rule, gradually try for a greater range of motion rather than for increased speed. When I do this exercise it is at the end of my stretching routine.

Chest/Shoulder Stretch

Group: Chest, shoulders
Equipment: None
Procedure:

(1) From a standing or sitting position, pull your elbows straight back behind you while keeping your forearms perpendicular to your trunk.
(2) Move your elbows back out to the front, touching your fists, and repeat.

Comments: This is a fine exercise for preceding or following a weight workout, especially one using chest and shoulder exercises such as bench press, parallel bar dips, etc., and I use it at such times. You can perform this exercise statically to begin with, and then do several ballistic motions concentrating on a good, even stretch of your chest and shoulder muscles rather than on exercise speed.

Arm Circling
Group: Chest, shoulders
Equipment: None
Procedure:

(1) Hold your arms straight out to the sides.
(2) With your shoulder joint serving as the axis and with your arms kept straight, slowly rotate your arms in a circular fashion.
(3) Continue with this range of rotation for several seconds or so and then vary it, gradually going through several ranges. You may also vary the rotational speed somewhat.
(4) Repeat, with your arms rotating in the opposite direction, also varying the rotational range and speed.

Comments: This simple exercise is good as a warm-up prior to sprinting, throwing, or heavy lifting. While you should rotate your arms at a good clip, do not get carried away with the speed aspects of this drill. I like to do it at slow to moderate speeds.

Throwing Motion
Group: Chest, shoulders
Equipment: None (football optional)
Procedure:

(1) Swing your arm up and back as if throwing a football.
(2) Move your arm forward in a throwing motion.
(3) Without hesitating, let the momentum of your forward throwing motion carry your arm forward, down, around, and back up for a continuous, nonstop throwing action.
(4) Repeat with the other arm.

Comments: This is a fine exercise for anyone who throws the football, and indeed it can be done while holding a football. Since I occasionally throw the football, I do it a few times a week.

Shoulder Stretch Cycle
Group: Chest, shoulders
Equipment: Towel
Procedure:

(1) Grip a towel or rubber cord with your hands somewhat wider than shoulder width. (You may have to experiment to get the correct gripping distance.)

(2) Locking your elbows and keeping your arms absolutely straight, raise the device over your head as far back behind you as you can.

(3) Next bring the device forward and back over your head to the original starting position, again keeping elbows locked and arms straight.

(4) Repeat this back-front, back-front sequence in a continuous cycle.

Comments: This exercise is a ballistic version of the static shoulder stretch exercise, and it's just excellent for flexibility in the shoulder and chest region. You should take care not to do this exercise too quickly, and you can make it harder by gripping the device with your hands closer together. As with the static version, I like to do this exercise with a rubber cord instead of a towel.

P.N.F.

After several months or more of flexibility training, you'll probably reach somewhat of a sticking point, a situation in which your flexibility stops improving. You might want to try something called proprioceptive neuromuscular facilitation, or P.N.F. This is a process that has been around for years, and yet only fairly recently have very many athletes used it.

In its simplest form, P.N.F. works like this. Do a regular static stretch for approximately 10 seconds. Next, perform an isometric contraction (maximum force vs. an object that cannot move) coming back the other way, also for about 10 seconds, and then follow this with yet another stretch. In other words, you have stretched, or lengthened, your muscles in one direction, tried to shorten them with the isometric contraction in the other direction, and then stretched them again in the original direction.

As a concrete example of P.N.F., let's say you are stretching your hamstrings by placing your palms on the floor from a standing position. You hold them there for about 10 seconds, and then you grab on to something for support and hook your ankles under an immovable object—for example, a very heavy barbell—and try to flex your hamstrings for about 10 seconds. You then go back to the original hands-to-floor stretch for 10 seconds to conclude the cycle. You can repeat this sequence several times.

The use of a stretching partner can be very helpful when you perform P.N.F. Your partner can, of course, aid you in achieving the desired stretching range when it is difficult to reach it on your own in certain stretching movements. Then in a procedure specific to P.N.F., your partner can provide the resistance in the isometric contraction phase of the P.N.F. movement. This latter advantage is significant, for with many stretches it is difficult to apply suitable isometric resistance in a direction opposite to that of the stretch.

If you perform P.N.F. properly, you should be able to stretch farther on your second stretching movement, or the one that follows isometric contraction. Yet you must be cautious, for the P.N.F. procedure interferes with your stretch reflex, rendering you less sensitive to whether you might be stretching too far. Accordingly, it must again be emphasized that P.N.F. is for the advanced stretcher who has reached a sticking point.

I work P.N.F. into about every other stretching routine, and I am convinced that it significantly aids both my strength and flexibility.

FLEXIBILITY WORKOUT SCHEDULE

You cannot include each and every one of these exercises whenever you stretch. Yet you should try to include exercises from each group at least a couple of times a week.

One strategy is to concentrate on stretching your lowest extremities (Zone 1), your quadriceps (Zone 2), your hamstrings (Zone 3), and to some extent your arms, chest, and shoulders (Zone 7) prior to running and/or any quickness/agility work, and then hit these groups again lightly after running while you also do exercises from each of the other 5 zones. This works out neatly, since you can catch exercises from the other zones while you walk it off after your running workout.

Another way you can work your stretch routine is by integrating it with your strength training. Stretch those same muscle groups that you are working that day, going with a light stretch before your strength workout and a heavier stretch after. This practice will keep you flexible as you gain strength, a desirable combination.

Here are the two mentioned flexibility workout strategies in summarized form:

Workout	Pre-workout Stretch	Post-workout Stretch
All running, quickness/ agility	Heavy stretch of muscle groups used (zones 1, 2, 3, and 7)	Light stretch of muscle groups used
Strength	Light stretch of muscle groups used (all muscles worked)	Heavy stretch of muscle groups used

FINAL WORD ON FLEXIBILITY

Flexibility training lacks the glamour of strength training and speed training. While the numbers for bench press and 40-yard dash are often on the minds of many football players, few are as concerned with their degree of flexibility. Nonetheless, in its own right flexibility is as important as strength or speed.

The good thing about flexibility is that is does not take grueling hours in the weight room or on the field to develop. It can be achieved with 20-minute workouts done during several full weekly workouts. As a football player, you should take the time to get flexible as part of your total football fitness routine. Such a practice will definitely help you.

3

A Game of Movement: Developing Quickness and Agility

"Football is a quickness game."

Bud Wilkinson, former head football coach, University of Oklahoma

AN OVERVIEW OF QUICKNESS/AGILITY

QUICKNESS/AGILITY DEFINED

Although they are related to each other, quickness and agility are actually different characteristics. Quickness may be thought of as speed of movement over very short distances, and agility may be defined as the ability to quickly and precisely change direction or body position. An individual who is agile is also quick with regard to the specific change of body direction he is implementing, and this same individual is also usually at least fairly quick in the strict sense of the word.

A quick person is usually agile, and yet there are some exceptions. There have been extremely fast football players who were not very agile. Because these people had to move well over the first 5 to 10 yards in order to have good dash times, they were examples of "pure quickness" without necessarily having a lot of agility.

Coaches use the term "football quickness," something that top players at all levels usually have in abundance. Football quickness is the ability to react and move very quickly in game situations. It involves not only "pure" quickness/agility but also visual recognition of football stimuli, as well as some football technique. Other things being equal, improvement in "pure" quickness/agility will result in better football quickness.

IMPORTANCE OF QUICKNESS/AGILITY

Good quickness/agility will obviously help you make the play in football, and at any position. Less obvious is the fact that it will aid you in resisting injury. The more quickness/agility you have, the more able you will be to apply the proper football technique as a protective mechanism. Good agility will also aid you in injury prevention because your body will be conditioned to quick changes of direction and will thus be less likely to be injured when you make such changes.

As with all other physical traits, quickness/agility can aid you psychologically. If you're quick and agile and you know it, you're going to have more confidence that you can play the game. You're also going to be less likely to "tense up" when performing any football activity. Your body is trained to move fluently and economically in all football situations, regardless of anything else.

All football players need quickness/agility regardless of position. It is as important a trait for an offensive center as for a defensive cornerback. The difference is that an offensive center and defensive cornerback need different types of quickness/agility. Each exercises different football movements requiring quickness/agility specific to their position.

MEASUREMENT OF QUICKNESS/AGILITY

Quickness/agility measurement is done through a time factor. Yet before timing any movement, certain considerations must apply. To begin, the actual movement must be thoroughly and precisely described in terms of its technique. All dimensions and distances involved must be given, and it must be stated at exactly which points the stopwatch starts and stops.

QUICKNESS/AGILITY STANDARDS

There are relatively few absolute standards for quickness/agility, largely because so many different drills exist that none have been singled out as commonly accepted for measurement standards. Thus it is not as meaningful to attach a number to a quickness/agility drill as it is to a sprint time or a weight lifted in a certain manner.

Some of the more commonly used drills do have time standards, and they will be referred to during the drill descriptions. Additionally, you can be timed over a number of drills, and work to beat your own times. Be sure to follow the correct timing procedures, as were stated, and time yourself both ways (that is, left and right, clockwise and counterclockwise), when applicable.

DEGREE OF QUICKNESS/AGILITY IMPROVEMENT

It is possible to improve your quickness/agility significantly if you work at it. When he coached at Alabama, the late Paul "Bear" Bryant felt that he could teach a player to have "quick feet." If you ever watched his teams play, you probably noticed that they definitely possessed this trait, and yet probably not all of his players possessed such quickness when they first came to him.

Quickness/agility can be developed more than sprinting speed, mainly because more "learning" is involved. A sprint involves a basically straight-ahead motion that is repeated over and over. Since this consistent sprinting motion pattern uses essentially the same groups of motor units (nerves plus muscle fibers), relatively few new muscle fibers are recruited to "learn" new motion patterns, and improvement is relatively less. By contrast, quickness/agility movements involve motion in many directions and use different groups of motor units. These movements involve the recruiting of new muscle fibers that learn these new motion patterns, and improvement results as this learning occurs.

Quickness/agility cannot be improved as much as strength or stamina. Although it is a trait that involves muscle learning, it nonetheless ultimately depends upon your speed of muscle movement. It is generally accepted that muscle speed can be developed to a lesser extent than muscle strength or stamina. (Chapter 4 covers this in more detail.)

FACTORS AFFECTING QUICKNESS/AGILITY DEVELOPMENT

Certain factors affect the development of quickness/agility, namely, flexibility, strength, and power. Flexibility can aid quickness/agility by allowing for greater ease of muscle movement (as covered in the last chapter), and a lack of flexibility can adversely affect quickness/agility. Strength can also aid quickness/agility development since stronger muscles provide a stabilizing influence that aids in changing directions more quickly. In any quickness/agility movement, you need to both brake your body's momentum in one direction and quickly change it to another direction. Stronger, more stable muscles will aid you in a quicker and more efficient braking action and in the reapplication of force in another direction.

The development of muscular power will aid your quickness (and thus perhaps your agility). Power is the rate at which work is done, and in any short, quick movement you are doing a relatively great amount of work per unit of time. Power development is particularly helpful in developing a quick start in a straight-ahead sprint.

Activities such as handball, racquetball, basketball, tennis, and volleyball, among others, will help to develop quickness/agility. Racquetball and handball are the best of these, and handball is particularly good. These games involve fast lateral movements with quick changes of direction, just as in football, and I personally enjoy playing them.

QUICKNESS/AGILITY WORKOUT PRINCIPLES

DRESS PROPERLY

Proper dress is needed for quickness/agility work. Basically, you should dress for your quickness/agility work as you would for a sprint workout on the same surface.

WARM UP THOROUGHLY

You should warm up properly before you begin your quickness/agility work. Start with a few minutes of jogging, stretch out well, take a few "runs" of gradually increased speed, and then ease into some basic light drill. As you get warm, move to your more taxing quickness/agility work.

BEGIN WITH GENERAL DRILLS

Essentially, you can begin your quickness/agility work with several of the general drills, and then perform those drills specific to your position. Yet always check with your coach, for if he is going to be emphasizing certain drills, you should work on them. This is especially true if certain drills are going to be timed.

PERFORM BEFORE WEIGHTS OR CONDITIONING

It is probably best to do any workout for quickness/agility before any heavy weight training or conditioning workout, and either before or after any workout for pure speed development. If you consider yourself fairly quick and agile but short on sprinting speed, do your sprinting first. If you are fairly fast but not so quick and/or agile, do your quickness/agility first. I'll go into more detail on how to integrate your various workouts in chapter 7.

WORK AT LEAST TWICE WEEKLY

Ordinarily you want to work on your quickness/agility at least twice a week during the off season, increasing this to 3 to 4 workouts weekly the last 6 to 8 weeks before the start of practice. Once practice begins, your coach will direct your quickness/agility work as part of the overall practice scheme. If you feel you are not getting enough drill, or if your coach is not including some particular drill that you know works for you, try to get in 1 or 2 brief sessions of such drill weekly. An extra 10 minutes a day can do it for you. Again, chapter 7 will go into more scheduling details.

SIMULATE FOOTBALL CONDITIONS

It's a good idea to do your quickness/agility work under conditions that simulate football playing as closely as possible. While it is not practical to dress in full football gear in the off season, you should wear football shoes and work out on a surface simulating the one you practice on, if the weather permits. During inclement weather, you may be forced to do your drills indoors, wearing shoes appropriate for the surface.

KEEP RECORDS OF QUICKNESS/AGILITY WORKOUTS

It is important to record all of the quickness/agility work that you do. This is necessary for overall workout planning, and particularly important when timing any drills. Your record sheet can be set up with the following headings:

Date   **Location**   **Exercise**   **Sets**   **Comments**

QUICKNESS/AGILITY DRILLS

Some quickness/agility drills are general, and some are more oriented to specific positions. The general drills are of value to everyone, and the position-specific drills are most valuable to those playing those positions.

You will need a couple dozen rubber or plastic cones (commonly called pylons) or similar objects for your quickness/agility work. Check with your coach to see if you can borrow some. If you can't, ask him where you can purchase them. If you are unable to secure these cones, use any bright, soft, upright objects of the same approximate size.

GENERAL QUICKNESS/AGILITY DRILLS

Following are general quickness/agility drills that apply to all football players. Of the 10 drills listed, 5 contain precisely laid-out diagrams, with time standards so that you can evaluate your performance. Observe the following legend for these drills:

———————————	forward
— — — — — —	backward
= = = = = =	lateral
O	cone
⊗	player

Cross-over Drill

Application: All players
Procedure:

(1) Line up in a good football ready position.
(2) Move sideways by stepping straight out laterally with your lead leg and then crossing your other leg in front of and past it.
(3) Continue this sideways movement of lead-step, cross-over step, lead-step, cross-over step, etc., for 10 to 20 yards.
(4) Perform the drill going back the other way.

Comments: This is a good general quickness/agility drill with some carry-over properties to game movements. It also serves as a good warm-up for more taxing drills, and I use it for this purpose.

Rope Drills

Application: All players

Procedure: Perform any of the following drills with the ropes.

(1) Run them hitting every other square, with left foot staying in left row and right foot in right row.

(2) Run them hitting every square, with left foot in left row and right foot in right row.

(3) Run them hitting every square, staying in 1 row with 2 steps taken in each square.

(4) Run them sideways, staying in 1 row; this requires 2 steps in each square.

(5) Run them sideways, hitting both rows; the pattern could be over-back-over-up, over-back-over-up, and so on.

(6) Jump them, hitting every other square diagonally.

(7) Jump them, hitting every square in the same row.

(8) Jump them, hitting every square in both rows.

(9) Jump them sideways, staying in one row.

(10) Jump them sideways, hitting every square in the pattern over-back-over-up, over-back-over-up, and so on.

Comments: These drills are done with training ropes suspended on a frame about 30 feet by 6 feet. The ropes are about a foot off the ground, and they tie onto the frame so that they form two rows of squares, each about 3 feet by 3 feet.

Rope drills are a lot of fun and quite popular in football practice sessions, and I enjoy them myself. They act as a good developer of fundamental quickness/agility as they "guide" your movement over every step. You can add a little extra challenge to your rope drills by raising the frame up on blocks of wood. If you do not have access to training ropes, you can stack used tires on top of one another.

Forward Roll (Somersault)

Application: All players

Procedure:

(1) Perform a forward roll, moving into the drill slowly and making sure your chin is tucked in.

(2) Come out of the roll on your feet.

(3) Repeat the roll several times.

(4) As you gain skill, increase the speed of your roll.

Comments: This simple exercise aids you in developing the body control agility to fall properly. Every year, many players are hurt because they do not fall the correct way; these injuries could have been prevented with just a little practice in falling. So if you repeat this drill just a few times each week, you can improve your falling skills and decrease your chances of injury. I like to do this drill with a football, particularly in pre-season training.

Shoulder Roll
Application: All players
Procedure:

    (1) Assume a 3- or 4-point stance, and perform a shoulder roll, being sure to hit the ground.
    (2) Come out of the roll back in your stance.
    (3) Repeat the roll several times.
    (4) Repeat several times back in the other direction.
    (5) As you gain skill, very gradually and slightly increase the speed of your roll.

Comments: This is another drill that teaches you how to control your body when you hit the ground. You should do it a few times a week, as it may someday prevent an injury. As with the forward roll, I like it with a football.

Circle Drills
Application: All players
Procedure:

    (1) Set up about 12 cones in a circle.
    (2) Perform any number of drills utilizing this circle, including:
        (a) sprinting the circle forward.
        (b) sprinting the circle backward.
        (c) sprinting the circle forward, weaving in and out between the cones.
        (d) sprinting the circle backward, weaving in and out between the cones.
        (e) weaving in and out of the cones while keeping your front squared to the center of the circle.
        (f) weaving in and out of the cones while keeping your back squared to the center of the circle.

    (g) sprinting half the circle forward, cutting across the middle of the circle backward, and sprinting the other half of the circle forward.

    (h) sprinting half the circle backward, cutting across the middle forward, and sprinting the other half backward.

Comments: You can use your imagination and make up your own circle drills. There are literally dozens of possibilities. Be sure your circle is the exact same size and has the same distance between the cones if timing any drill.

Boomerang Run (see Fig. 3–1)

Application: All players

Procedure:

    (1) Set up the cones as shown, with a uniform 5 yards between them.

    (2) Sprint to and around the far cone (#2) and then sprint back to the middle cone (#3).

    (3) Sprint around the middle cone (#3) and then sprint to cone #4.

    (4) Sprint around #4 and then sprint back to and around cone #5.

    (5) Sprint from cone #5 back to and around the middle cone (#3).

    (6) Sprint from the middle cone back to the finish line.

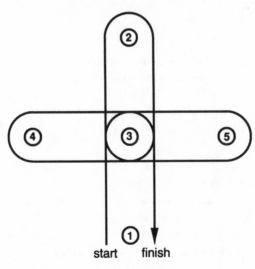

Fig. 3-1

Comments: This drill has a fairly complicated pattern, so you might go through it several times at less than full speed. Once you do run it all out, a time of 11.5 or less is good, and 10.9 or less is outstanding. It is a good drill to do indoors over the winter months.

Shuttle Run (see Fig. 3–2)

Application: All players
Procedure:

   (1) Set up 4 cones, as shown.
   (2) With your back to the cones, shuffle laterally from the first cone to the second.
   (3) Backpedal from the second cone to the third.
   (4) Sprint from the third cone to the first.
   (5) Backpedal from the first cone to the fourth.
   (6) Sprint from the fourth cone to the second.
   (7) Shuffle laterally from the second cone to the first to finish.

Comments: This drill incorporates lateral movement, backward movement, and changes of direction, making it an excellent all around drill. A time of 11.5 or less is good, 11.0 or less is excellent, and 10.7 or less is truly outstanding. It is another drill that you can do indoors.

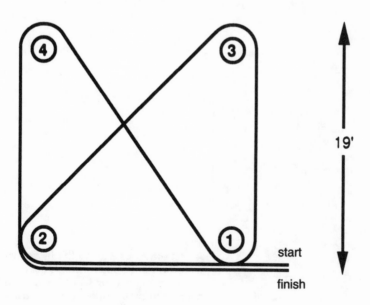

Fig. 3-2

Lateral Run (see Fig. 3–3)

Application: All players
Procedure:

(1) Sprint the pattern shown, being sure to touch each outside line with your foot.
(2) Run the drill in the opposite direction.

Comments: A time of 4.4 is good for this drill, and 4.2 or less is excellent.

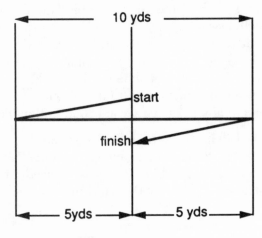

10 yds

start

finish

5yds   5 yds

Fig. 3-3

An effective way to do the lateral run is with the item shown, which keeps you from crossing your feet. The device is called the sidewinder, and it is available from Speed City, Inc.

Maze Run (see Fig. 3–4)

Application: All players
Procedure:

(1) Place 5 cones 5 yards apart as shown.
(2) Sprint the indicated pattern.
(3) Run the drill the opposite way, performing the same pattern but starting at "finish" and finishing at "start."

Comments: A time of 12 seconds is good for this drill, and 11.5 seconds or less is outstanding. Since the pattern for this drill is fairly complicated, you might want to first go through it several times at less than full speed.

start   finish

Fig. 3-4

Illinois Agility (see Fig. 3–5)

Application: All players
Procedure:

(1) Set up 4 cones as shown.
(2) Sprint from the starting point to the far cone.
(3) Circle the cone, and weave through the cones to the opposite far cone.

(4) Circle this cone, and weave through the cones back to the original far cone.
(5) Circle this cone, and sprint to the finish.
(6) Repeat the drill in the other direction.

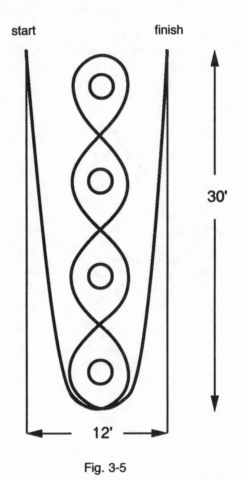

Fig. 3-5

Comments: A time of 14 seconds or less is very good for this drill, and 13.8 seconds or less is exceptional.

OFFENSIVE LINEMAN QUICKNESS/AGILITY DRILLS

The following quickness/agility drills are particularly applicable for offensive linemen.

Lineman's Pull (see Fig. 3–6)

Application: Offensive linemen
Procedure:

(1) Line up the cones in the approximate pattern shown, with about 5 yards between cones.
(2) From a good lineman's stance, sprint the indicated pattern.
(3) Repeat the drill in the other direction.

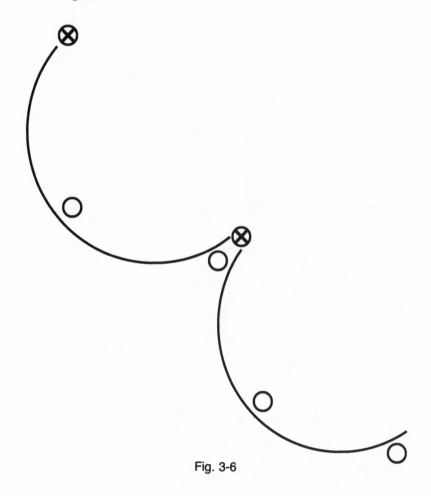

Fig. 3-6

Comments: This drill simulates a lineman pulling to lead interference. You can set up several groups of cones, simply extending the pattern shown, to get repeat action on it. Be sure to run it both to the left and to the right, regardless of which side of center you play on.

Pass Block Shuffle (see Fig. 3–7)

Application: Offensive linemen
Procedure:

(1) Set up the cones in an arc pattern, as shown, with about a 5-yard distance between the outside cones.
(2) Shuffle back and forth between the outside cones, keeping square and not crossing your feet.

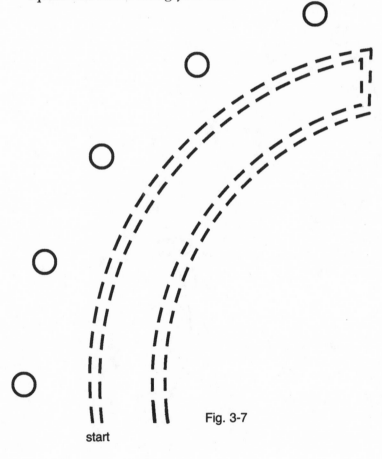

Fig. 3-7

start

Comments: This drill simulates the lateral, circular movement required in pass blocking. You should vary the pattern considerably for best results, always keeping the same basic arc shape. Once you get some practice on this drill, you can have someone shout "out," in which case you break your shuffle and sprint past the far cone in a simulated effort to catch an escaped pass rusher. I do this drill myself because at times I have to pass block.

Out and Back

Application: Offensive linemen
Procedure:

(1) From an offensive lineman's stance, fire out for about 4 steps, or 5 yards.
(2) Upon hitting the fourth step, immediately recoil back to your lineman's stance and repeat.
(3) Repeat the drill several times.

Comments: This drill teaches you agility out of a stance. By practicing it, you will develop a sense of balance and movement from a down stance.

Stance to Stance

Application: Offensive linemen (also defensive linemen)
Procedure:

(1) Place 2 cones 5 to 10 feet apart.
(2) Assuming a good lineman's stance, move laterally from your stance for 5 to 10 feet and very quickly assume your stance again.
(3) Move back laterally from your stance in the other direction for the same 5 or 10 feet and begin the drill over.
(4) Continue this pattern of stance–lateral movement–stance–opposite direction lateral movement, for several repetitions.

Comments: This drill teaches you an agile stance, from which you can move laterally to trap block or pull. You do not need to shuffle when moving laterally. Rather, move the way that results in the most speed for you.

BALL-CARRYING DRILLS

Next are some drills that apply to anyone who carries the football. They mainly apply to offensive backs, but are also of value to tight ends, wide receivers, and punt and kickoff returners. They are even valuable for linebackers and defensive backs, and to anyone else who carries the ball after a fumble or interception.

Integrated Weave (see Fig. 3–8)
Application: Ball carriers
Procedure:

(1) Set up the cones in the approximate pattern shown.
(2) Sprint in and out between the cones while carrying a football.
(3) Repeat while carrying the ball in the opposite arm.

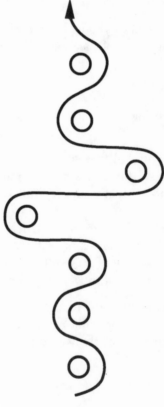

Fig. 3-8

Comments: There are many variations to this integrated pattern, and you can use your imagination to practice them. I work on this drill consistently, especially in the pre-season.

Offset Weave (see Fig. 3–9)
Application: Ball carriers
Procedure:

(1) Set up the cones as shown, with any reasonable spacing between them.
(2) Sprint in and out between the cones while carrying a football.
(3) Repeat while carrying the ball in the opposite arm.

Comments: You can use a wide variety of cone placements and spacings for this drill. If you time it and later compare times, make sure you use the exact same setup. This is another drill that I have often used.

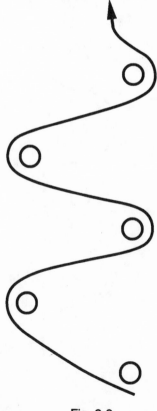

Fig. 3-9

In-line Weave (see Fig. 3–10)

Application: Ball carriers
Procedure:

(1) Set up the cones as shown, with any reasonable spacing between them.
(2) Sprint in and out between the cones while carrying a football.
(3) Repeat while carrying the ball in the opposite arm.

Comments: Here again, you can use a wide variety of cone placements and spacings while carrying the football.

Fig. 3-10

Lateral Stepping

Application: Ball carriers

Procedure:

(1) Carrying a football, sprint straight ahead for 4 steps.
(2) Move laterally off the fifth step.
(3) Sprint straight ahead for 4 more steps.
(4) Move laterally off the fifth step, in a direction opposite to the original lateral movement.
(5) Continue this step-step-step-step-over, step-step-step-step-over sequence for about 20 to 30 yards.
(6) Repeat while carrying the ball in the opposite arm.

Comments: This drill will aid you in developing quick lateral movements as a ball carrier. You can do this drill with a "barrier" that you must cross when you make your lateral movement. You can use a rope, aligning it a couple of feet away from a yard-line marker and increasing this distance as you gain skill. You can also vary the number of steps you take before you move laterally. I like to do this drill as part of my warm-up before practice.

Circle Sweep and Weave (see Fig. 3–11)

Application: Ball carriers

Procedure:

(1) Set up the cones as shown, with any reasonable spacing between them.
(2) Sprint the pattern shown, switching the ball as you change directions.

Comments: You can set things up so that you have 2 or 3 sweeps in each direction over 1 repetition of the drill. You can vary the arc and the length of each sweep. Carry the ball in your right arm when sweeping right and in your left arm when sweeping left. This is another drill that I rely on, especially in the summer months preceding training camp.

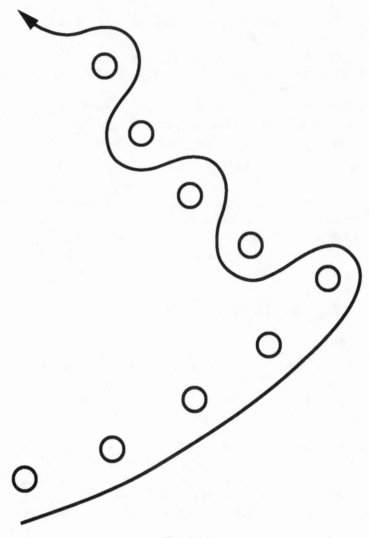

Fig. 3-11

RECEIVER QUICKNESS/AGILITY DRILLS

The following drills are for wide receivers and tight ends. They may also be run by offensive backs with some adjustments.

Head Swivel
Application: Pass receivers
Procedure:

    (1) Work up to a controlled sprint, preferably along a straight line.
    (2) While making sure you maintain your speed and continuing to run in a straight line, practice turning your head from side to side.
    (3) Eventually work up to a full-speed sprint when performing this drill.

Comments: A major problem of pass receivers is twisting the body too much in an attempt to see the ball in flight. This excessive twisting has a slowing effect, and as a result passes that could possibly be caught are sometimes not even reached. To counteract this twisting tendency, this drill should be performed with care taken to turn the head only. A good place to do the drill is on the yard-line markers that extend across the field.

Up and Over (see Fig. 3–12)
Application: Pass receivers
Procedure:

    (1) Set up the cones as shown, with 8 to 10 yards between them.
    (2) From the appropriate pass receiver stance, sprint up for about 8 or 10 yards, over for 8 or 10, up for 8 or 10, over the opposite way for 8 or 10, and so on.

Comments: This basic movement is part of some pass receiving patterns, and it should be mastered. The spacing of the cones can vary.

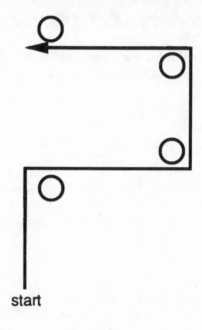

Fig. 3-12

Z Movement (see Fig. 3–13)

Application: Pass receivers
Procedure:

(1) Set up the cones as shown, with 8 to 10 yards between them.
(2) From the appropriate pass receiver stance, run the Z pattern as indicated.

Comments: This is another basic movement that should be learned. Over each phase of it, you can practice looking over your shoulder at a fixed object. Vary the angles and the distance between cones for best results.

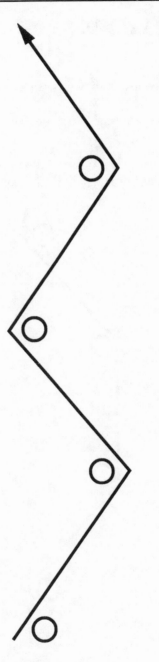

Fig. 3-13

Up and Slant (see Fig. 3–14)

Application: Receivers
Procedure:

(1) Set up the cones as shown, with about 8 to 10 yards between them.
(2) From the appropriate pass receiver stance, run the pattern indicated.

Comments: This up-and-slant movement is yet another basic move that is part of some complete routes. Vary the cone spacing and angles for best results.

start

Fig. 3-14

Complete Pass Routes

Application: Pass receivers
Procedure:

(1) Line up in a 3-point stance and practice running various complete pass routes.

(2) Practice running these routes from both sides of center, taking your stance with your head turned in toward the center if you are a wide receiver.

Comments: One of the greatest assets a receiver can have is the ability to run precise pass routes. So many receivers have good speed and good hands but run their routes in a sloppy manner. Consistent, exacting practice on running them correctly is necessary to keep this sloppiness from occurring.

The routes that you practice and the specific techniques for each one should depend upon what your coach emphasizes. You might go to him and ask which routes to emphasize, as well as the particulars of each route. Try to get him to diagram each route on paper, showing the actual steps to take and specifying where fakes are to be made. Some of the routes he might diagram, including combinations and variations, are:

Hook	Flag
Curl	Drag
Quick out	Out and up
Slant in	Z-out
Post	Z-in

Training Tips: Mark off your routes by placing a cone or some other object at the point of each step. Practice them diligently this way, and they will become second nature to you.

Do not have anyone throw you the football when first learning your routes. Too many receivers concentrate so much on catching the football that they never learn to run routes correctly.

Once you are running your routes sharply and catching the ball well, you can set up some cones to practice ball-carrying cuts, as covered in the section on drills for ball carriers. You can first practice these drills separately and then integrate them with your pass routes, placing them on the tail end of your routes.

DEFENSIVE LINEMAN/LINEBACKER QUICKNESS/AGILITY DRILLS

The following quickness/agility drills are basically of value for defensive linemen and linebackers, although they have some application for all football players.

Play the Piano (see Fig. 3–15)

Application: Defensive linemen, linebackers
Procedure:

(1) Set up the 2 cones as shown.
(2) Shuffle back and forth between the cones, squaring your shoulders and making sure you do not cross your feet.

Comments: This is a basic but effective drill that simulates lateral movement along the line of scrimmage. It can be started from a defensive lineman's stance. An excellent way of doing this drill is with a device called the Sidewinder, a rubber shock cord with its ends attached to each of your ankles. The Sidewinder keeps you from crossing your feet when "playing the piano," and it simultaneously strengthens the all-important abductor muscles as you work against its resistance. It is available from Speed City, Inc., P.O. Box 1059, Portland, Oregon.

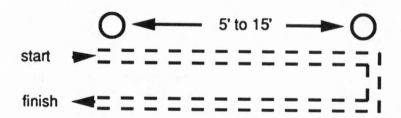

start

finish

5' to 15'

Fig. 3-15

Over and Out (see Fig. 3–16)

Application: Defensive linemen, linebackers
Procedure:

(1) Set up a number of cones in a straight line, as shown.
(2) Shuffle laterally over the first 10 feet, squaring your shoulders and not crossing your feet.
(3) Turn and sprint the next 20 feet.
(4) Continue this shuffle 10–sprint 20 pattern the entire drill.
(5) Repeat the drill in the opposite direction.

Comments: This drill simulates the defensive lineman "playing the piano" along the line of scrimmage and then breaking into a pursuit sprint. Doing it correctly requires concentration since the shuffle and sprint portions are each done over stipulated distances. The number of cones and the distances between them can be varied, yet the sprint distance should remain greater than the shuffle distance.

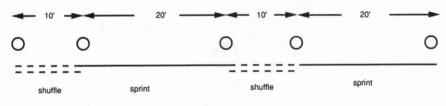

Fig. 3-16

Over and Up (see Fig. 3–17)

Application: Defensive linemen, linebackers
Procedure:

(1) Set up the cones as shown with about 10 feet between them horizontally and 10 feet vertically.
(2) Shuffle laterally over the first 10 feet, squaring your shoulders and not crossing your feet.
(3) Cut up between the first pair of cones, moving forward on through the second pair of cones.

(4) Continue to shuffle laterally after passing through the second pair of cones, maintaining this over/up pattern throughout the drill.

(5) Rearrange the cones and repeat the drill in the other direction.

Comments: This drill is comparable to over and out, with the exception that the sprint portion is up instead of out. Notice that the sprint portion is shorter here since a lineman usually sprints less across the line of scrimmage than he does laterally. For variety, the "up," or sprint, portion can be done at various angles.

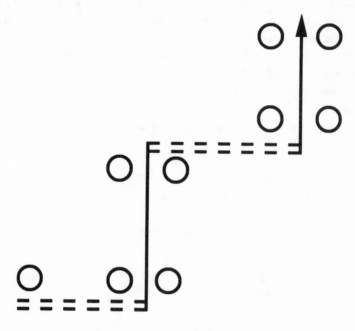

Fig. 3-17

Circle Pass Rush Drill (see Fig. 3–18)
Application: Defensive linemen, linebackers
Procedure:

(1) Set up the cones in a circle with about a 10-yard diameter and place a cone in the middle.

(2) From a defensive lineman's or linebacker's stance, sprint clockwise around the outside of the circle.

(3) At 90 degrees, cut into the circle and sprint toward the cone in the center, tagging it.

(4) Continue sprinting to the other side of the circle.

(5) Upon reaching the outside of the circle, sprint counterclockwise and cut back into the circle at 90 degrees.

(6) Sprint toward the cone in the center, tag it, and continue to sprint to the other side of the circle.

(7) Repeat the drill beginning in a counterclockwise direction.

Comments: This is essentially a pass-rush drill, with the center cone simulating the quarterback. This is a good drill to do with a partner, as one of you can sprint the circle and the other can yell "cut," in which case you react by cutting into the circle to the cone in the center.

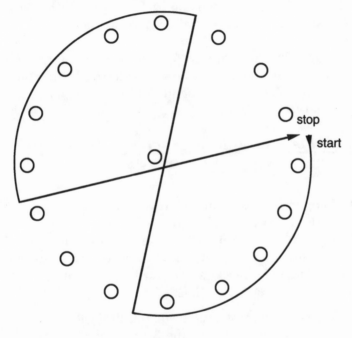

Fig. 3-18

LINEBACKER/DEFENSIVE BACKS QUICKNESS/AGILITY DRILLS

The following drills apply basically to linebackers and defensive backs, with some application to all football players.

Backward Sprinting

Application: Linebackers, defensive backs
Procedure:

(1) Line up in upright defensive stance; you might check with your coach as to the stance he prefers you to use.
(2) Sprint backward at full speed for 20 yards, staying on the balls of your feet.

Comments: For linebackers and defensive backs, backward sprinting speed is perhaps as important as forward sprinting speed, at least over short distances. A time of 3.0 or less is excellent for 20 yards, and 3.1 or 3.2 is good. You can improve your time on this drill since it is a new activity for your muscles, and they will perform it better as they adjust to it. Although as a running back I seldom sprint backward in a game, I still enjoy this drill and do it on occasion.

Training Tips: Just for fun, start 5 or so yards ahead of your training partner and sprint backward as he sprints forward. Race for 25 to 30 yards or any distance that is competitive, based on your abilities. Switch positions and race again.

Backward/Forward Sprinting (see Fig. 3–19 to 3–21)

Application: Linebackers, defensive backs
Procedure:

(1) Line up in an upright defensive stance.
(2) Sprint backward for 5 to 10 yards.
(3) Upon reaching a pre-established marker (such as a cone or yard line), immediately sprint forward for 5 to 10 yards.
(4) Continue this backward/forward movement for 2 to 3 sequences in each direction.

Comments: For variety, you can begin this drill with a forward sprint. You should probably emphasize the 5- to 10-yard distance since the idea is to learn to change from one direction to the other. This is a good drill to time since it is so straightforward.

Training Tips: For variety, practice this same backward/forward movement from different angles. You can sprint backward at an angle and forward straight, backward straight and forward at an angle, and both

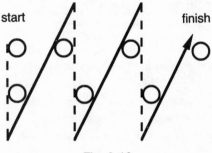

Fig. 3-19

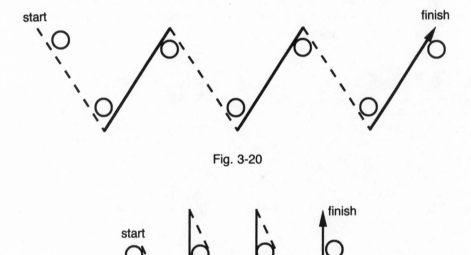

Fig. 3-20

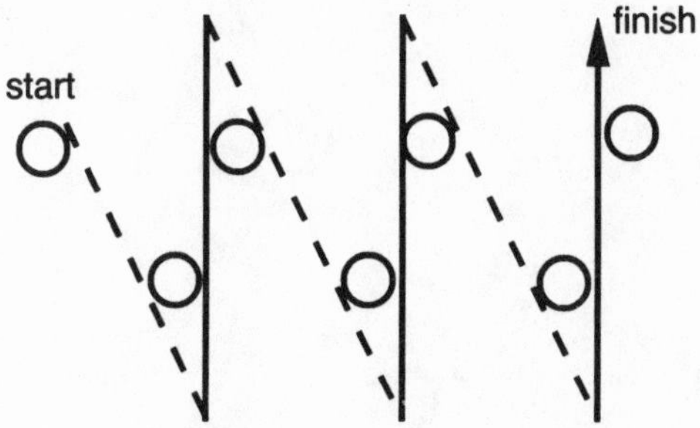

Fig. 3-21

backward and forward at an angle. You can use cones to set up perimeters for these maneuvers, emphasizing 5- to 10-yard sprinting distances and setting up a series of cones so that several consecutive repetitions of the drill can be done. See the three examples above.

Backward Angle Sprinting (see Fig. 3–22)

Application: Linebackers, defensive backs
Procedure:

(1) Set up the cones in the approximate pattern shown, with about 5 yards between them.
(2) From an upright defensive stance, sprint in and out between the cones in a backward direction.
(3) Repeat the drill in the opposite direction.

Comments: Mastering this drill requires practice since you must make your cut at the right angle en route to the next cone. For this reason, it is perhaps best to use only one or two basic angle patterns for this movement, and to run it at less than full speed until you get used to making your cuts at the correct angle.

Fig. 3-22

DEFENSIVE BACK QUICKNESS/AGILITY DRILLS

The next group of drills applies mainly to defensive backs, since they emphasize defensive "patterns" to counter offensive pass routes. They are also of value to linebackers, who are involved in man-to-man coverage. Those pass routes not covered in these drills are covered indirectly with other quickness/agility drills.

Fly (see Fig. 3–23)
Application: Defensive backs (linebackers)
Procedure:

(1) Set up the cones as shown.
(2) From a good upright defensive stance, sprint backward for about 10 yards.
(3) After passing the second cone, pivot in the direction of the cone and sprint forward for about 20 yards.
(4) Also work the drill from the other side, pivoting in the opposite direction.

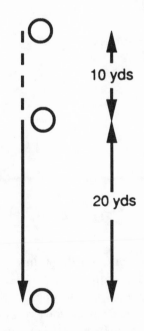

Fig. 3-23

Comments: This drill is designed to defend against the fly pattern. It can be practiced over various distances for both its backward and forward portions, and you can change the angle of the cone slightly. You can also do this drill for 2 or 3 consecutive repetitions by setting the cones up accordingly, using both shorter distances and an adjustment distance between reps.

Quick Out Defender (see Fig. 3–24)

Application: Defensive backs (linebackers)
Procedure:

(1) Set up the cones as shown with about 8 to 12 yards between them.

(2) From a good upright defensive stance, sprint the pattern indicated.

(3) Repeat, with the cut made in the opposite direction.

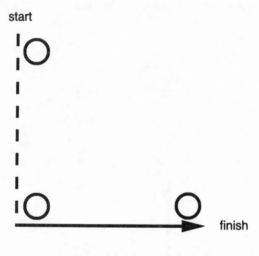

Fig. 3-24

Comments: This drill works on defending against the quick out, and is especially valuable for cornerbacks. An advantage to this drill is that you "react" to the cone. You can change the distance between the cones to keep from "pre-setting" your response to them. You can set the cones up to do this drill for several consecutive reps, with your cuts made in the same or alternating directions.

Post (Slant in), Flag (see Fig. 3–25)

Application: Defensive backs (linebackers)
Procedure:

(1) Set up the cones as shown, with about 8 to 12 yards between them.
(2) From a good upright defensive stance, sprint the pattern indicated.
(3) Repeat, with the cut made in the opposite direction.

Comments: This drill should also be done with different angles and distances between the cones. It can also be done for consecutive reps, with the cuts made in the same or alternating directions.

Fig. 3-25

Out and Up (see Fig. 3–26)

Application: Defensive backs (linebackers)
Procedure:

(1) Set up the cones as shown, with 5 to 15 yards between the cones.
(2) From a good upright defensive stance, sprint the pattern indicated.
(3) Repeat with the cuts made in the opposite direction.

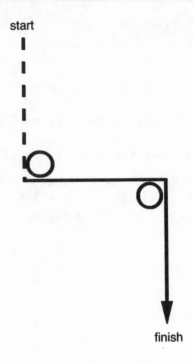

start

finish

Fig. 3-26

Comments: You should do this drill with the cones set at various distances and slightly different angles. You can set the cones for consecutive reps, making the cuts in the same or alternating directions.

Z in, Z out (see Fig. 3–27)
Application: Defensive backs (linebackers)
Procedure:

(1) Set up the cones as shown, with 5 to 15 yards between the cones.
(2) From a good upright defensive stance, sprint the pattern indicated.
(3) Repeat the drill while starting from the opposite direction.

Comments: Once again, vary the cone angles, the distances between them, and run the drill with consecutive reps, if desired.

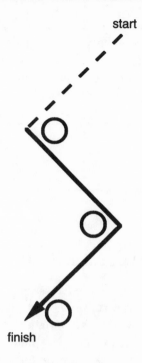

Fig. 3-27

QUICKNESS/AGILITY WORKOUT SCHEDULE

When planning your quickness/agility workout schedule, you must decide which drills to do. Generally speaking, you could pick 2 or 3 drills from the general section and 2 or 3 more from the section that gives drills for your position, and then work on these drills for several weeks before making any changes. You could then substitute for any or all of these drills, following the same format of 2 or 3 general drills and 2 or 3 position-specific drills.

It is a good idea to have your coach help you select which drills to do, for these are likely the ones he will be emphasizing in practice anyway. If you are absolutely sold on certain drills, you can incorporate a couple of them into your program in addition to the ones your coach gives you.

I work on quickness/agility 2 to 4 times weekly, which, as stated, is about what it takes to make progress. I do it before any sprinting or lifting work, and I recommend the same sequence for you. Following is a brief summary of a quickness/agility workout schedule.

Days	Drills
2–4 times weekly	2–3 general
2–4 times weekly	2–3 position-specific

A FINAL WORD ON QUICKNESS/AGILITY

Quickness/agility work is neglected by a lot of football players. They might lift weights, do some running, and even play a little handball or basketball. Yet those with a systematic football-specific off-season program are the exception. Thus if you take the time—only about 2 hours a week overall—to work on your quickness/agility, you'll have a definite advantage on your competition. And remember: In most instances football quickness is every bit as important as raw sprinting speed.

4

Speed Is Needed:
Improving
Your Sprinting

"I taught myself how to run, and if people tell you that's
not possible, they're full of it."
Mark Gastineau, former All-Pro Defensive end,
New York Jets

"Speed kills."
American colloquialism

AN OVERVIEW OF SPRINTING SPEED

SPRINTING SPEED DEFINED

Just about everybody knows that sprinting speed is how fast you can
move from point A to point B. Of course the distance must not be so
short that you are measuring quickness or so long that you are measuring stamina. For football purposes, a distance of 40 yards is most
commonly used to measure speed.

Although sprinting speed is related to quickness, the two are not
the same thing. A quick individual may move very well over the beginning of the race and still lack real speed. There have been cases of
top-strength athletes running with world-class sprinters for 10 to 15
yards before falling back. One world-class powerlifter—with a record
squat lift and an outstanding 38-inch vertical jump—was said to actually
tie up at 10 yards, unable to maintain the speed he generated over
this short distance.

Even though a quick person is not always fast, a truly fast individual must always be quick. As mentioned in the previous chapter, anyone with a really good dash time—be it 40 yards, 60 yards, or 100 yards—must move very well over the first 10 to 15 yards.

THE IMPORTANCE OF SPRINTING SPEED

The importance of sprinting speed to football is pretty apparent. While the game involves short, high-speed movements (quickness) and rapid changes of direction (agility), situations inevitably arise where pure speed is the deciding factor, when the football is out in the open field and it's all a matter of who can turn on the juice.

Speed can serve as a great equalizer for a team that is outmanned physically. A club might run 70 plays and be chewed up and spit out on 65 of them. It's the other five that do the damage, the ones where the 4.4 sprinter—bullied around by bigger and tougher defenders all day—winds up carrying the ball with a step on the slower defenders and a grin on his face.

In football, sprinting speed is like a loaded gun, and this is true for two reasons. It not only acts as an equalizer—it kills!

Improved sprinting speed will also help you to generate more focus upon impact. It's really just simple physics, since the initial force you apply to your opponent in a block or tackle is the weight you hit with times your velocity. So, with the same technique and the same weight, upping your velocity is going to add a little "mustard" to your greeting.

SPEED MEASUREMENT FOR FOOTBALL

As was stated earlier, your speed in football is measured by how fast you run the 40-yard dash. This is done by lining up in a starting stance and firing when ready with the stopwatch operator reacting to your movement. So common is this test that when someone talks about a player's speed, he is referring to his "40 time." A reference to "4.6 speed" or "4.8 speed" is simply the time in which a player can sprint 40 yards under the procedure indicated.

Your 40-yard dash time is certainly not an indicator of your football playing skills. It also says nothing about such physical attributes as football quickness, agility, strength, size, stamina, power, and balance.

Nor does it measure mental or physical toughness in any way. Perhaps its major value is that, in the extreme, it can be used in eliminating certain people from playing certain positions.

SPRINTING SPEED STANDARDS

Forty-yard dash standards vary according to position and level of play. For high school linemen, 5.1 to 5.2 is average, 5.0 is good, and anything less is excellent. For linebackers and tight ends, 5.0 is about average, 4.9 good, and 4.8 or less excellent. For backs and receivers, 4.8 to 4.9 is close to average, 4.7 good, and anything under 4.7 excellent. These standards will vary a little bit depending upon the size of the school and the level of play.

College standards are generally about .1 second faster than those given for high school. They will also vary somewhat from small college to major university.

FACTORS AFFECTING SPRINTING SPEED DEVELOPMENT

Sprinting speed development is affected by sprinting technique, flexibility, strength, percentage of body fat, anaerobic conditioning, present level, age, and heredity.

Technique. It is obvious that you must utilize the correct technique if you wish to maximize your sprinting speed. Improved technique can result in both a faster and a longer stride through the elimination of nonproductive motion. There will be a detailed discussion of sprinting technique later in the chapter.

Flexibility. Flexibility is important for two reasons. It can aid your sprinting by allowing for a longer, more economical stride, and this is especially true when it is combined with increases in strength. It can also indirectly aid your sprinting by helping to prevent injuries so that you can continue to work out.

Strength. Increased strength usually results in increased power, and this can help your acceleration (remember those strength athletes) and aid you in the later stages of a sprint or series of sprints. Like increased flexibility, strength can aid you in lengthening your stride, as it gives you a stronger, more stable base from which to launch each stride that you take. Better strength can also aid you in preventing injury.

Keep in mind that improved strength will not, in and of itself, result in improved muscle speed. Rather, it is one of several factors that, in combination with sprint training and stretching, can improve your overall sprinting.

Percentage of Body Fat. The less fat you have on your body, the faster you can run, everything else being equal. I have always been fortunate in this regard, possessing a low percentage of body fat naturally. Fat is simply excess baggage, and 10 pounds of fat around your gut has the slowing effect of sprinting with a 10-pound weighted belt. Proper diet and workouts will help to reduce body fat, and remember that this does not necessarily mean weight loss.

Anaerobic Conditioning. Superior anaerobic conditioning can aid your sprinting by increasing the interval over which you maintain your speed. It can also aid your sprinting by enabling you to do more productive work in your training sessions before tiring, thereby increasing the effectiveness of your training.

Present Speed Level. The slower you are right now, the more room for improvement you have. A slower sprinter is probably not as developed in technique, flexibility, strength, and low body fat. He can also improve more because he is not as close to the limits of how fast man can run.

Age. There is a certain age span during which sprinting speed can be maximized. Generally, this begins around the time full physical growth is achieved and extends into the middle twenties or beyond, varying with the individual. If you are now playing high school or college football, you probably fall within this range.

Heredity. There can be no denying that heredity is an important factor in fast sprinting. Probably all of the great sprinters were born with the ability to contract their muscles very quickly, and as a guy who has run a 9.3 hundred while concentrating mainly on football, I was born with a lot of inherent sprinting ability myself. Yet there is really no reason to be concerned about your heredity since you cannot do anything about it.

While few, if any, coaches downplay the importance of heredity to top sprinting speed, some of them feel it is something that can be worked around to some extent. One coach in particular stated that in his opinion almost any healthy football player could learn to run at 4.8 or 4.9 speed with proper training.

DEGREE OF SPEED IMPROVEMENT

Of all the physical traits covered in this book, sprinting speed is the most difficult to improve. Ordinarily once an athlete has reached his full natural growth and physical maturity, an improvement of 5 percent is considered good and one of 10 percent truly outstanding.

Why is sprinting speed so tough to improve relative to, say, the trait of strength? Consider for a minute what would happen if an individual doubled his speed. Suppose someone went from a 5 flat 40 to a time of 2.5. The forces generated in sprinting 40 yards this quickly would result in severely pulled muscles and perhaps ripped tendons and even broken bones.

To guard against such effects, we all have a built-in limit on muscle speed, a sort of governor that won't let our muscles move any faster. This limit is said to be determined by the percentage of fast-twitch, as opposed to slow-twitch, muscle fibers that we are born with. These fast-twitch fibers contract more quickly and powerfully, and theoretically, the more of them that are present in an individual the greater the potential for fast sprinting.

Although it is relatively tough to improve sprinting speed, consider one way of looking at the difference between a slow sprinter, one averaging 4 steps per second, and a fast sprinter who averages 5 steps per second. This is a substantial difference of 25 percent. Yet 4 steps per second is .25 seconds per step, and 5 steps per second is .20 seconds per step. This is a difference of only .05 seconds per step. How much of this .05-second difference can be made up with hard work is what makes sprint training so interesting.

One thing is for certain with regard to improving sprinting speed: You must consistently train in a scientific, systematic manner to reach your potential. You cannot simply run sprint after sprint and expect top results.

EXAMPLES ON SIGNIFICANT SPEED IMPROVEMENT

An inspirational story on sprinting improvement—and one that contradicts the extremist position that great sprinters are strictly born and not made—is the achievement of Britain's Alan Wells. In 1970, at the age of 18, he ran 100 meters in 11 seconds even, a respectable enough time but hardly world class. In 1980, at age 28, he brought home an Olympic Gold Medal with a time of 10.02. That's nearly a 1-second improvement over 10 years of hard training, something few of the born-and-not-made school would have predicted.

Then there is the example of former Pittsburgh Steeler Rocky Bleier. He ran a 5.0 forty in 1968 at the age of 22 while weighing 205 pounds. Four years later, after being wounded in Vietnam and told that he would never even walk correctly again, he clocked a 4.6 at a bodyweight of 210. Again, this contradicts the idea that sprinting speed is strictly inherited.

There is also the high school athlete who went from 11.2 to 9.8 in the 100-yard dash in a single season. A college lineman improved his 40 time from 5.5 to 4.9 and another from 4.9 to 4.5. A back went from 4.8 to 4.4. Finally, another player utilized intensive weight training, sprint training, and flexibility work over several years to improve from a 5.8 time in high school to 4.7 in college, totally refuting the theory that sprinting speed cannot be significantly improved.

SPRINTING TRAINING EQUIPMENT

You don't need a lot of equipment to embark on a training program for sprinting. You basically need a method of monitoring your stride length as you sprint. This can be achieved by cutting up used bicycle inner tubes into 12- to 18-inch strips, painting them white, and then nailing them into the ground at both ends with a designated distance between each strip. Be sure that the distance between each marker is exactly what you want it to be; very carefully measure this distance from the edge of one marker to the same side edge of the next marker. To make sure you have aligned all of the markers in a straight line, run a string between 2 stakes in the ground and square the ends of the markers up to the string. (The various sprinting drills will go into more detail on how to use this stride-gauging device.)

Other drills require you to get your knees up when you sprint, and you can stretch rubber shock cord across vertical supports to get this effect. You want to measure not only the height of the cord but the distance between each of the cords as well, and you can adjust both as you gain proficiency.

Another effective training device is rigging your running shoes so that your heels cannot touch the ground when you run. You can do this by raising the front part of your shoe by fastening tape all around it, or you can go to a shoemaker for something more permanent. Another idea is to place foam or rubber padding in the heels of your shoes. You won't be able to come down quite as much on your heels, and the shock absorbing effect of the material will cause you to work harder when you do so.

You can purchase a ready-made device called the Strength Shoe; this consists of a pair of shoes with raised rubber platforms attached to their front halves. You can get information about the Strength Shoe from Strength Footwear, Inc., 2701 Independence St., Metairie, LA 70006. Their telephone number is 1-800-451-5867.

Sprinting with your heels raised can be an effective training aid. (A high school coach in Texas reported an average 40 time improvement of .3 seconds when his team incorporated this method.) Yet since this type of training is new and not a lot is known about it, you should ease into it very gradually and continue to do at least as much sprinting in your regular football shoes, always ending your workout in regular football shoes. Later on, those sprinting drills that most effectively utilize the raised heels method will be given.

Another sprint training device is a unit called the Speed Builder, which will be covered in the section on overspeed.

A highly acclaimed piece of equipment for sprint training is a device called the Speed Chute. This unit amounts to an actual small parachute that is pulled behind you as you run, offering greater wind resistance. The main thing about the Speed Chute is that the faster you sprint the more wind resistance you generate. Additionally, the load is such that your sprint form is minimally affected, resulting in greater carryover to actual free sprinting motion.

The Speed Chute is currently used by a good many professional teams, and not just in football, but in basketball, baseball, soccer, and hockey, among other sports. Additionally, a good number of individual athletes use the device, including sprinters, quarter milers, long jumpers, triple jumpers, and even boxers.

The results with the Speed Chute have been encouraging. Stanley Morgan, who was a wide receiver for the New England Patriots and then the Baltimore Colts, improved his forty-yard dash time from

4.53 to 4.35. As if this is not a remarkable enough achievement by itself, consider that Morgan accomplished this at the age of thirty-six. Blake Ezor, a running back with the Denver Broncos, went from 4.77 to 4.63 after a month of training with the chute. And in eight to twelve weeks of work, a number of college athletes improved from .2 to .4 of a second, and high school athletes from .2 to .6, according to the manufacturer.

The Speed Chute comes in three different sizes; the larger the size the greater the wind resistance to the sprinting motion. Thus, the size or combinations of sizes that you use will depend upon which element of your sprinting you wish to work on. The manufacturer includes an instructional booklet on how to incorporate the various size chutes into a workout program, and included is advice on using the chute only two or three times weekly and finishing each chute workout with some regular sprints.

The Speed Chute is not only good for improved sprinting speed, but works as a conditioning device as well. Accordingly, the later chapter on conditioning recommends the device for use in load-pull sprinting.

The Speed Chute is available from All-Star Athletic Systems, Inc., P.O. Box 751622, Memphis, TN, 38175-1622, and their phone number is 1-800-828-5047.

Stanley Morgan

SPRINT TRAINING WORKOUT PRINCIPLES

DRESS PROPERLY

There is no secret here. You simply want to wear traditional workout clothes that are appropriate for the weather and shoes that are appropriate for the surface. Generally, the softer the surface you will be sprinting on, the longer the cleats of your shoes should be, and the harder the surface, the shorter the cleats. Don't be afraid to experiment in order to find out what shoes work best. Try to wear only 1 pair of socks with your shoes when doing serious sprint work. You want your shoes to fit snugly but not to pinch your feet.

WARM UP THOROUGHLY

This emphais on warm-up will begin to sound like a broken record before you are through with this book. And well it should, for, again, the importance of proper warm-up cannot be overemphasized. This is particularly true when it comes to sprinting, and you should never—repeat, never—sprint without thoroughly warming up, except in an emergency situation. This chapter's section "Warm-Up Drills" describes the appropriate means for warming up before sprinting.

INCREASE INTENSITY GRADUALLY

This axiom applies to all strenuous training. You simply have to give your body time to adjust to the new workload you are placing on it, particularly with something as taxing as sprinting. To do otherwise invites injury and hinders progress. The section "Sprint Training Workout Schedules" reinforces this concept of gradually increased intensity.

SPRINT UNDER THE BEST CONDITIONS

You can't always do your sprint work on the latest track surface when it is 70 degress and there is little wind blowing. Yet you should try to simulate those conditions that will allow you to run your fastest. You can start by picking the best possible running surface and then matching your shoes to it. Basically, if you play and practice on grass, your coach will—or, at least, should—time your 40 on grass, so you should do your working out on a grass surface. Conversely, if your games and practices are on artificial turf, do a good share of your training on this surface.

You can't control the weather when you sprint, and if you live in certain sections of the country, this means working out under less than ideal weather conditions. What you can do, time permitting, is try and work out during the part of the day when the weather is the best for training, relatively speaking. Of course, in certain climates this does not offer you much choice at all, so simply do the best you can under the given circumstances.

DO SPRINT WORK BEFORE CONDITIONING

You want to perform your pure sprinting work while you are still fresh, and this means getting it in before your heavy conditioning. The reasoning here is that in order to run faster you must literally run faster, and you cannot run faster when fatigued from stamina work. Thus do your pure speed work first.

KEEP ACCURATE RECORDS

You must keep a thorough, accurate training log for your sprint training. By knowing exactly what you did during each workout, you can effectively plan your succeeding workouts. You can also correlate the effects of certain training approaches to your improvement.

Your training log should be organized using the following headings:

Date	Drill	Distance	Stride	Apparatus	Recovery	Comments

The distance, stride, and apparatus categories do not apply to every drill, and "time" must be added for any drill that you time. Under apparatus, you should list any device you used, such as extra weight, shock cord, or elevated heels. Under comments, mention things such as where you worked out, the weather, field conditions, and so forth.

SPRINTING TECHNIQUE

Sprinting technique is so important that it rates a section of its own. Correct technique can be defined as those body mechanics that result in the best combination of stride length and stride frequency for maximum sprinting velocity at any instant. There is some controversy regarding the term since certain coaches claim that technique is a precisely defined manner of sprinting, and others feel it to be more of an individual issue. If the mechanics that define technique are those traits that should be common to all sprinters (these will be explored later), then technique is most definitely a precisely defined way of running. If the mechanics that define it include stride length and knee lift—with stride frequency so affected—then it is to some extent an individual thing. Stride length and knee lift depend upon height, weight, strength, flexibility, muscle speed, muscle origin and insertion points, nerve and muscle coordination, bone lengths, and the like. It is plain that since these traits vary greatly from person to person, sprinting technique will likewise vary greatly.

There are a few fundamentals of sprinting technique that you should master. First, your stride length should be such that your foot hits the ground directly under the center of gravity, or with your lower leg at 90 degrees to the ground. If your lower leg is not at this 90 degrees—say your foot is out ahead from overstriding—a braking action results. You must wait until your lower leg is at 90 degrees before you can begin the pushing action for your next stride.

Another important aspect of sprinting technique is knee action. You bend your knee more in sprinting than in other types of running, and you raise your heel until it almost touches your buttocks. This action will aid you in moving your knee forward with greater angular velocity since, as you rotate your leg from your hip, you have a much shortened radius. Also, the higher you raise your knee in front, the more your opposite (rear) leg can extend. This reduces its angle with the ground and increases the force of its extension, which increases stride length.

The momentum of a high, powerful knee lift can also help the extending action of your opposite leg by, in effect, lightening the load on its extensor muscles. The more force you use in swinging your knee, the less the force required to straighten your opposite leg and the faster the rate at which the muscles that straighten this opposite leg can contract. Yet keep in mind that those previously mentioned anatomical traits are going to influence any knee action, and thus stride length, to some extent. Once more, there are a number of good sprinters who run with other than "textbook" knee action form. Whether they would be faster if they adhered to it is a matter of debate.

Some additional items of technique are maintaining proper head alignment (hold it steady and look about 5 yards straight ahead); relaxing the jaw; relaxing the shoulders and squaring them to the direction of the run; and relaxing the hands and bringing them to a point somewhere in front of the chin and inside the shoulder on the upswing. On the downswing, extend the elbows slightly and keep them fairly close to the body. Another basic but important fundamental is to sprint on the balls of your feet, keeping your heels from touching the ground.

These very basic technique principles are practiced by almost all good sprinters, and it is generally accepted that deviation from them will have a slowing effect. It requires a good amount of practice to master them, and yet they can be mastered by all, regardless of ability. (Drills to improve technique will be given later in the chapter.) Although I have always had good natural speed, I have worked hard on sprinting technique to take full advantage of it. I strongly recommend that you do the same.

SPRINT TRAINING DRILLS

WARM-UP DRILLS

All sprint work must begin with a proper warm-up. As stated previously, unless it is an emergency you should never run at full speed without being completely warmed up. To do otherwise is to invite muscle pulls, strains, and other serious injury.

The colder the weather, the longer your warm-up period should be, and you should always extend your warm-up if you don't feel ready. No one knows as well as you do whether your body feels ready for sprinting.

A good warm-up sequence is to jog, stretch, and run. Usually several minutes of jogging followed by 10 or 15 minutes of stretching and several "runs" should be adequate. Each run can be done at a slightly faster pace until the last one is just under an all-out sprint. The runs can be for distances of up to 100 yards, and you should walk back after each one.

The following warm-up drills can be effectively integrated with your runs. They are strenuous, and each takes only a short time to practice. They also work on various aspects of the sprinting act itself.

Sprint Statue
Procedure:

(1) Grab a solid object at shoulder height for balance.
(2) Rise up as high as possible on the ball of one foot.
(3) Simultaneously raise the knee of your other foot as high as possible.
(4) Hold this position for about 10 seconds, concentrating on getting your knee higher and higher while staying on the ball of your foot.
(5) Switch legs and repeat.

Comments: This "static" drill is simple yet effective, requires no warm-up, and can be done nearly every day. For really top results, keep track of how high you can get your knee up. You can do this by running a rope or string horizontally and keeping track of the height at which you can touch it. I do this drill in such a manner periodically.

Training Tips: One alternate way of doing the sprint statue is by raising one knee and holding for about 1 second, then raising the opposite knee and holding. This process can be repeated for 8 or 10 reps per knee. You can also do the sprint statue against resistance, stretching a bicycle inner tube or some other flexible device between 2 vertical posts and bringing your knee up underneath it. You can lower and/or tighten the inner tube for more resistance and raise and/or loosen it for less.

Arm Action
Procedure:

(1) Stand upright and, starting slowly, swing your arms as you do when sprinting.
(2) Gradually increase your speed while maintaining good form, doing about 20 reps for each arm.

Comments: This is another fine warm-up drill, and yet you should probably do some jogging and upper-body stretching before you do it (see chapter 2). Keep your hands and jaw relaxed, and pick up your pace only if you can maintain good form. I do this drill regularly as part of my warm-up before sprinting.

Training Tips: Check your form by doing this drill in front of a mirror.

Stride Switcher
Procedure:

    (1) While standing upright, place one foot several feet in front of you.

    (2) Staying on the balls of your feet, switch the position of your front and rear feet.

    (3) Continue this switching action for about 20 repetitions total.

Comments: This is a fine warm-up drill that also aids you in coordinating the muscles used in sprinting. You can keep track of your stride length when doing this drill by placing a couple of 2-by-4s exactly parallel to each other and a given distance apart. Place the boards at a distance you are sure you can clear when you begin this drill, for you won't be able to see the board that your rear foot must clear.

Training Tips: Move the boards slightly farther apart as you gain proficiency. Occasionally add a weighted belt or vest to make the muscles of your calves, ankles, and feet work harder.

Knee Lifts
Procedure:

    (1) Grab a solid object (such as a football goalpost or cyclone fence) at shoulder height for balance.

    (2) Bring one knee up to your chest, consciously bending your leg in the process and emphasizing a vertical lift.

    (3) Lower your foot back to the ground, and repeat the sequence for 10 or 15 reps.

    (4) Repeat the drill with your other leg.

Comments: Do this drill slowly at first to get the feel of it, and be sure to jog and stretch beforehand. You can start with 10 reps per leg and work up to 15 or more.

Training Tips: I like to rise up on the toes of my ground leg when doing this drill, and I am able to do so without support. Once you are warmed up and acclimated to it, you can use a more vigorous action, bringing your knee up against your clavicle and letting your leg bend naturally. You can also do this drill against resistance in a manner similar to the sprint statue.

TIMING AND DIAGNOSTIC DRILLS

The following drills involve establishing times and speeds, and are used to diagnose the strong points and weak points of your sprinting. Some of them test your "top in" speed and others test your starting and accelerating ability.

Maximum Velocity Test
Procedure:

(1) Find a good sprinting surface of 100 yards or more that a vehicle can gain access to.

(2) After warming up thoroughly, accelerate to top speed at your own pace while the vehicle driver stays even with you. (Stay at least 10 feet to the side of the vehicle.)

(3) The driver calls out the vehicle's speed as you run.

(4) Rest 5 minutes and repeat.

Comments: It is good to do this drill at the beginning of your sprint training so you can note the improvement your training brings. Take your time in accelerating to top speed as this will help you to run relaxed. I do this drill in the off season to check how my speed is holding up.

Training Tips: When you do this test again at a later date, use the same workout area, car, and driver, if you can, and try to pick a day when the weather and ground conditions are as close as possible to those of your first testing day. This will minimize any variation in testing accuracy and help you to better note any improvement.

Maximum Velocity Test (Alternate Method)
Procedure:

(1) After warming up thoroughly, take a running start and sprint for time over a 20-yard stretch.

(2) Rest 5 minutes and repeat.

Comments: You can set this drill up so that you're running just a hair under top speed about 10 yards before beginning the 20-yard stretch, and then "gather" to reach top speed from there. Have the timer stand to the side and be sure the 20-yard distance is clearly marked so that he can gauge when you enter and leave it. If need be, you can help the timer by giving an audible sound when you enter the stretch and again when you leave it.

Training Tips: Try to use the same workout area and timer when you repeat this test at a later date, having him stand in the exact same place. Also try to retest on a day when the weather and ground conditions are as similar as possible to those of your first testing day.

If no one is around to time you, with practice you can time yourself. You can try this out during warm-up, and then check your accuracy by timing yourself 2 or 3 times over the 20-yard stretch (taking 5 minutes between runs). Theoretically, you can get an accurate time this way, since you are in the best position to observe just when you cross the lines. Sprinting with a stopwatch might have a slight slowing effect, however.

Forty Timing Drill
Procedure:

(1) After warming up, have someone time you over 10, 20, 30, and 40 yards from the starting line.
(2) After warming up very thoroughly, sprint 40 yards from a good stance.
(3) Each person starts their stopwatch on your movement and stops it when you reach the yard line they are standing on.
(4) Record the time of each stopwatch. Rest 5 minutes and repeat the drill. Rest 5 minutes and repeat again.

Comments: Once you have recorded the times from each stopwatch, you can calculate the time it took you to run each 10-yard segment. For example, if the watches read 1.7, 2.8, 3.85, and 4.85, respectively, then your 0 to 10 time is 1.7, your 10 to 20 time is 1.1, your 20 to 30 time is 1.05, and your 30 to 40 time is 1.0.

Training Tips: You might run a 40 at 3/4 speed and another at 7/8 speed as part of your warm-up, and perhaps work in a couple of 10-

yard starts. Try to retest with this drill about every 6 weeks, and do so under conditions as close as possible to the original ones (same shoes, sprinting surface, testers, and, if possible, weather conditions).

Forty Timing Drill (Alternate Method)
Procedure:

    (1) After warming up very thoroughly, have someone time you over 10, 20, 30, and 40 yards, recording each time.

    (2) Rest a few minutes between each dash.

    (3) Rest 5 minutes and repeat the entire drill. Rest and repeat again.

Comments: This method is just as effective as the prior one, and is more practical since only 1 timer is needed. The disadvantage is that 4 separate dashes must be run, but if adequate rest is taken between them, your times should not suffer.

Training Tips: Sprint a good 5 yards past the finish line with each dash; this will prevent you from "reaching" to get across the line, a practice that will slow you down over the post-dash distance. Remember that you want to sprint each dash as part of your 40, and just as you would not "reach" when sprinting your overall 40, you should not reach when sprinting any part of it.

    You can time yourself over 40 yards in the same manner that you did when testing for your maximum velocity. Simply start the stopwatch as your hand leaves the ground when coming up out of a stance, and stop it when you reach the finish line.

GENERAL SPRINTING DRILLS

The upcoming sprint drills work on the direct development of actual sprinting skill. They emphasize gradual acceleration, relaxed running, and, to some extent, anaerobic conditioning.

Fly-ins
Procedure:

    (1) At your own rate, accelerate to your top sprinting speed.

    (2) Hold this speed for several seconds.

Comments: The best way to do fly-ins is by sprinting alongside a vehicle that monitors your velocity, utilizing the same procedure as in the earlier-covered maximum velocity test. The major advantage of doing fly-ins this way is that you have instant feedback as to your sprinting effectiveness, which is the best teaching system possible. A good training technique is to work up to a sprint about one mile per hour under your best recorded speed, hold for 3 or 4 seconds, and then "gather" in an all-out effort to beat the car. (You can have the driver maintain this speed to see if you can leave the car behind.)

Training Tips: Do your fly-ins in a relaxed, almost lazy manner, taking your time in reaching full speed and then maintaining it with the least possible effort. Pretend that you are putting on a clinic for onlookers on how to sprint with perfect form at "just under" top speed. One method is to run a given distance or number of steps with so much covered at 3/4 speed, so much at 7/8 speed, and the last segment at a relaxed "99 percent" speed. You can use about 20 steps per segment, if measuring by steps. (Note that in the section that covers actual sprint routines, any reference to distance for the fly-in drill refers only to the actual distance over which top speed was attempted.)

Fly-ins are one of my very favorite training drills, as I find it very relaxing to run at near top speed without "really trying." I do them on a regular basis.

Ins-and-outs
Procedure:

    (1) Work up to just under a full sprint and hold for a given interval.
    (2) Shift to a full sprint and hold for the same interval.
    (3) Continue this up and down shifting over the duration of the sprint.

Comments: Think of this drill as if you were driving a car with a 4-speed transmission. You go into third gear for a given interval, shift into fourth gear for the same interval, shift back into third, back into fourth and so on. This is a tough, effective drill that takes great concentration.

Training Tips: You can sprint a given distance or a given number of steps over each interval before shifting, with 10 to 20 steps per interval effective. You might keep your number of overall steps per rep constant—say at 60—and go with 6 "shifts" of 10 steps apiece, 4 "shifts" of 15 steps apiece, or 3 "shifts" of 20 steps apiece. For best results, try to do some of each.

Stride Monitored Fly-ins
Procedure:

(1) Set the earlier-mentioned stride-gauging apparatus (p. 114) with the distance between each marker equal to your sprinting stride length.
(2) Perform the fly-in sprint drill while using this apparatus to gauge your stride.
(3) Very gradually increase the distance between each marker while maintaining your stride rate. (See text below on how to best do this.)

Comments: This is one of the best aids to sprinting development there is. When each stride is monitored, you have instant feedback as to whether you are striding the correct distance. In addition, since the stride markers "tell" you exactly where to place each foot, this aid to your neuromuscular system allows you to concentrate on the stride marker (sensory orientation) rather than on your own movement (motor orientation). Since conscious control of motor movement interferes with the reading of nerve impulses, sprinting to a visual stimulus can aid you in going faster.

Training Tips: Research has shown that new motor skills are learned most effectively when the training action is modified in small steps. Sprinting with a longer stride amounts to a new motor skill, and for it to be learned most effectively the change from your regular stride to a longer one should occur in small steps. Thus you want to increase your stride length very gradually, perhaps by 1 inch per month or two, in order to maintain your sprinting form and stride frequency. After a period of 6 months of consistent work at this, you will have increased your stride rate by the substantial amount of 3 to 6 inches.

Even though I have good natural speed, I do stride-monitored fly-ins as part of my program, which concentrates on keeping me fast. My feeling is that I need every edge I can get, and I think you should have the same attitude about this drill.

Stride-Monitored Ins-and-outs
Procedure:

(1) Set up the earlier-mentioned stride-gauging apparatus.
(2) Perform the ins-and-outs sprint drill while using this apparatus to gauge your stride.

Comments: You can do your stride-monitored ins-and-outs in the same manner as your regular ins-and-outs, covering a given number of steps per shift interval. The mentioned sequence of 10 to 20 steps works well.

An alternate way of doing your stride-monitored ins-and-outs is to set up a given number of markers 2 or so inches under your regular sprinting stride length and a like number 2 or so inches over your regular sprinting stride length. For example, you could set up 10 markers under, 10 over, 10 under, 10 over, 10 under, and 10 over, giving you a 60-step workout. You then sprint and hit each marker, adjusting your stride length every 10 steps. This quick, shocking shift will aid you in coordinating a feel for maximum stride length with maximum stride frequency.

Training Tips: For top-notch results, mix this latter drill in with all regular, constant-length stride-monitored sprints whether they are fly-ins or ins-and-outs, a mixture that I have found works very well. This will require 2 sets of stride markers, but the benefits make it worthwhile. Remember to gradually increase the distance between your markers when you perform any stride-monitored ins-and-outs. An increase of 1 inch every month or two is good.

SUPPLEMENTARY SPRINT DRILLS

The following supplementary sprint drills work on improving the various parts that make up the overall sprinting action. The idea is that by improving its parts, the overall sprinting action will be improved. These drills should generally be performed for distances of 50 to 60 yards or more as you gain experience with them. Some of these drills suggest that you monitor your stride length when doing them, utilizing the apparatus described earlier.

Speed Stepping

Procedure: Sprint with a deliberately shortened stride, moving your
    legs as fast as you can.
Comments: The idea behind this drill is to feed nerve impulses to your
muscles at a faster than usual rate. Be sure to stay up on the balls of
your feet.

Training Tips: You can begin doing this drill at a stride of 1 foot less
than your sprinting stride and then time it over a given distance. You
can then work to beat your time; when you reach a sticking point,
increase your stride very slightly while trying to maintain the same
stride rate. If you increase your stride length by 1 inch a month and
maintain your initial speed-stepping frequency, after 1 year you will
be sprinting with your regular stride rate at this faster frequency.

High-knee Sprinting

Procedure: Sprint while raising the knees as high as possible.
Comments: The idea behind this drill is to assure that correct knee
lift occurs automatically when you sprint with your regular form. You
should do it in 3 stages, particularly as you are getting used to it.
During the first stage, simple concentrate on getting your knees up as
high as you can and don't worry about stride length. During the second
stage, continue to concentrate on getting your knees up as high as you
can, and go for a stride length about a foot to a foot and a half under
your normal sprinting stride. During the third stage, once again concentrate on getting your knees up as high as you can, and attempt a
stride length as close as possible to your normal sprinting stride. When
you can do this drill at your normal sprinting stride length, you are
performing one of the smartest and most valuable supplementary sprinting
drills there is.

Training Tips: To practice this drill systematically, use the earlier-
mentioned rubber shock cords stretched across vertical supports. Decide how high you want your knees to be, and then raise the cords to
a corresponding height that requires your knees to be this high to clear
them. Then adjust the horizontal distance between the cords to cause
your stride to be a certain length. Begin with moderate heights and
distances, and increase gradually but steadily over the months, always
keeping track of these variables. When working out with any given
horizontal distance between the cords, begin your movement perhaps

10 or 15 yards away from the cords and with shorter high-knee strides. Then steadily increase your high-knee stride length as you approach the cords, building up enough momentum that you are "high kneeing" it at your working stride length when you reach the cords.

You can also elevate your heels with this drill. Combining this with the earlier-mentioned knee-lift and stride-length monitors works well. Be sure to do plenty of high-knee sprinting in conventional shoes.

I have done high-knee sprinting on a consistent basis since junior high school. I enjoy this drill and believe that it has been instrumental in my developing a longer, smoother, more powerful stride.

Bounding
Procedure:

    (1) Run down the field with an exaggerated stride length, not necessarily staying on the balls of your feet.
    (2) Gradually increase your stride length until it is maximum.
    (3) Cover a distance of 50 to 60 yards.

Comments: In contrast to high-knee sprinting, which works on the vertical component of sprinting, this drill emphasizes the horizontal component. It is an excellent drill to do while elevating your heels. The natural tendency is to come down on your heels when bounding, and elevating them counteracts this somewhat.

You should monitor your stride length with this drill, gradually working up to a stride of 1½ feet or more beyond your regular sprinting stride.

Training Tips: Give yourself a 10-yard running start and time this drill over a set distance at a monitored stride length. Work to beat this time; once you reach a sticking point, lengthen your stride and begin the process again. You can do this drill between sets of high-knee sprinting. This will integrate the drills that work the horizontal and vertical components of your sprinting.

Knee-lock Run
Procedure:

    (1) Lock your knees and run with a "goose step," staying on the balls of your feet.
    (2) Gradually increase your stride length as the run progresses.

Comments: This very effective drill might seem a little awkward at first. You have to really concentrate on keeping your knees locked since the tendency is to bend them. You must also concentrate on staying on the balls of your feet and not letting your ankles hit the ground.

You can start this drill with short strides, emphasizing technique instead of speed, and work up to a stride length close to that of your regular sprinting stride. Actually, you want to increase your stride as much as possible with this drill, maintaining proper form. Thus, you can at times monitor your stride with this drill.

Training Tips: To aid you in staying on the balls of your feet, perform this drill with your heels elevated. You may have to modify your form a bit to do this. I do the knee-lock run this way and find it beneficial.

Caution: Although this drill has been widely used, some medical authorities believe that keeping your knees in a locked position creates too much stress; they recommend keeping your knees slightly bent during all such exercises.

Toe-rise Walk
Procedure:

(1) Rise up on your toes and walk down the field, taking steps as long as possible while staying high on your toes.

(2) Walk for 20 or 30 yards.

Comments: This simple drill can be used in any phase during which you are recovering from another drill, and it can also be done with your knees locked. Make every effort to walk in a straight line, and swing your arms for rhythm and balance. Do not attempt to walk particularly fast, and be sure to stay completely up on your toes. You can work up to distances of 50 yards or more.

Training Tips: Add a weighted belt or vest when doing this drill, concentrating with great intensity on staying on the balls of your feet and elevating your heels, if you have to. You can also perform this drill inside while weight-training. Place a barbell across your shoulders (make sure the plates are well secured) and perform the drill in any open area you can find. Start with a moderate weight and increase gradually, again always staying on the balls of your feet.

STARTING AND ACCELERATING DRILLS

Starting and accelerating ability is very important to the football player. In fact, the first 10 yards of a sprint is the most important distance in football. This is the period of your most rapid acceleration (up to about 85 to 88 percent of your maximum velocity), and you must be fairly quick over this distance to be an effective football player, regardless of position.

Beyond this 10-yard distance, you will continue to accelerate, reaching about 90 percent of your top speed at 15 yards and about 95 percent at 20 yards. Some sprinters reach their top speed at around 30 yards, while others continue to accelerate slightly up to 50 or 60 yards.

The following drills are designed to help you improve your starting and accelerating ability. They are particularly valuable for 40-yard dash work since this distance is largely a test of starting and accelerating. Some of the drills work on specific segments of your 40-yard dash, and you should particularly emphasize those segments in which you need work, based upon your diagnostic times for each 10-yard segment.

You can use the combination of a weighted vest or belt, along with raised heels, when you work these drills. This works well because the tendency is to come down onto your heels when wearing extra weight, and the raised heels setup prevents this. If possible, do your drills this way on the days you do your strength training for your legs, and be sure to do as many without extra resistance, closing your starting/ accelerating workout with nonresistance drills.

It is possible to monitor your stride length when practicing starting/ accelerating drills, but to do so you have to get a stride-length pattern for your acceleration. Find a surface that leaves footprints, and then accelerate from a standstill or a near standstill for 20 or 25 steps. Then measure and record the exact distance between each step, and set the stride markers accordingly. When you do your drills, try to match or slightly surpass each stride marker on every step. You can repeat the entire process while wearing extra resistance and with your heels elevated.

For those drills that are applicable, you can use a sprinter's stance. Place your fingertips just behind the starting line at about shoulder width, and place your front foot 14 to 21 inches behind the line. Place your rear foot anywhere from having its toe 12 inches behind the heel of your front foot to where your knee is even with the heel of your front foot. Your weight is well balanced, and your buttocks are about

3 inches higher than your shoulders. Have your coach check your stance. He may also want you to practice some starts from a football stance, and if he does, have him show you the stance he wants.

Ten-yard Starts
Procedure:

  (1) Line up in a good starting stance.
  (2) Sprint 10 yards down the field.
  (3) After slowing, walk to another starting point and repeat the drill.
  (4) Perform repetitions this way.

Comments: Start on the goal line, sprint to the 10, slow down and walk to the 20, start again from the 20, and so on, moving right down the field. Be sure to sprint a good 10 yards each repetition; to insure this, count the number of steps it takes you and then always sprint an extra step. You can also practice your 10-yard starts on an unmarked field when you know the number of steps you need.

A good time for this 10-yard distance is 1.6 to 1.65, and anything less than this is very good. You can improve your time with practice, and there are cases of players improving by .2 seconds or more over several months of hard work.

Training Tips: Run this drill from both a sprinter's stance and from the football stance for your position. Work on this drill more extensively if your 10-yard time is weak. I do this drill regularly, since as a running back my first 10 yards from a stance is extremely important.

Twenty-yard starts
Procedure: Same as for 10-yard starts, except the distance used is 20 yards.
Comments: Be sure to sprint at least 20 yards on each repetition. Again, count the steps it takes you to do this and then sprint an extra step. You should work on this 20-yard distance and try to get your time down to at least 2.8. A time of 2.7 is very good, and 2.6 or less is excellent.

Training Tips: As with the 10-yard start drill, run this drill from a football stance as well as from a sprinter's stance.

Shortened Ins-and-outs

Procedure: Same as for the ins-and-outs drill covered under "General Sprinting Drills," with the exception that each interval uses only 5 to 10 steps.

Shortened Stride Monitored Ins-and-outs

Procedure: Same as for the stride-monitored ins-and-outs drill covered earlier, with the exception that each interval uses fewer steps and the stride length shift is different. (Set up 5 to 10 stride markers at about 6 inches under your full-sprint stride length, and then set up 5 to 10 right at your full-stride length. Set up 30 to 60 stride markers this way.)

Jog and Explode

Procedure:

(1) From a slow jog, explode into a sprint for a given distance or a given number of steps.
(2) From this sprint, slow completely back to a jog.
(3) Perform repetitions this way.

Comments: This drill gives you practice on accelerating, and it is most effective if done for distances of 10 to 40 yards. Obviously, if you perform this drill for 10 yards, you are working on the first 10 yards of your sprint; if you perform it for 20 yards, you are working on the first 20 yards; and so on. Thus you should emphasize working on that part of your sprint that is weakest. Be sure to slow to a complete jog between repetitions of this drill. To assure this, you can use a partner and explode to his verbal command.

Training Tips: You can explode for a designated number of steps instead of for a given distance; as a general rule, you should sprint 5 steps for every 10 yards of distance that you simulate. Thus if you are going by steps, each separate rep should be between 5 and 20 steps. It is a good idea to count steps even if you have a marked field, always exploding for 1 more step than is needed to cover the distance. For example, if you cover a 20-yard explosion in 9 steps, sprint for 10 steps to be sure you do not let up over this 20-yard distance.

Explode for a good 50 steps over your last rep or two, especially if you are wearing extra weight and/or your heels are elevated.

Forty-yard Dash

Procedure: From a good stance, sprint 40 yards.

Comments: You should include some simple 40-yard sprints in your starting and accelerating workout. This drill puts together everything you have been working on. I generally run some forties 2 or 3 times a week.

Training Tips: Count the number of steps it takes you to sprint 40 yards and work on taking one less step. With the same stride rate, one less step will improve your time from .2 to .25 seconds.

OVERSPEED SPRINT TRAINING

INTRODUCTION TO OVERSPEED TRAINING

Overspeed is a new frontier in sprint training. It consists of using an external device (such as a car or rubber cable that pulls you) to aid you in sprinting faster than you can sprint by yourself. There have been reports of dramatic success with this type of training, with 40-yard dash times said to improve by several tenths of a second in just one off season of working out.

A major advantage of overspeed training is that it helps to develop proper sprinting technique. This makes sense, since good technique is by definition that sprinting action by which you can run your fastest. Using overspeed, you cannot help but run your fastest (and then some) and consequently you "cannot help" but run with good technique.

THEORY OF OVERSPEED TRAINING

It is not completely understood why overspeed training works. One theory has it that since overspeed lightens the load on your muscles while you sprint, certain slow-twitch fibers that ordinarily lie dormant during sprinting are activated. Using these slow-twitch fibers this way causes them to take on the characteristics of fast-twitch fibers and improve the speed of muscle contraction.

Another idea is that overspeed improves the ability of your central nervous system to sort out impulses. During unaided sprinting, your central nervous system cannot sort the messages (such as extend, flex, and relax) beyond a certain speed. When overspeed is used, the messages are apparently sorted and thus delivered faster; this may be the result of the rerouting of certain nerve impulses because of the lightened load on those muscles that these nerves innervate (connect with). This improved sorting ability seems to carry over when unaided sprinting is performed, provided enough overspeed work has been done and continues to be done.

Still another theory is that overspeed work teaches you to utilize fewer muscle fibers when you sprint, because of the lightened load. This "learned" ability then transfers to unaided sprinting, resulting in faster muscle contractions.

Regardless of exactly why overspeed works, the underlying principle is that in order to run faster you must run faster. With overspeed, you are able to circumvent your inborn speed governor and thus run faster.

DIFFERENT METHODS OF OVERSPEED TRAINING

There are several different methods of overspeed training. You can sprint downhill, sprint while being towed by a car or other mechanism, sprint on a high-speed treadmill, or sprint while being pulled by a large rubber cord. Of these, the last one is probably the safest and least expensive, and most of the overspeed drills offered will feature this piece of equipment.

Many of the given overspeed drills utilize a device called the Speed Builder. It consists of a 25-foot cord with a waistbelt or harness. You can order it from Speed City, Inc., P.O. Box 1059, Portland, OR 97207. Their phone number is 1-800-255-9930. You might want to ask about an extra length or two of cord, as well as extra belts needed for certain drills done with a partner. When you use your Speed Builder, you should not stretch the cord to more than 3 times its length (a 50-foot cord should never be extended to more than 150 feet). To do so would weaken it, causing it to lose some of its effectiveness and perhaps break. A cord that breaks could catch your eye, so you might want to wear goggles or safety glasses.

If you cannot afford such a custom-made overspeed training unit, make your own. Check out a bicycle repair shop and ask them for used inner tubes. (These should not be too worn, because they must be able to withstand a great deal of pressure.) Then very securely tie the tubes together until you have 50 or 60 feet or more of them. Tie one end to your anchor and the other to you. Be very careful that these tubes are sturdy, otherwise they could snap and hit you in the face. Again, always protect your eyes with safety glasses.

In your Speed Builder drills, you might have to experiment with the amount of cord stretch as well as cord length and strength. The length can be altered by adding one cord lengthwise to another, and the strength can be increased by using 2 cords in parallel, which is a good idea for moving-anchor sprinting. This is because as your training partner sprints away from you as the "moving anchor," he will keep the cord from unwinding as fast as it would if it were fastened to a stationary object. The result is that you will lose force and thus speed from this slower rate of cord contraction. The two parallel cords compensate by doubling the cord's contracting force and thus increasing the speed you are able to generate. Be sure to also experiment with the distance you stretch the cords when using them this way, starting out moderately and increasing gradually.

OVERSPEED TRAINING CONSIDERATIONS

Although overspeed work can definitely aid you in running faster, you must consistently continue its use in order to maintain your faster rate. Essentially, it can bring about a quite rapid and significant increase in unaided sprinting speed. However, if you discontinue its use, you will start to taper off to your initial, pre-overspeed level of sprinting speed.

Another characteristic of overspeed is that in order to realize its maximum benefits you must do plenty of strength and power work with it. Let's say you can sprint at 20 m.p.h. with an overspeed pulling force of 10 pounds and you wish to transfer this 20 m.p.h. speed to unaided sprinting; this roughly amounts to keeping the same 20 m.p.h. speed while carrying an extra 10 pounds. This means doing more work in the same time period, which requires more power. Since power is the product of strength and speed, and since speed is already maximized here (at 20 m.p.h.), any increase in power must come from an increase in strength.

You should be in excellent sprinting condition before using overspeed. This type of training involves an overexertion, so to speak, of the sprint action. To prepare for this, you must have your sprinting muscles ready for all-out work, and over a fairly lengthy interval. You can gauge your readiness by sprinting 220 yards for time. Then take your best 100-yard dash time and multiply it by 2.25; your 220 time should be in this vicinity. As an example, if you run 100 yards in 11 seconds, your 220 time should be around 24.75 seconds (11 times 2.25) in order to be ready for overspeed work.

It is an understatement to say that you must be thoroughly warmed-up for overspeed work. Your warm-up should consist not only of the usual jog, stretch, and gradually faster runs, but you should work up to several full-speed sprints as well. In fact, you should never do any overspeed training before doing unaided full-speed sprints. In effect, you must precede overspeed work with some general sprint work.

If you have any soreness, even a slight muscle pull, or otherwise do not feel up to par, neglect overspeed training for that day. If the weather is unusually cold or the running track in poor condition, do not use overspeed. This type of training demands good conditions all the way around in order to maximize safety.

A final consideration with regard to overspeed is that it can easily be overdone. Overspeed is not conditioning work, as each repetition is relatively short in duration, and ample recovery time between reps is encouraged. Since it is not as painful as pure conditioning and since it is such a fun way to train, the tendency is to do too much. Guard against this by doing no more work with overspeed than with your general sprint work.

OVERSPEED TRAINING DRILLS

The overspeed method of training requires a select series of drills. The following drills apply when using this method.

Moving-anchor Sprinting
Procedure:

    (1) Both you and your partner don the Speed Builder at opposite ends of the cord.

    (2) Using your partner as the anchor, stretch the cord (not exceeding 3 times its natural length).

    (3) On command, both you and your partner begin sprinting, your partner acting as a moving anchor.

    (4) Work up to your top speed and hold for several seconds, signaling your partner when you are through.

    (5) If desired, switch roles with your partner and repeat the drill.

Comments: This is the preferred way to do your overspeed work with the Speed Builder. In fact, some coaches perform only moving-anchor sprinting movements with it, totally neglecting stationary-anchor sprinting. It is the way that I do my overspeed work unless I cannot find a partner.

You do not have to force things with the moving-anchor sprinting drill. Instead, concentrate on sprinting in a loose, relaxed manner. Pretend that you are demonstrating proper sprinting technique to a group of onlookers.

Training Tips: You can sometimes alternate moving-anchor sprinting with unaided fly-in sprints. The theory here is that right after overspeed work, your body is "primed" to sprint faster, and you can take advantage of this by mixing in unaided sprint work. You should always begin with a few unaided sprints (remember they must be part of your pre-overspeed warm-up anyway), and then you can mix the two, alternating every other sprint, every two sprints, or what have you.

Stationary-anchor Sprinting
Procedure:

(1) Don the Speed Builder harness or belt, and anchor the other end of the cord to a solid object at waist level.
(2) Stretch the cord out a specific distance (not exceeding 3 times its natural length).
(3) Work up to a full-speed sprint and maintain for several seconds, letting the cord pull you.

Comments: You should do stationary-anchor sprinting only if you can't find a partner for moving-anchor sprinting. In stationary-anchor sprinting, the cord retracts over a shorter distance than it does with moving-anchor sprinting; the result is that your neuromuscular system does not get as much time to "learn" the new speed.

Training Tips: If you do not have a training partner and must do stationary-anchor sprinting, try using a longer cord. This will give you a greater distance over which your system will get the benefits of overspeed work. You can experiment with different lengths of stretch.

Supplementary Anchor Sprinting Drills

Procedure: After a thorough warm-up that includes a little unaided sprinting, perform applicable drills from the section "General Sprint Drills," using the Speed Builder. Use the moving-anchor style if possible.

Comments: Set the tension of the cable to whatever feels comfortable (do not stretch it beyond 3 times its length), varying it as you see fit. These drills are a good adjunct to any overspeed sprinting workout, and they may be done before, during, and after your regular overspeed sprinting. I do them regularly as part of my overspeed work.

Training Tips: Do these drills both unaided and utilizing overspeed, alternating back and forth the same as with overspeed/fly-in alternations.

Towing

Procedure: Perform overspeed towing drills with the appropriate apparatus (usually a vehicle).

Comments: Never attempt towing except under the direct supervision of your coach. This drill can be dangerous, and your coach must be there to oversee the procedure. It is for this reason that detailed instructions for towing are not given here.

PLYOMETRIC TRAINING

INTRODUCTION TO PLYOMETRICS

Plyometrics are select hopping and jumping exercises that work your neuromuscular system in a unique and beneficial manner. They are often referred to as the link between strength and speed, and as such they serve to develop explosive power for sprinting and jumping. The Russians pioneered plyometric training in the 1960s, and a number of American coaches have begun to use it in recent years.

When properly done, plyometric training will decrease the time each foot spends in contact with the ground while sprinting. Studies have shown that the major difference between fast sprinters and slower sprinters is this ground contact time.

PLYOMETRIC THEORY

Plyometric drills involve a pre-stretching, or lengthening, of your muscles before they are contracted, a practice that brings about forceful and efficient muscular contractions. Also, the greater the rate of the lengthening, the greater the rate of the contraction. With the jumping drills (of which sprinting is one) that make up plyometrics, when your foot hits the ground during a rebounding motion your muscles lengthen with great speed. This lengthening is called an eccentric contraction. When you push off the ground with your foot, you have reversed this muscle-lengthening process, and your muscles shorten with a concentric contraction. Plyometric training will improve this eccentric to concentric "switching" efficiency, reducing the time it takes for your muscles to switch from the lengthening to the shortening phase, and developing a stronger contraction in the latter. In effect, they convert your downward motion to upward motion more quickly, allowing you to get airborne sooner and with more distance.

The fast contractions that result from plyometrics amount to one of your body's protective mechanisms at work. Since overstretching a muscle can damage it, when a muscle "senses" it is going to be overstretched because of a rapid rate of stretch from a plyometric drill, it contracts automatically in a direction opposite to that of the stretch in order to protect itself. This contraction is faster than a willful contraction, and apparently takes place by an altering of the nerve impulse pattern that is being sent to your motor units to contract your muscles.

PLYOMETRICS AND OVERSPEED

Plyometrics actually amount to a special form of overspeed. With conventional overspeed work, your muscles are able to contract faster because there is less of a load on them. With certain plyometric drills, your muscles contract faster but under the same load: your body weight. This means that you are doing more work per unit of time for the leg that is being used. Since work per unit of time is power, plyometrics serve as a power builder, and at the speed end (as opposed to strength end) of the power spectrum.

If you can sprint regularly with 4.5 steps per second and can manage 3 steps per second with a one-legged hopping drill, your sprinting rate in steps per second for one leg (2.25) is less than your hopping rate for the same leg (3). When you are sprinting at 4.5 steps per second, one leg will hit the ground, contract eccentrically, switch, contract positively, and recover while in the air to hit the ground again. Yet this will occur at the rate of 2.25 times per second, since the other leg involved in the sprint action moves at the same 2.25 times per second rate to make up the 4.5 steps per second sprint motion, which consists of both legs.

When you are hopping on one leg at 3 strides per second, this one leg must hit the ground, contract eccentrically, switch, contract positively, and recover while in the air to hit the ground again, but at the faster rate of 3 strides per second. In fact, this faster overall rate brought about by plyometric drill is said to develop the ability to anticipate ground contact. This is a neuromuscular skill of great difficulty that will carry over to regular sprinting.

Your neuromuscular system must also recruit enough muscle fibers to generate the force needed to propel your body upward. Ordinarily, the faster your muscles move, the more difficult it is to produce force. Yet to a good extent, the "short circuiting" effect of plyometrics counters this problem.

PLYOMETRIC DRILLS

Although there are a lot of plyometric drills around, the following should be adequate to develop your sprinting power. They should not be attempted before a month or so (12 to 15 workouts) of general sprinting, preferably with a like amount of work on strength development. Perform these drills on a relatively soft surface if possible, avoiding concrete, ice, hard ground, etc. Perform those plyometric drills that utilize extra resistance on the same days you do strength training for your legs, if you can.

Note that it is very easy to overtrain with these drills. Thus you should limit yourself to only 2 sets of any drill at one training session. Perform your plyometrics generally only twice and never more than 3 times weekly.

Sprinting in Place
Procedure: Sprint in place for about 30 repetitions, staying on the balls of your feet and raising your knees as high as possible. Utilize good arm action.
Comments: This is a good drill to do inside when inclement weather affects outdoor workouts. For extra resistance, or assistance, utilize the shock cord.

Training Tips: Stretch a rubber cord or a rope horizontally at a specific height and fasten a bell to it. Then ring the bell with your knees as you sprint in place. Just as with the overhanging bell and rope suggested for vertical jumping, you can adjust the height of this unit as you progress, and time yourelf over a given number of "rings." Do your sprinting in place in front of a mirror to check your form.

Vertical Jump
Procedure:

(1) From a standing position, jump as high as you can for about 10 to 15 reps.

(2) Perform each jump by rebounding off the ground at maximum speed.

Comments: Improved vertical jumping ability is not only an asset in itself (some coaches feel it is as important as 40-yard dash time for receiver and defensive backs), it also correlates positively with improved 40-yard dash time. You can work on your vertical jumping with regular jumps, with deeper jumps in which you touch your palms to the ground each rep, and with jumps in which you alternately touch each knee to the ground. Be sure to spring up from the ground as quickly as possible when jumping, minimizing ground contact time.

I do each style of vertical jump with extra resistance, using either weights or rubber shock cord. I also jump with assistance, using a trampoline and/or using the shock cord so that it helps to pull you up. This assisted method will increase your muscle contraction velocity. For best results, end your workout with regular jumps using neither resistance or assistance.

Training Tips: There has been a recent trend to do vertical jumps utilizing an approach called depth jumping, in which you jump off a platform from a designated height (usually 29½ inches) and spring back up immediately, thus affecting your stretch reflex for the desired plyometric effect. The problem with depth jumping is in choosing the optimal height. It must be higher than you can ordinarily jump or the platform does not help you, but it should not be so high that you are injured. (Go for a few inches over your best vertical jump.) You should also do more than one depth jump at a time to involve the "learning" effect that successive jumps have on your neuromuscular system. This involves setting up several platforms so that upon jumping off one you immediately rebound onto another, and so on, in effect turning the exercise into a vertical hopping drill.

Two-legged Hopping

Procedure: Hop forward on both legs as quickly as you can for 10 to
15 reps, swinging your arms for assistance.

Comments: Here you are hopping (jumping) for distance rather than
height. For maximum distance, your takeoff should be around 45 degrees. You should try to stay on the balls of your feet when doing this
drill, elevating your heels for this purpose. Start with shorter, more
controlled hops, and increase as you get the feel of the movement.

You can do your hops with extra resistance, hopping up hills or
steps, or using a weighted belt or vest so that your arms remain free.
You can also do them with assistance, featuring the Speed Builder
device used for overspeed. Finish your hopping work with some regular
hops.

Training Tips: Hop over rubber shock cords, keeping track of horizontal and vertical distances and attempting to minimize ground contact
time. Hop onto and off of platforms in quick succession, proceeding
in a straight line with as many platforms as you have and keeping track
of the distance between each one. I utilize both of these methods.

One-legged Vertical Jumping
Procedure:

(1) Staying on the ball of your foot, jump up and down on one
leg 15 to 20 times, trying to keep your knee straight each time
your foot touches the ground.
(2) Perform each jump as quickly as you can, striving for maximum
height.
(3) Rest and repeat with the other leg.

Comments: You should gain some mastery of this drill before you
attempt one-legged hops. You should try to keep your heels from
touching the ground when doing it, and you can elevate your heels
for this purpose. You can perform one-legged vertical jumps with assistance, a method that, as mentioned, will increase muscle contraction
velocity.

Placing one foot on a sturdy bench, perform your jumps off your
other foot. A trampoline will also give you assistance, as will a shock
cord setup. For extra resistance, utilize a weighted vest or belt, or rig
the shock cord. Finish your workout with jumps using neither assistance nor resistance.

Training Tips: For variety, try skipping rope when performing your one-legged vertical jumps. You can shorten the rope so that your foot must come up higher to clear it on each rep. Try to maintain the same rope-jumping speed when you do this.

One-legged Hopping
Procedure:

(1) Staying on the ball of your foot and concentrating on keeping your knee relatively straight, hop forward on one leg as quickly as you can for 15 to 20 steps.
(2) Rest, then repeat with the other leg.

Comments: If you had to restrict yourself to one plyometric drill for sprinting improvement, this would be the drill. Accordingly, it is the plyometric drill that I do most often, having emphasized it since my high school days. It is a difficult exercise to perform since it takes time for your body to adjust to the demands of hopping around on one leg. Yet the results can be amazing. There was a high school football player in Florida born with one leg who could outrun many of his teammates and dunk a basketball. He developed this incredible dynamic power by the constant demands placed on his one leg.

One-legged hopping lends itself to the raised-heel method as well as any other drill, because it is difficult to stay up on the balls of your feet when doing this drill. Perform at least as many sets of one-legged hopping with your heels raised as you do with regular shoes.

You can perform one-legged hopping with extra resistance; however, be sure your weighted belt or vest is not so heavy that your heel touches the ground. Hopping up hills and steps works well as extra resistance, for you can stay on the balls of your feet when doing these drills. You can also utilize overspeed hops with the Speed Builder, but be sure to begin with just a moderate amount of tension on the cord so that you do not lose your balance.

For variety, do some hops for a given number of steps; then, without stopping, switch to the other leg for the same number of steps. You can switch off like this several times per set.

Training Tips: Place 15 to 20 rubber shock cords about 5 feet apart and hop over them, making sure you stay on the ball of your foot. Increase the distance 1 inch every 10 workouts. Do the drill with extra weight and then with the overspeed cord, adjusting the distance between the cords accordingly.

String out about 10 solid platforms (around 18 inches square for the top surface, preferably covered with a rubber gripping material, and around 12 inches high) in a straight line with the boxes about 5 or 6 feet apart. Hop up onto the first box, back to the ground, and then up onto the second box, and so on, moving as quickly as possible through the entire course. Increase the distance between the boxes gradually.

Gauge improvement in your one-legged hopping by timing yourself over any drill variation, always making sure the variables are the same when comparing times. You also want to time yourself over a given distance (20 to 40 yards is good), working to improve this time.

SPRINT TRAINING WORKOUT SCHEDULES

Your first approach to a sprint-training program is to set up an accurate training log, as covered earlier in the section "Sprint Training Workout Principles." You might review that procedure at this time.

Once your training log is organized, you should determine your maximum velocity and your 40-yard dash time, utilizing those procedures given in the section "Timing and Diagnostic Drills." (Try to take your 40 time in the manner described, which results in times for each 10-yard segment.) Record the results in your training log; then repeat the procedure every 6 weeks or so, recording the results again and noting any improvement.

BEGINNING SPRINT ROUTINES

After establishing your diagnostic times, you are ready to begin your sprinting program. If at all possible, start with a month (12 to 15 sessions or more) of general sprinting and supplementary sprinting drills. This establishes a solid foundation in sprinting fundamentals to both prevent injury and maximize overall training effectiveness. Following are some examples of beginning routines that might be done 3 to 4 times a week:

BEGINNING SPRINT ROUTINE #1

Warm-up

Several minutes jogging
Complete stretching routine
Several "runs"
Other warm-up drills as needed (from sprint statue, arm action, knee up, and stride switcher)

General Sprinting

Fly-ins	2–4 × 50–60 yards
Ins-and-outs	2–4 × 60–120 yards
(Can be stride-monitored, done with heels elevated)	

Supplementary Sprinting

High knee	2–4 × 50–60 yards
Bounding	2 × 50–60 yards
Speed stepping	2 × 50–60 yards
Knee-lock run	2 × 50–60 yards
(All can be stride-monitored, done with heels elevated)	
Toe rise walk	2–4 sets; do between other drills

Warm-down

Several minutes jogging

BEGINNING SPRINT ROUTINE #2

Warm-up

Several minutes jogging
Complete stretching routine
Several "runs"
Other warm-up drills as needed (from sprint statue, arm action,
    knee up, and stride switcher)

General Sprinting

Fly-ins	2–4 × 50–80 yards
High knee	2–4 × 50–60 yards
Ins-and-outs	2–4 × 60–120 yards

(Can mix above three drills in any pattern; can be
    stride-monitored, done with heels elevated)

Supplementary Sprinting

Bounding	2 × 50–60 yards
Speed stepping	2 × 50–60 yards
Knee-lock run	2 × 50–60 yards

(All can be stride-monitored, done with heels
    elevated)

Warm-down

Toe rise walk	2–4 sets; do between other drills

INTERMEDIATE SPRINT ROUTINES

After you are acclimated to general sprint and supplementary sprint work, a good intermediate off-season routine for football speed is one featuring 4 workouts weekly. You can emphasize general and supplementary sprint drills along with overspeed on 2 days, and starting/accelerating drills along with plyometrics on the other 2 days, a method that I have found to be successful. Another method is to go with general and supplementary and starting/accelerating on 2 days, with overspeed and plyometrics on the other 2 days, another method that has worked for me. Yet if you use any resistance with any routine, do so only 2 days a week.

INTERMEDIATE SPRINT ROUTINE #1

Days 1 and 3
(A: General/Supplementary Sprinting plus Overspeed)

Warm-up

Several minutes jogging
Complete stretching routine
Several "runs"
Other warm-up drills as needed (from sprint statue, arm action,
   knee up, and stride switcher)

General Sprinting

Fly-ins	2 × 50–60 yards
Ins-and-outs	2 × 60 yards

(Can be stride-monitored, done with heels elevated)

Overspeed Sprinting

Anchor sprinting	2–4 × 80–100 yards
High-knee anchor sprinting	2–4 × 50–60 yards

(Use moving anchor if possible)

Supplementary Sprinting

Bounding	2 × 50–60 yards
Speed stepping	2 × 50–60 yards
Knee-lock run	2 × 50–60 yards

(All can be stride-monitored, done either with
   overspeed or with heels elevated)

Warm-down

Several minutes jogging,
   light stretching

Days 2 and 4
(B: Starting/Accelerating and Plyometrics)

Warm-up

Same as days 1 and 3 plus fly-ins	2 × 50–60 yards

Starting/Accelerating

10-yard starts	2 × 2–3 reps per set
20-yard starts	2 ×

Starting/Accelerating

Ins-and-outs	2 × 2–3 reps per set
Jog and explode	2–4 × 2–3 reps/set
40-yard dash	2–4 ×
(Can be stride-monitored, done with resistance, elevated heels)	

Plyometrics

Vertical jump	2 × 10–15 reps
Two-legged hopping	2 × 10–15 reps
One-legged vertical jump	2 × 15–20 reps each leg
One-legged hopping	2 × 15–20 reps each leg
(Can elevate heels, use resistance, assistance)	

Warm-down

Several minutes jogging, light stretching

INTERMEDIATE SPRINT ROUTINE #2

Days 1 and 3
(A: General/Supplementary Sprinting plus Starting/Accelerating)

Warm-up

Several minutes jogging
Complete stretching routine
Several "runs"
Other warm-up drills as needed (from sprint statue, arm action, knee up, and stride switcher)

General Sprinting

Fly-ins	2 × 50–80 yards
Ins-and-outs	2 × 60–120 yards
(Can be stride-monitored, done with heels elevated)	

Starting/Accelerating

10-yard starts	2 × 2–3 reps per set
20-yard starts	2 ×
Ins-and-outs	2 × 2–3 reps per set

Starting/Accelerating

Jog and explode	2–4 × 2–4 reps/set
40-yard dash	2–4 ×
(Can be stride-monitored, done with	
resistance,	
elevated heels)	

Supplementary Sprinting

High knee	2 × 50–60 yards
Knee-lock	2 × 50–60 yards
(Can be stride-monitored, done with heels	
elevated)	

Warm-down

Several minutes jogging,
   light stretching

Days 2 and 4 (B: Overspeed and Plyometrics)

Warm-up

Same as Days 1 and 3 plus fly-ins	2 × 50–60 yards

Overspeed Sprinting

Anchor sprinting	2–4 × 80–100 yards
High-knee anchor sprinting	2–4 × 50–60 yards

Plyometrics

Vertical jump	2 × 10–15 reps
Two-legged hopping	2 × 10–15 reps
One-legged vertical jump	2 × 15–20 reps each leg
One-legged hopping	2 × 15–20 reps each leg
(Can elevate heels, use shock cord	
assistance)	

Warm-down

Several minutes jogging, light stretching

ADVANCED SPRINT ROUTINES

The advanced sprint routines are merely extensions of the intermediate sprint routines; they feature the drills and exercises contained within the intermediate routines, but are done more frequently. You can perform more sets of these drills and exercises per training session, perform more sprint training sessions per week, or perform more sets per session and more sets per week, with the latter method ordinarily not recommended.

The preferred method is a very gradual increase in the number of sets per session. Start out by increasing 1 single drill by just 1 set, and then increase another drill by 1 set a week or so later. Do this until you have very gradually increased each drill in your program by 1 set. This will have gotten you into an advanced sprint training routine.

If you are still not making progress with your sprint training and feel the need for further change, you can continue to gradually increase the number of sets that you do, again going up by 1 total set a week or so. You can also increase your number of weekly training sessions, although this should be done with caution. If you go for more than 4 training sessions per week, give yourself at least 1 light session weekly in which you do fewer sets. Your best bet is to add an extra session of moderate general sprinting work where you "lazily" work up to "just under" full speed and maintain it as effortlessly as possible, concentrating on perfect form and preferably monitoring your stride. You can then work overspeed sprinting and supplementary sprinting into your extra session, adding drills gradually and probably staying with 2 or, at the most, 3 sets per individual drill.

Ordinarily you want to refrain from adding more training sessions per week where you are doing starting/accelerating and plyometric drills, particularly when doing them in the same session. These training methods are very taxing, and 2 sessions per week should be enough. Of course, if you have tried the other methods of moving into advanced sprint training and are not making progress after a solid 4 to 6 weeks of training, you might look at first adding an extra day per week in which you do starting/accelerating drills. See how this goes before adding another session featuring plyometrics. Under no circumstances should you feature more than 3 days weekly when drills from either group are done.

Finally, don't fail to consider the possibility that you are doing too much sprint work. Sprint training is very taxing, and more often than not a slight decrease in your overall training load will be just what you need to aid your progress, particularly when you are working hard on your other physical traits. Although such a decrease is not really part of an advanced sprint training routine as such, it can have the effect of advancing your sprinting results. You might want to give this approach a try before anything else. I remember in my early high school years I had a tendency to do too much sprinting. Not only did I go stale and suffer some slight losses in speed, but I neglected some of my other training work. When I decreased my sprinting work load a bit, my times improved and I also increased my other training work.

IN-SEASON SPRINT ROUTINES

Although the outlined 4-day routines are for off-season work, you can utilize them during the season by cutting them to 2 days a week. This schedule works out effectively as a supplement to the conditioning sprints you do in practice and the sprinting you do during the games. You can do 1 sprint workout the day after a game and another around the middle of the week, utilizing either routine #1 or routine #2.

SPRINT DRILL SUMMARY

Following is a summary list of each drill, along with a rating of how accessory methods apply to it. Each method is rated as:

1	Very applicable
2	Applicable
3	Somewhat applicable
4	Not applicable

Drill	Stride-monitored	Heels elevated	Speed Chute	Resistance	Assistance/ Overspeed
Fly-ins	1	1	1	4	1
Ins-and-outs	1	2	1	3	4
High knee	1	3	3	4	1
Bounding	1	1	2	2	3
Knee-lock run	2	1	4	3	2
Speed stepping	3	3	4	4	2
10-yard starts	2	2	1	2	4
20-yard starts	2	2	1	2	4
Ins-and-outs (shortened)	2	2	2	1	4
Jog and explode	2	2	1	1	4
40-yard dash	1	2	1	2	3
Vertical jumps	4	2	4	1	1
Two-legged hopping	1	2	4	1	1
One-legged vertical jumping	4	1	4	2	1
One-legged hopping	1	1	4	2	1

A FINAL WORD ON SPRINTING

By now you should have enough technical information to carry out a systematic sprinting program. Yet sprint training often requires more than just technical information. While you must be motivated to train for football in general, you must be particularly motivated to train for improved sprinting speed.

Progress in sprinting is hard to come by. You might train consistently and correctly for months on end, and then get timed and show no measurable improvement. You must discipline yourself to continue to train if this happens. You have to keep on with the same methodical work without any guarantee of getting any faster. You tell yourself that a speed improvement breakthrough can occur at any time . . . any time . . . any time.

Then suddenly you're down a tenth of a second! And just as suddenly, all the painstaking work and discipline seem worth it. You attack your sprint workouts with a renewed vigor, for you never know when you're going to knock off another tenth of a second, or another tenth of a second after that.

Actual progress in sprinting has always been somewhat difficult for me to achieve. As one who had excellent natural speed, it was tougher for me to improve than it was for a slower guy who had more room for improvement. I recall working out for months and months with no improvement in my times. Yet I kept on training, consistently and systematically, eventually improving my times to 4.3 over 40 yards, 9.3 over 100 yards, and 20.8 over 220 yards. And I have kept on training ever since, the major benefit of which has been that I can still run 40 yards in 4.3 as I approach my thirtieth birthday.

The overriding axiom with regard to sprinting training is really quite simple: Regardless of how fast you can sprint at present, or how much improvement you have shown, if you want to run as fast as you can . . . you must train like a champion for years on end.

5

Strength Makes the Difference: Building Your Power

"One of the most important elements in a football
player's ability is strength."
> *The late Woody Hayes, former head football coach,*
> *Ohio State University*

AN OVERVIEW OF STRENGTH

STRENGTH DEFINED

Strength is the amount of force or tension that your muscles can exert.
The more raw force you are capable of applying, the stronger you are.

Strength is a little different from power, although the two are
related. While strength is force application regardless of the time involved, power is force application over a time interval. If two athletes
can each press 300 pounds, both are equally strong. Yet the athlete
who makes this lift in less time has exhibited more power.

As you gain in strength, you will also increase your power. Let's
say that you are a beginning lifter capable of pressing 150 pounds one
time in a maximum effort. With hard training, you eventually increase
this to 200 pounds. Then you can take the same 150 pounds and press
it for 8 to 10 repetitions. In so doing, you will move this weight at a
much greater speed than when you were pressing it for 1 rep in a

maximum effort. Since you are lifting the same weight in less time, your power has increased.

Strength gains also correlate with gains in local muscular endurance, or endurance related to your muscular system rather than to your "wind." In effect, such increases in strength develop muscular endurance indirectly. If you can press the same 150 pounds for 8 to 10 reps, up from the one repetition maximum you performed in the beginning, you have increased your muscular endurance as well as your strength and power. This increased muscular endurance is valuable for football and other sports.

THE IMPORTANCE OF STRENGTH

There is quite a long list of the benefits of strength for football, headed by the fact that strength aids you in preventing injury, and nothing is more important to you as a football player than remaining injury free. Other things being equal, when your muscles and tendons are stronger, they are less susceptible to pulls and tears, and the bruises, contusions, and general soreness they sustain do not adversely affect their function as much. Your muscles form a protective sheath around vital body parts, and the stronger your muscles, the tougher and often larger this sheath is. The result is that stronger muscles will both better absorb the shock of contact and also protect your bones and internal organs from it. There is even some evidence that added muscular strength makes your bones stronger, and possibly larger.

Strength development will also aid you in recovering faster from injury, particularly if the injury is to the muscles themselves. Your body is used to rebuilding itself as a result of being constantly "injured" through the intense strength-training exercises you have given it, and to a great extent this will carry over to other "real" injuries.

A big advantage of extra strength is that you can generate more force upon contact, and in football this is the name of the game. Much of this extra force comes from the gain in body weight strength training can give you. Recall from the last chapter that force is mass times velocity. So if you up your weight (mass) and maintain your velocity, the "explosion" you cause is going to be that much more powerful.

Extra strength can also aid your hitting power even though you don't gain any body weight, essentially because you retain a greater velocity component throughout your hitting technique. In other words, the stronger you are, the less you will slow upon impact, and the more force you will maintain. This strength, in effect, can better aid you in driving "through" your man. So extra strength with the same velocity and technique can make you more of a "hitter."

Strength training enables you to perform the same or even more work per unit of time without getting as tired, in effect increasing your muscular endurance. Suppose you can handle 120 pounds in a pressing motion for 5 reps. Performing these 5 reps will leave you breathing hard, with your muscles temporarily tired. So you train steadily and increase this lift to 160 pounds for 5 reps. Now when you pick up the 120 pounds and "toy" with it for 5 reps in a warm-up type of movement, you are doing the exact same work you did earlier, with less stress on your breathing and with less muscle fatigue. This has a direct carryover to the work you do on the football field.

One distinct advantage of strength training is that it aids you in getting bigger, in packing slabs of muscle onto your body to better play the game. Other things being equal, a good big man beats a good smaller man hands down in football (remember that equation for force). This probably doesn't seem fair to those of you not blessed with great size, and you're right. Yet instead of moping around about it, get on a good lifting program to pack on some muscular body weight, and read or reread the section in the first chapter on gaining weight, while you're at it. You may not become the Incredible Hulk of your ball club, but any extra weight at no loss of speed, quickness, and agility has got to help you. So go for it.

A good strength training program can also help you maintain your sprinting speed while you gain body weight, and this is particularly true if you simultaneously do an adequate amount of sprinting and stretching. While some guys complain about "slowing down" after adding muscle, it's almost always the case that they have neglected their sprinting and stretching while they lifted. Actually, a good strength program is like adding extra shielding to your body (remember that protective muscular coating) while upping your body's horsepower. If you train the wrong way, the extra shielding becomes so much extra baggage, since your increase in horsepower is not enough to overcome the extra weight.

As mentioned in chapter 4, increased strength can aid you in sprinting faster, when it is used in conjunction with flexibility and sprint training. Some guys have used strength training to put on 20,

30, even 40 pounds, and still knocked time off their 40-yard dash. Of course, these kinds of gains are possible only with years of intense, systematic training.

As mentioned in chapter 3, strength training can improve quickness/agility. Essentially, stronger muscles are able to give you a little extra "boost" for more rapid starts and direction changes. Yet again, a lot of actual quickness/agility work must also be done, as strength training merely supplements quickness/agility development.

Heavy strength training involves subjecting your body to some pain, and this is good training for football because the game involves pain. By increasing your pain threshold in the weight room, there should be some carryover to the football field. If you have the guts to take the pain of heavy, "sell out" sets of squats, this will help you take the pain of football contact.

Finally, strength training gives you a psychological advantage due to the results you get from it. Since you are stronger, you're going to play stronger. In other words, you're strong, you know it, and you want to kick some tail. You've paid the price with all those tough hours in the weight room, and now it's time for your opponent to pay his price.

One way of thinking about what strength training can do for you as a football player is to view the game of football as a demolition derby, with your body the car to be used. The car that is structurally stronger, can be repaired faster, can hit with more force, can carry more gasoline, is heavier, can add more weight without slowing, is faster, is more maneuverable, can stand more damage, and "has confidence in" and "enjoys" what it does will—to say the least—have an advantage. It should be crystal clear that strength training is a must if you want to reach the top of your game.

STRENGTH MEASUREMENT AND DEVELOPMENT METHODS

When you talk about strength measurement and development, you're usually talking about dynamic strength, or strength featuring movement. The technical term for dynamic strength is isotonic contraction, and there isn't anything fancy about measuring it. The measurement is simply how much weight you can lift (usually using a barbell or dumbbells) through a complete lifting movement. In effect, you are really measuring the force, or strength, necessary to overcome and thus move the weight.

The purest form of isotonic strength measurement is the amount of weight you can lift for one repetition. Yet for football, some coaches think that the weight you can lift for 4 to 8 or even 10 reps is more applicable. In fact, some studies (which will be discussed later) show that handling maximum weight for 4 to 6 reps is the best measurement and developer of muscular power, and power is what you are primarily concerned with developing through your strength training work. Also, doing reps like this develops not only strength but some of the local muscular endurance required for football.

You can also measure (and develop) what is called static strength, or strength without movement. The term for static strength is isometric contraction, and it is measured with a gadget called a dynamometer, a scale that shows the force that you apply against it. A good dynamometer has a dial that moves to the position of maximum force application and stays there until it is reset. It is helpful in getting an accurate reading to diagnose strength levels at different positions of a particular lift.

Additionally, you can measure and develop strength with what is called isokinetic contraction. Briefly, this is a type of strength exercise movement in which the speed of motion is limited regardless of the force applied. The result is that you can exert maximum force through the entire range of lifting motion without accelerating the load. Most isokinetic devices have dials that show the maximum force generated, much like a dynamometer. Some really fancy (and expensive) ones contain mini-computers that average out your exerted force and add it up over each repetition, counting the reps and giving you your total work effort in foot pounds.

Isokinetic strength is a form of dynamic strenth and can probably be measured more accurately than isotonic lifting strength. The isokinetic machines take little technique, minimize cheating, and are generally quite accurate, at least within the same machine.

Yet isotonic strength is probably the best gauge of strength for football application. Since football is a dynamic (motion-involving) game, isometric (static) strength is not as applicable as isotonic (dynamic) strength. Isokinetic strength, while dynamic in nature, does not require the balance, timing, or coordination of isotonics. Additionally, the various resistances presented on the football field are probably more isotonic than isokinetic in nature.

Since measured increases in strength are largely specific to the type of strength training done, the major focus of this chapter will be on isotonic strength development. Yet later sections will cover isometric and isokinetic strength training methods, as both are excellent supplements to isotonics.

FACTORS AFFECTING STRENGTH DEVELOPMENT

Your strength development is affected by a number of factors, among them heredity, age and physical maturity, stage of training, diet, and training methods.

Heredity. Heredity definitely affects strength development. Some people seem to have a greater potential (or at least an easier time) in getting strong. Nearly every football team seems to have at least one guy who was always strong, who seemingly never had to endure the process of beginning with moderate weights to get where he is now. Yet, by contrast, every team has the guy who started out with nothing and went on to develop outstanding strength.

My own inherent ability to develop strength is probably better than average, but I know of a number of athletes who are—for whatever reasons—stronger than I am. I have been able to develop a good level of strength over the years, but I have had to work hard for my development, since strength has never come as easily to me as has sprinting speed.

Age. Your age and physical maturity will affect your strength development. Your rate of strength increase should be higher when you are younger. It is at this time that your body can recover more quickly from intensive strength workouts.

Yet most guys don't reach their peak in strength until their late twenties or early thirties, at least if they keep on training. I am 29 at the time of this writing, and I am still gaining strength and expect this to continue over the next several years. Since there is so much room for strength improvement, it takes considerable time to realize your maximum strength development. Thus you should keep on getting at least a little stronger over a long period of time.

Stage of Training. The stage of lifting you are in will influence your rate of strength development. Generally, you will make the fastest gains at the beginning of your lifting program, and your gains will slow somewhat as you progress. As an example, if you are a beginning high school lifter who can bench press 150 pounds, you should improve from 150 to 200 faster than you improve from 200 to 250. Many beginning lifters will improve specific lifts as much in a month of training as very advanced lifters do in a year.

Diet. To say that diet is important to strength development is like saying oxygen is important to life. For no matter how hard you work out, or how sound your routine, you won't benefit fully unless you eat good food, and plenty of it. If you're a junk food junkie, content to skimp on a real meal in favor of Twinkies and a soda pop, forget it! Go play Ping-Pong or Frisbee because, with regard to strength training (and all other training as well), eating this kind of garbage will not get the job done. If you have not read chapter 1, now is a good time to do so.

Training Methods. The final factor in getting strong is how you train. You have to use the correct lifts in a workable sequence, perform an effective number of sets and reps with them, and take your workouts over the right frequency and with the right intensity. Unfortunately, it's not quite as simple as this, mainly because there is a lot of disagreement over exactly what is "correct." The section on actual workout routines will get into this controversy a little bit more.

DEGREE OF STRENGTH IMPROVEMENT

Strength can probably be improved more than any other physical trait. Improvements of 50 percent or more in a year's time are not uncommon, as are improvements of 100 percent or more from the time a guy first starts training. In fact, I have improved all of my major lifts by more than 100 percent since I first started strength training many years ago. This should make it pretty obvious that consistent strength training will pay off.

STRENGTH TRAINING TERMINOLOGY

It is important that you understand basic strength training terminology in order to work out properly. First, any one bout of a strength exercise is called a set. Each set then consists of a certain number of repetitions.

For example, if you bench pressed a certain weight 8 times, you would have done one set of 8 repetitions. If you then rested a bit and bench pressed the weight another 8 times, you would have done 2 sets of 8 repetitions. If you again rested and bench pressed the weight yet another 8 times, you would have done 3 sets of 8 repetitions.

The abbreviation for 3 sets of 10 repetitions with the bench press is: bench press–3 × 10, or something reasonably similar. The weight to be used is generally not given since it varies so much with individual strength levels. Actually, even the number of sets and reps are merely estimated. For if you work your sets to failure (to be covered), it's impossible to say exactly how many sets of a given number of reps you will do.

The strength training program in any sample routine may contain up to a dozen or more exercises, sometimes offered in suggested order of performance and/or divided up by body part. Additionally, reference is ordinarily made to the days of the week on which the various exercises are to be done. There will be examples of such programs later on.

STRENGTH TRAINING EQUIPMENT

The major tool for any strength program is the barbell, a solid bar a bit over an inch in diameter and about 5 to 7 feet long. Plates are loaded onto the barbell from both ends, and the load should always be balanced. An Olympic barbell, which is generally about 7 feet long and uses plates with 2-inch holes, is considered the Rolls-Royce of barbells.

Another basic strength training tool is the dumbbell, which is really just a shorter version of the barbell. Dumbbell bars, around 10 to 12 inches long, are usually gripped with just one hand for exercising. They are often used in pairs and for more specialized exercises than barbells. Dumbbells are not as effective overall as the barbell for strengthening large muscle groups. A guy just can't use as much weight when he exercises with dumbbells.

The flat bench is a fundamental item for strength training since quite a few exercises can be done with it. If the bench has supports to hold the bar for bench pressing and/or if it is adjustable for pressing at different angles (called an adjustable-incline bench), so much the better.

One piece of equipment that is nearly indispensable is the power rack. It consists of 4 vertical pieces (usually angle irons) often fastened at right angles to a horizontal platform and then also connected together at the top. Two of the pieces are located on one edge of the platform about 1 to 2 feet from each other. The other 2 vertical pieces are located about 4 feet over on the opposite edge of the platform, also about 1 to 2 feet from each other. Each of the 4 pieces has matching holes drilled in it every couple of inches or so, and "pins" made from solid round stock are then inserted through the holes. The pins are then set to support the barbell for various lifting movements, acting as a safety catch for lifts not completed. On the newer models, a device that holds the barbell is lodged into the pin holes from the inside. This way the bar can be lifted off the holder with the exercise movement then started from the "up" position, the pins still acting as a safety catch.

The power rack can also be used for isometrics by simply pressing the bar up against the lodged pins. Other advanced exercise techniques done with it are isometronics, partials, and lockouts, which will be discussed in more detail later.

With just the 4 pieces of equipment mentioned thus far—the barbell, dumbbell, flat bench, and power rack—the quality of strength workout you can get is amazing. You can perform all of the major big muscle group movements, and most of the supplementary movements,

The all-around press machine, which is also called the Smith machine, can be used to perform any pressing movement. Some people also like it for high pulls. *Photo courtesy of Jubinville Health Equipment.*

in complete safety. Thus these 4 units form the core of any strength program. If you were limited to just 4 pieces of equipment, these would be the 4 to go with.

There are a number of other strength training devices that can be considered basic, and many of them are applicable to training for football strength. Yet the design and function of each device will not be covered now. Instead, these units will later be shown in action featuring the various exercises done on them.

While still on the topic of equipment, you have probably heard of the Nautilus machines. These are a series of exercise machines, each of which works basically on one body part. Nautilus equipment is extremely well built, but also very expensive, running in the range of thousands of dollars per machine.

Besides being well made, the Nautilus machines are extremely safe and therefore valuable for injury rehabilitation. Additionally, the machines are good because the famous Nautilus cam varies the resistance throughout the movement, increasing it as the mechanical advantage of your lifting muscles increases. Nautilus was the first to come out with many of the specialty devices you see on the market today, and their thigh extension and leg curl devices, among other units, are thought by some to be the best available anywhere.

Extravagant claims have been made with regard to the Nautilus machines, their manufacturer feeling that they are superior to regular isotonic barbell and dumbbell lifting. Yet it is questionable whether Nautilus workouts will add the kind of bulk and raw strength that heavy-duty free-weight workouts will. They do not stress the large muscle groups of your body as much as free weights do. Accordingly, most football strength programs emphasize power movements with free weights, and some of them use Nautilus in a supplementary manner.

If you have access to Nautilus equipment, you might want to try to supplement your regular isotonic routine. Their manufacturer suggests you use only 1 set of 8 to 12 reps per exercise, do them very strictly with no cheating, hold the movement for a few seconds at the point of full contraction, and lower the weight slowly to get some of the benefits of negative exercise. You may, of course, wish to vary from these suggestions, depending on how you feel your body is responding.

Another popular piece of equipment is the universal gym, commonly referred to as the universal. Technically, this name describes equipment originally manufactured by a company of the same name, yet the basic design has been duplicated by so many manufacturers that any equipment resembling it is now called "universal." What it amounts to is a device with several to a dozen or more different exercise stations, each designed essentially for 1 or 2 exercises, although with some imagination more can be thought up.

The universal has some distinct advantages. It takes up very little space for the variety of exercise movements that it offers and is safer than barbells and dumbbells. The larger units can accommodate a dozen or so people simultaneously with stations to work every major muscle group. The universal is also good for quick workouts since the amount of weight used can be altered in seconds with a simple change in key placement. Some universals also feature a very effective exercise concept that they term "dynamically variable resistance," which is much like the Nautilus but with different exercise movement applications. This concept will later be discussed in detail.

An increasingly popular piece of equipment is the Smith machine, a barbell rigged to a rack so that it can only go straight up and down. The Smith machine can be used for a wide variety of exercises, which you must do in a strict, efficient manner since the bar moves only vertically. This machine is also quite safe, employing safety catches to rack the bar at various heights.

Certain exercise gadgets feature a friction brake, hydraulic fluid, or compressed air as the resistance. These units employ the earlier mentioned concept of isokinetic contraction, which is discussed in greater detail later in the chapter.

One item that you should definitely invest in is a lifting belt, a heavy-duty leather support belt that is several inches wide over its support area. It offers good lower-back protection for lifting and should be worn snugly and low on your back for all heavy lifts.

STRENGTH TRAINING WORKOUT PRINCIPLES

DRESS PROPERLY

Proper dress for weight training is mainly a matter of common sense. In other words, do not do your deadlifts in your new designer jeans. Instead, take 5 minutes to put on a jock, sweat socks, appropriate shoes, and shorts or sweats, depending upon the weather and your personal preference. The jock is a must if you want to have kids; as for shoes, any good gym shoe will do. There are weightlifting shoes on the market, but you do not really need them. You should also wear a lifting belt, particularly when doing any exercises that place stress on your lower back.

WARM UP THOROUGHLY

Proper warm-up is a necessary part of any good strength training routine. It will not only help to prevent injury, but will help you to lift more productively. A weightlifting warm-up involves beginning with light weights and increasing to progressively heavier ones over several sets. As an example, you might begin with 30 to 50 percent of your projected workout weight and perform 10 or more reps with it. You can jump up to 60 or 70 percent on your next set, and do 4 to 8 reps. Your last warm-up set can be at 80 to 90 percent of your workout set, and you can do 2 to 4 reps.

Note that warm-up sets do not count as part of your official routine. If your workout calls for 3 sets of incline presses, for example, you count only those sets on which you are working to failure.

You might go through a complete warm-up routine like this and still not feel ready to "lift heavy," especially in colder weather. If this is the case, take more warm-up. How your muscles feel is a more important indicator of being ready to "go heavy" than is working through a prescribed routine.

You should need less warm-up as you progress from one exercise to another one that works much of the same muscle group. If you move to one pressing movement shortly after completing another pressing movement, you should not need as much warm-up for the second pressing movement. Again, be in touch with how your body feels in deciding how much warm-up you want.

BREATHE CORRECTLY

Proper breathing is essential when strength training. You should inhale when lowering the weight, and exhale when raising it. It is easy to keep these procedures in order by remembering to "blow the weight up" as a means of boosting your lifting power.

USE SPOTTERS

Spotters are people who help you when you cannot complete your lift. They assist you in finishing your lift and getting the bar safely back on the rack when you are unable to do so. If your equipment has a safety catch (as with the power rack, for example), you can generally perform your lifts without spotters.

There are certain lifts where you absolutely must use either spotters or a safety catch. These lifts are the squat, bench press, and incline press. To perform heavy sets of these exercises without spotters or a safety catch is to invite serious injury. If no spotters are available to assist you, your best bet is to do these movements inside a power rack with the safety pins set just below your lowest lift movement point, a practice that I rely on when no one is spotting me.

Spotters can be helpful in aiding beginners with their form in various heavy lifts. Guiding the lifting form of the novice installs confidence, and the resulting correct form serves as a safety technique by itself.

You should always communicate your needs to your spotter. Tell him how many reps you are going to try for. You should be within 1 or 2 reps either way on your estimate; this way your spotter will be less likely to break your set by assisting you too soon. You should also tell your spotter what to do if you can't make your lift, and whether you want him to just help you rack the weight or to make you work in getting it back up. Tell your spotter if you want a lift off, which is help in unracking the bar to start your lift, especially applicable to the bench press.

INCREASE YOUR INTENSITY GRADUALLY

This is another important strength training principle that is often violated; this is unfortunate because by "going up slowly" you will progress better in the long run. A slow, gradual increase gives your body a chance to adapt to the stress you are placing on it, and this means lessening your chance of sustaining any injuries that will halt your training. A gradual increase also means steadier strength gains since you will minimize your periods of staleness and the related sticking points in your strength gains. It is also psychologically beneficial since you are more confident of performing the desired number of reps when you have increased your weight ever so slightly from the previous time. I have always concentrated on fairly slow, steady gains in strength, and I feel I have benefited accordingly.

An example of a gradual increase in intensity is as follows. Suppose you can handle 205 pounds for 5 reps maximum in a given exercise. You then increase to 206 pounds over your next training session instead of jumping to the conventional 210. Although you might well have handled the 210 for 5 reps, the 206 gives you the mentioned benefits of a gradual increase.

If you increase your body weight by an average of just 1 pound every 3 workouts, and if you work out 105 to 120 times a year (not counting your in-season workouts), this amounts to a 35- or 40-pound increase annually. Multiply this by each year that you lift and you can see how slow, gradual increases add up to substantial long-term gains in strength. Obviously, a maximum level of increase will be reached for each individual.

Since weight sets traditionally do not have the plates needed for 1-pound jumps, you have to improvise. Your best bet is to haunt a garage sale for some old 1¼-, 2½-, and perhaps 3- to 5-pound plates. Then take them to a machine shop (perhaps your school has one) and have them shaved down so that you have 2 one-half pounders, 2 one pounders, 2 two pounders and maybe a couple of three pounders, while you're at it. For best results, make sure the holes are centered and the plates balanced, and by all means go with holes that fit the bar you will be using. If you use an Olympic bar, you can take plates with 1⅛-inch holes and expand them to 2 inches as part of the shaving-down process.

The mentioned assortment will allow you to take 1-pound jumps within any 5-pound range. For example, if you have 205 on the bar, add a ½-pound plate to each end to get 206. To get 207, add a 1-pound plate to each end of the 205. For 208 add a 1-pounder and a ½-pounder to each end, and for 209 add a couple of 2-pound plates. Then add your conventional 2½-pound plates to each end to get 210, and for 211 add a couple of 3-pounders, if you have them.

WORK YOUR SETS TO FAILURE

To maximize the strength-gaining process, you must do as many reps as you can in each and every set, excluding warm-ups (a practice that

I invariably adhere to when doing serious strength training work). This is one of the most fundamental principles of strength training, and also one of the most violated. If you don't work your set to failure, you're performing what amounts to a heavy warm-up set; you just have to do those last tough reps to obtain maximum benefit. One all-out set done to failure is more productive than 4 or 5 sets that are not done to failure. Anything less than an all-out set for strength development is like less than an all-out sprint for speed development; it helps, but not to the maximum.

USE A MAXIMUM OF THREE SETS TO FAILURE PER LIFT

This is also probably one of the most violated principles of strength training. The average guy will reach a plateau in strength development and reason that he has to perform extra sets to get over the hump. In doing them, he will work his body to a state where it cannot recover fully between strength training sessions, and the result is a continued lack of improvement or perhaps even a loss of some strength.

I remember back when I first started lifting weights how I would pile on set after extra set whenever I would reach a sticking point. I would then be surprised when my strength would not only fail to increase but would actually decrease somewhat, and I would compensate by adding even more sets and then continue to not make progress. It was not until I learned that it is sometimes better to do fewer sets (particularly when the quality of each set is increased, as with the "Advanced Methods of Strength Development," which will be covered later) that my progress picked up.

Three sets to failure for any single lift is a lot. While there are programs that call for more sets than this, consider that they might not be talking about sets done strictly to failure. Consider also that as a football player, you have to save some time and energy for other types of training.

As a beginner, you can actually make gains with just 1 set to failure, and 2 sets to failure is plenty. As you advance, rather than extend beyond 3 sets to failure, try some of the advanced forms of strength development that are covered later in this chapter.

EMPHASIZE THE CORRECT NUMBER OF REPS

You must perform within the range of the correct number of repetitions for the various exercises. This general range is 4 to 10 reps for large muscle group (Big 6) exercises, 6 to 12 reps for supplementary exercises, and 8 to 20 reps or more for body part exercises.

CYCLE YOUR TRAINING

Using cycles is a fairly recent trend in lifting circles and what it means is to periodically vary the intensity and perhaps the frequency of your workouts, a process also known as periodization. It is necessary to do this because your body and mind simply can't handle "killer" workouts every time you hit the iron.

A lot has been written about how to cycle your training, including some precise charts and formulas telling you to lift a certain percent of your maximum for so many sets and reps over so many workouts, and then switch to a new percent for so many sets, reps, and workouts. A problem with this approach is that by confining you to, say, 4 sets of 5 reps with 85 percent of your maximum, you won't always work to failure. For if you get 5 reps with a given weight while working to failure, it is very unlikely that you can get 3 more sets of 5 with the same weight.

One way to cycle your workouts is to train hard for a given period of, say, 4 to 8 weeks; take a week off or work out lightly for a week; and then begin another cycle for the same 4- to 8-week period, perhaps with a new, or at least altered, routine.

You can also cycle within your cycle, so to speak. You might alternate heavy and light workouts within your period, going, say, heavy-light-heavy on a 3-days-per-week routine. Another method is to begin your cycle with 1 set to failure and end it with 3 sets to failure, which would entail adding a set every so many weeks, depending upon the length of your cycle. You could also use a pyramid scheme, starting your cycle with 1 set, progressing up to 3 sets by the middle of your cycle, and decreasing back down to 1 set by the end of your cycle.

An additional approach is to cycle your repetitions, perhaps beginning your cycle with sets of 8 to 10 reps for your heavy power movements and working down to sets of 4 to 6 reps by the end of your cycle. You can pyramid your reps during your cycle, either going high reps–low reps–high reps, or low reps–high reps–low reps for the beginning, middle, and end phases.

During the week or so between your cycles, you can work out moderately with isokinetics if you feel up to it. Isokinetics do not cause the muscle and joint soreness of isotonics and can serve as an effective change of pace. You can also supplement your isotonic lifting with isokinetics during your cycle, as will be discussed in a later section. You can also perform moderate amounts of resistance exercise that does not require barbells. (See the later section on "Strength Training with Limited Equipment.") Naturally, you can always simply skip resistance exercise during your week between cycles. This practice is particularly effective if you are an intermediate to advanced lifter who has been training hard. You can work on your other training (speed, quickness/agility, stamina) during the week that you do no lifting.

The idea with these cycles is to temporarily "peak" during or after each period, recuperate over the layoff or light workout period, and then reach a slightly higher peak over the next cyclic period. It is felt that this gradual, up-and-down method of training will minimize those sticking points that inevitably occur when you train super hard, workout after workout. I have found this to be the case in my own strength training work.

While cycling is important, it is actually secondary to your making progress. In other words, if you are making steady strength gains with your routine, you don't have to drop everything and rest for a week just because you have been doing your routine for a certain time. Yet keep in mind that sooner or later you're going to need a rest and probably a change in routine, so you want to be thinking about a cycling approach to some extent.

TRY NEW METHODS AND ROUTINES

If you want to maximize your strength gains, you must keep your mind open to new methods and routines. You never know if something is going to work for you until you try it. So don't be one of those narrow-minded guys who refrains from trying something different just because it is new to you. This kind of attitude can cost you in strength gains, something that I learned the hard way.

GIVE YOUR METHODS AND ROUTINE A CHANCE

This might seem a little contradictory to the last guideline. Yet although you must be willing to change routines and methods, you must also give your new routines and methods a chance once the switch is made. In essence, you have to strike a balance between staying with one system to the point of being closed to everything else and switching things around to the point of not giving them a chance to work for you.

Ordinarily you should give any change a good several weeks or so. If you have made no progress over this time, the routine is probably not right for you and should be changed, or at least modified.

TRAIN CONSISTENTLY

One of the most important principles in strength training is that of consistency. You simply must train with consistency in order to make the most of your workouts. A consistent pattern of moderately thorough workouts is far better than sporadic killer workouts followed by periods of loafing. Remember that strength is gained in small steps and that you must consistently be in the gym to take those small steps.

GET IN AND GET OUT

Many guys spend too much time in the weight room. They take 2½ or 3 hours to accomplish what could be done in an hour and a half. They talk about their grade on a history test or the girl they're chasing, and their workout takes longer than it should and is less productive. (I must admit that I was guilty of this myself in years past.)

The weight room is not a place to socialize. It is for the sole purpose of preparing your body for football action. So do your socializing elsewhere.

Another cause of marathon workouts is too many exercises and sets. If your workout is taking much longer than 90 minutes, you might adjust your exercises and sets accordingly. There may be some occasions when workouts of 2 hours or so are productive, but this happens mainly with fairly advanced routines.

Regardless of what lifting stage you are in, the underlying principle is this: get into the weight room consistently, work out intensely, and get out.

KEEP ACCURATE RECORDS

Accurate record-keeping is important for all training and is particularly important for strength training. In order to select a good working weight for an exercise, you must know what weight you have handled in that exercise previously. Thus if you wish to do a couple of sets to failure with the high pull, getting about 5 or 6 reps, you must select the correct weight. Accordingly, you must know the weight and reps you handled during your previous high pull workout. A written lifting record keeps such information readily available.

Some of the things to include in your lifting records are: date, type of lift, weight, reps, grip, style, device used, and comments. You can list these 8 factors horizontally in a notebook and then simply fill in under them accordingly. Keeping records like this shouldn't really extend your lifting time since you can fill it in while you're resting between sets.

Date	Lift	Weight	Reps	Grip	Style	Device	Comment
6–12	seat press	95	8	med.	touch go	Olym. bar	warm-up
"	"	115	4	"	"	"	" "
"	"	135	2	"	"	"	" "
"	"	155	6	"	"	"	fine set
"	"	155	5	"	"	"	failed 6th
"	"	155	5	"	"	"	did not try 6th

STRENGTH TRAINING EXERCISES

BIG 6 LIFTS

How would you like "baseball" biceps, "horseshoe" triceps, "coconut" deltoids, "barn door" lats, "washboard" abs, "treetrunk" thighs, "diamond" calves, "pyramid" traps, and a neck that would make a bulldog jealous? As "totally awesome" as these things sound, they should not be the desired result of your football strength program. Your goal should be the development of functional strength for football rather than building a body beautiful. In effect, any "show" development you achieve through your training can be considered a side effect that is secondary to your goal of pure strength and power.

The major lifts for football are the following Big 6 movements: squat, deadlift, high pull, bench press, seated press, and incline press. These movements work the large muscle groups of your body, building functional strength and power for football. It is necessary that you emphasize these lifts in your strength program, generally doing them first in your workout and closely scrutinizing the weights you handle with them. You should perform sets of 4 to 10 repetitions with these lifts, and you might work your weaker Big 6 lifts first, increasing your chances of gaining more strength with them relative to your stronger Big 6 lifts.

Squats. Squats are probably the most effective football strength training exercise known. They will develop your raw leg power more than any other exercise and are also tops for helping you gain muscular body weight. This is because they both work the largest muscle groups of your body (frontal thighs, lower back, buttocks) and stimulate overall muscular growth. Squats will also help your wind (anaerobic capacity) a little bit if worked hard in fairly high reps, and they can aid you in running faster if done along with a good sprint and flexibility program. They can be particularly beneficial during the accelerative phase of your sprint.

Squats are also very valuable in helping you to resist leg injury. A properly done squat program will strengthen your legs and make them less susceptible to injury from football play. One strength coach has equated the consistent and correct use of squats to an "insurance policy" against injury.

Although I hate a tough set of squats as much as the next guy, I do this exercise on a regular basis. The benefits are simply too great to bypass.

The squat movement is performed by stepping under a racked and collared barbell that is slightly lower than shoulder height. You dip slightly and place the center of the back of your neck directly under the center of the bar, even marking the center of the bar in some way, if you have to. You then support the bar with your shoulders as it rests against the base of the rear of your neck. You should have your feet a little wider than shoulder width apart and your hands out and gripping the bar in any position that is comfortable. You then back out of the rack very carefully, taking about one short step with each foot and keeping your feet the same shoulder width distance apart. You may point your feet slightly out, if you wish.

Once your position is established, slowly bend at your knees until your thighs are parallel to the floor, and then come back up to your original position. You should keep your head up through the duration of the lift (perhaps concentrating your eyes on a spot in front of you) and inhale while going down and exhale while coming up.

It is imperative to have complete control of the bar when you squat. Thus you must always lower the bar at a speed at which you can control it, and always only to the parallel or just under the parallel position. Too fast a descent can cause injury or, at the very least, cause you to miss your lift.

Squatting technique can vary a bit. Some guys like to place the bar a little lower, or slightly below where their neck meets their shoulders, and they then lean forward more as they do the lift. Often they spread their feet a little wider as well. This type of squatting puts more stress on your lower back and doesn't work your frontal thighs as much. Thus although the higher bar and straighter back method is good for pure quadricep development, you can handle more weight with your feet a bit wider. You might want to experiment a bit to develop your own "feel" for placement.

One good pointer when squatting is to try and get exactly under the center of the bar. You can use your hands to roughly measure the distance from common markings on either side of the bar to your shoulders. You don't have to be exact since the weights on either side of the bar aren't going to balance out perfectly. Yet get it as close as possible.

Another tip is to avoid taking extra steps away from the rack. This energy-robbing motion will move the plates, hurting your alignment and putting changing pressure on your body. You want to keep the bar as silent and controlled as possible, and the one careful step back with each foot is your best bet for this.

As mentioned previously, you should never squat alone unless you use a safety catch to stop the bar if you should miss your lift. An excellent example of using a safety catch is, of course, to squat inside a power rack with the pins set just below the position to which you lower the bar. Another safety catch device is the "staircase" squat rack, which has a similarly placed support rack for missed lifts.

If your gym does not feature a safety catch item, you must use spotters on all but your warm-up sets. Ideally you will want one on each side of you, although some people work squats with a single spotter behind them.

When using a spotter or spotters, give instructions on what you wish done, and then purposely "fail" during a warm-up set to test reaction. If the spot was not done properly, very tactfully correct them and try it again.

You should always wear a sturdy, snugly fitting lifting belt when squatting, to protect against lower-back injury. A lot of people wear their belt too high. Wear it as low as possible for squats and other power movements that stress the lower back.

It is important to warm up thoroughly with lighter sets in all weight-training exercises, and this is particularly true with squatting. As a beginner, you probably shouldn't go up more than 50 pounds a set until you know what you're doing. You might also stretch your upper hamstring muscles, right where they meet your buttocks, and particularly if you're squatting with a fairly wide stance. (See those chapter 2 stretching drills that are applicable.)

Since squats are the primary leg exercise in any program that includes them, you should ordinarily do them before any other leg work. Naturally, there should be some training sessions in which you will want to emphasize other leg exercises to keep from going mentally and physically stale from the demands of squats. For example, you might emphasize leg presses followed by thigh extensions once every 3 or so workouts where you hit your legs.

Deadlift. The deadlift exercise mainly works your lower back, also hitting your legs, buttocks, upper back, traps, and grip. It is performed by gripping a barbell that is placed on the floor and straightening up with it. Although the movement is basically simple, there are some important points to consider in order to both maximize deadlifting efficiency and reduce the chance of injury.

The deadlift has tremendous value for football, adding strength and development to that most important link in your body: the lower back. Strength in this area can aid your squatting in the long run, and can additionally help you in handling the stress of seated presses and high pulls. It can also aid you in preventing injury on the field.

With my long arms and fairly good natural strength in my legs and back, I have always been a good deadlifter. The first time I tried to lift I was able to perform 22 repetitions with 375 pounds.

The deadlift movement begins with the position of your feet relative to the bar. You want them a bit more than shoulder width apart and actually under the bar. Leave an inch clearance at most between the bar and your shins, and don't worry about the bar rubbing against you on the way up. Some contact cannot be avoided.

Then crouch low enough to grab the bar with a reverse grip, with one palm facing toward you and the other facing away. This is to keep the bar from rotating out of your grasp as you pull it up, and it's not a bad idea to sometimes alter your grip from set to set to maintain "balanced" grip development. A lot of lifters like to chalk their hands for better gripping traction when deadlifting, especially if they are sweaty.

With your grip and your stance all set, next position your back and your legs for your lift. Ordinarily you want to keep your back as straight as possible, but there is a trade-off with your legs here. The less you bend your legs, the better leg leverage you have to move the weight. Yet the less you bend your legs, the more you must bend your back to grip the bar and the worse back leverage you have. It is easy to see how a long-armed guy has a deadlifting leverage advantage; when he grips the bar, he does not have to bend either his back or his legs as much.

Your best approach is to try to keep your back relatively flat and let your legs do most of the work, at least in your early stages of deadlifting. Later, you can bend your back a bit as you gain strength, and you might even reach a point where the amount of weight you handle would not permit your back to stay flat, even if you wanted it to. You can also do special deadlifts in which you intentionally keep your legs straight and thus really isolate your lower back. These are called stiff-legged deadlifts, and they'll be covered later.

When you have established the right back and leg position, you're ready to pull. You want to keep your head level or slightly up and bring the bar up forcefully without jerking it. If you unduly jerk the bar, you're susceptible to injury in your lower back and hamstrings.

You should refrain from straightening out your legs immediately after getting the bar off the floor. Keep them slightly bent, as this will both better distribute the force of the lift and give you some leverage advantage later in the movement. Also, keep the bar close to your thighs as you bring it up to aid you in locking it out. If it gets out in front of you, your lockout suffers. You should rotate your torso a bit to keep the bar near you, moving your hips forward and your shoulders back. You might also wish to arch your neck slightly, as this can help keep the bar in the right groove. Remember to exhale as you make your pull and inhale between deadlifting reps.

In your beginning deadlifting, it's probably a good idea to have an experienced deadlifter check you for form. You might even have him "spot" your form by actually physically aiding your lift. Have him go to the side of your underhand (palm up) grip, and place one hand on your lower back. He then hooks his other arm under your armpit. When you pull, he gives a slight tug up (armpit) and/or back (belt), as needed, to see that your form is correct. If doing this drill, first try it with light weights to coordinate things with your helper.

You must wear a snugly fitting lifting belt when deadlifting, and warm up very thoroughly. It would not hurt to stretch your lower back as part of your warm-up, and you should increase by no more than 50 pounds per set when lifting, at least as a beginner.

It is also necessary to increase your set weight slowly as a beginning deadlifter. If you jump up too quickly, you can unintentionally use bad technique in your desire to make your lift, and this invites injury. You should increase by no more than 5 pounds or so from one workout to another in your actual workout weight, using lower increases if necessary.

Many deadlifters have their grip give out before their lower back, causing them to end their sets prematurely. To circumvent this you should work on strengthening your grip for deadlifting. This can be done with general grip strengthening work (covered later in this chapter) and with some special exercises utilizing the deadlift movement. Place a load on the bar that you can deadlift about 10 times, deadlift it once, and simply hold the bar at the top of your lift for as long as you can. Keep track of how long you can hold the bar like this; once you reach a sticking point in terms of time, add another 5 pounds.

Another way of doing the same drill is taking a little lighter load and trying to squeeze the bejeebers out of the bar. You won't be able to grip it for as long this way.

Some lifters like to wrap a foam rubber padding around the bar and do some deadlifts, as well as the aforementioned grip exercises, this way. If employing this method, you probably want to do some regular bar deadlifts as well to keep a feel for them. Also, be sure to alter your grip when doing deadlift grip-strengthening movements, using both of the reverse grip positions. Then just for fun, use a palms-down grip as well.

A very important point about deadlifting is that if you feel any unnatural pain in your back—or anywhere else—while doing the lift, drop the weight immediately. Many gyms have special platforms for deadlifting, but even if this is not the case, a building is easier to fix than your back. The key here is to distinguish between really damaging pain and the normal pain of lifting. As you gain deadlifting experience and learn what normal lifting pain feels like, you should have no trouble in making this distinction. With proper warm-up, gradual weight increases, and good technique, you probably will never have to.

High Pull. The high pull movement is also called the upright row, and is perhaps the best developer of the deltoid and trapezius muscle groups there is. It also works your forearms and your grip. The high pull is a tremendous football strength exercise, and yet is neglected by a lot of people, perhaps because it lacks the glamour of the bench press. It is possibly the most demanding of all upper-body movements, requiring intense concentration and great willpower to perform prop-

The high pull—or upright row—should be done very strictly. Try to pull the weight using only your traps and deltoids, keeping the rest of your body as motionless as possible.

erly (the latter reps of this exercise hurt). It is a must for any football strength program, and is an integral part of my own.

The high pull movement is quite simple. You stand upright with your feet about shoulder width, and grip the bar evenly with your hands about 6 to 12 inches apart and your arms fully extended in front of you. Then pull the bar straight up as high as you can, all the way to your chin if you are able to. Lower the bar all the way back down again, fully extending your arms, and repeat the upright pulling movement. You should make every effort to do the movement as strictly as possible, attempting to keep your feet firmly on the floor and trying not to rock your body. (On your latter reps, you might need to "cheat" a little, and this is permissible as long as you have first done as many strict reps as possible.)

You can vary your grip somewhat when doing high pulls. The wider you space your hands, the more you work the outside and rear of your deltoids; with a narrower grip, the more you hit your frontal delts. When you use a very narrow grip—your hands 6 inches or less apart—and pull that bar to your collarbone or above, the exercise can be called an upright row.

A lot of people have a dead area beginning around two-thirds of the way up with their high pull movement, a place where the weight wants to stop moving. Once the bar makes it through this spot, which seems to extend for several inches or so, the lift can generally be completed. A training partner can help you here by giving you just enough assistance that you can get the weight through the dead spot, although this should be done only when you feel you can't make your rep. This "helping" principle, called forced reps, can be used on all major exercises. It will be covered later in this chapter, and is mentioned here only because it works especially well with high pulls.

You should use a weight that you can pull to your collarbone. Occasionally you can go heavier and pull the bar to your nipples, but mainly emphasize a movement to at least your collarbone area.

Bench Press. The bench press, probably the most popular lift of all, is a favorite of many football players. It is an excellent upper-body bulker since it works so many muscle groups—pectorals, triceps, deltoids, and, to some extent, lats—and because you can handle more weight with it than with any other upper-body movement. It is also a good indicator of all-around upper-body strength and is an important part of any good football strength program.

Some people tend to put too much emphasis on the bench press, neglecting their other lifts and training methods in the process. It should be remembered that it is just one lift in the overall strength training program. As much as I do bench pressing myself, I do not employ this lift to the detriment of my other strength movements.

The bench press is executed while lying with your back on a flat bench and your feet firmly on the floor. You then reach up and grab the bar, which is supported on a rack that is above and slightly behind you. You want to space your hands evenly and probably a bit wider than shoulder width. You then lift the bar off the support rack, or have your spotter assist you in lifting it off, and briefly extend it at arm's length. Next, lower it under control to your chest at around your nipple area, and then push it back up until your arms are again fully extended. Do not bounce the bar off your chest as this invites injury. You also must keep your feet flat on the floor when performing the lift. To do otherwise will only rob you of power when driving up the weight. Remember to exhale as you drive the weight up and inhale as you lower it.

Certain lifters tend to "bridge" when bench pressing, and this means arching the back in an effort to assist the weight up. Bridging brings other, supplementary muscle groups into play, and it also works by reducing the distance the weight must travel (as you arch your back, your chest moves up). It is also a natural reaction when struggling with a weight that you cannot quite get in good form. Yet it should be avoided because it creates bad habits. A more effective technique is to have your spotter slightly assist you with a weight that won't quite go. (This again gets into forced reps, mentioned earlier with high pulls.)

You can vary your hand spacing when bench pressing, as the closer together they are, the more you work your triceps. The more you move your hands out, the more you get your pecs. I like to vary my grip to emphasize both muscle groups. Yet notice the 2 grooves around the bar, each one about 6 inches in from the end. You don't want to place any part of your hands past these grooves while benching, since this would defeat the purpose of the lift.

A golden rule of bench pressing safety is to never bench press alone unless you have a safety catch. You must always use a spotter unless there is equipment available upon which to rest the weight should you miss a lift. A power rack (mentioned earlier) is excellent for this, and some benches also come with a special setup for accomplishing the same thing.

You should warm up thoroughly when benching, and add weight gradually, and it's a good idea to wear a lifting belt.

Seated Press. The seated press movement works your triceps, trapezius, and all-around deltoid (anterior, medial, and posterior heads) muscle groups. It also hits your upper pectorals slightly, especially when done behind your neck. The seated press is a fine football strength exercise because it works muscle groups that are used extensively on the gridiron. It isn't as good a "bulker" as the bench press since it doesn't work your pectoral muscles nearly as much and since you cannot handle as much weight with it as with the bench. Yet it works your total deltoid group better, and it gets your traps more.

A lot of guys neglect the seated press movement, perhaps because they cannot handle as much poundage as with benches. This is unfortunate, since seated presses will aid your bench press if done correctly and consistently, and probably more than bench presses will aid your seated press. Another probable reason why it is often avoided is that the seated press is a tougher movement than the bench press.

In its simplest form, the seated press movement is performed by gripping the bar with your hands spaced evenly at shoulder width or wider, with your thumbs facing in. Then, starting with your elbows down and the bar resting against your clavicle and frontal deltoid area, press the bar overhead while sitting on a sturdy bench, your feet firmly on the floor. You can get the bar to this beginning position by either cleaning it on your own or by taking it off a rack at just the right height. Be sure you exhale while pressing the bar up and inhale while lowering it.

The basic movement used in the seated press can be called the Olympic press or military press if it is done while standing up. Yet less cheating is possible when the lift is done seated since you cannot sway your body as much to assist the lift. The result is that your tris, traps, and delts do the work basically unassisted, and they also reap the benefits.

You will still move a little from the waist up when doing seated presses, especially during the latter reps in a set. Here your movement is almost automatic in an effort in involve other supporting muscle groups. This "arching" movement puts a little more strain on your lower back, so be sure you're wrapped tightly in a solid lifting belt. If you want to keep your back as straight and motionless as possible, you can brace your back against something solid (there are special benches

The seated press bench may be used for both barbell and dumbbell seated presses. To do them strictly, glue your back against the upright support and keep it there.
Photo courtesy of Jubinville Health Equipment.

for this) and concentrate on leaving it "cemented" there as you lift. I do my seated presses this way on occasion. You can also have your spotter assist you with those reps you can't quite get, thus keeping you from having to arch.

A popular variation of the barbell seated press is to do the movement from a *behind-the-neck* position. You simply begin your movement with the bar in a position as if you were going to squat with it and blast it right up overhead. This version works essentially the same muscle groups, probably in different proportions, and you can use a little wider grip with it. You might not be able to handle quite as much weight with presses behind the neck—or press rear, as it is also called. This is because you can't arch as much at the beginning of the movement. If you arch your back before the bar clears at least your head, you will lose leverage and perhaps the bar as well. This formula for strict form is part of what makes the press behind the neck such a fine movement, preferred by many to the regular barbell seated press.

Seated presses may also be done quite effectively with dumbbells. Here you simply bring the bells up to the same beginning position and press them overhead. You don't have to pay too much attention to palm position, as it will come naturally. Dumbbell presses offer a little more range of motion than barbell seated presses and add variety to your routine.

There are three basic variations of the dumbbell seated press. The first of these, *the straight dumbbell press*, is to press the bells up simultaneously. This is the strictest method, requiring the most balance and coordination. You can still arch your back a little when pressing them up together, but you can't sway from side to side as in the other two methods. This method also puts the most strain on your lower back since, at any given time of the lift, you are handling twice the weight overhead as you are with the other two.

The second method is called the *alternate dumbbell press*, and it is done by pressing up one bell, returning it, then pressing up another bell, returning it, and so on, a method I like for my dumbbell presses. As mentioned, you can lean one way when pressing one bell and lean the opposite way when pressing the other bell. This enables you to handle a little more poundage. You get excellent triceps involvement with this alternate method. One dumbbell helps you to balance the other, and since you do not need as much muscle involvement to balance the weights, you can use your triceps to do more work.

The third method is called the *see-saw dumbbell press*, and here you press up one dumbbell and, while returning it, you press up the other, a procedure that takes some coordination. You can handle the most weight with this method, but it also takes the most out of you overall, since you're doing more work per unit of time. You cannot rest for a few breaths since you have to match that descending dumbbell with a rising one.

One way to do your dumbbell press work is to perform an all-out set with all three methods. Do the first set with the straight dumbbell presses, pushing them strict and then arching a little as you have to over the last reps. Rest a few minutes and then catch your second set with alternate dumbbell presses, probably with the same weight. You're still fatigued but you can handle more weight with this alternate method, and you want to concentrate on snapping each one up from its dead-weight position. Rest a few more minutes and get your third set see-saw, using about the same weight. This should be right on time since the muscles involved are quite fatigued. Yet put mind over matter and start singing those bells up/down, up/down, putting it in your mind that you're never going to stop. Do a couple of workouts like this weekly and you will develop pretty good tri, trap, and delt strength to help you slam people around out on the field.

When doing any type of seated presses, warm up thoroughly and increase in weight gradually. Use a snugly fit lifting belt, placing it low on your trunk, and refrain from excessively arching your back. Also, it is a good idea to use a spotter since some people have blacked out when performing this movement, although this is rare.

Incline Press. The incline press movement is a hybrid of the bench press and seated press combined. It primarily works your anterior and medial deltoids, your triceps, and your upper pectorals where they tie into your anterior delts. It hits your deltoids all around more than the bench press does, and your pecs more than the seated press does. The incline press is not only a fine movement in and of itself, but its steady

This is the seated press done with dumbbells. Note how the dumbbells are alternated.

use will aid both your bench and seated press lifts. These factors make it a fine strength training exercise for football, and I use it regularly.

The incline press is performed at a position between the bench press and seated press. You brace your back against a bench that is set at a 15- to 45-degree angle, grip the bar the same as with a bench or seated press, and, with possible assistance from your spotter, remove it from its overhead rack and fully extend your arms with it. Then lower the bar under control and touch it to your upper pectoral area —somewhere around your collarbone perhaps—and press it back up, exhaling as you do so. You should concentrate on keeping your feet firmly on the floor, your buttocks firmly on the seat of the bench, and your back glued to the bench proper. You will have a tendency to arch your back and try to get more pec into things when you can't make a rep. Yet a better policy is to keep your form and have your spotter assist you slightly, as was covered.

There are a few variations of the incline press, among them the spacing of your hands. The wider you space them, the more you hit your upper pecs; the narrower, the more you get your tris. You might plan your spacing based on this information, along with how it feels to you, and also periodically vary your spacing for the two different effects and a change of pace.

Another variation is the angle of the bench you use for the lift. The more you increase the angle from the horizontal, the more you move toward the seated press range and thus utilize more deltoid. The more you decrease the angle with the horizontal, the more you move toward the bench press range and thus utilize more pectoral. You can handle more weight with the incline press as you decrease the angle with the horizontal.

Most people like to perform their incline presses at just one angle during any one workout. Yet there are some who adjust the angle from set to set, feeling it gives them a better all-around workout. There was one guy who took the interesting approach of increasing the angle with each set rather than going up in weight.

A third way to vary your incline press is to use dumbbells, and of course this may be done in conjunction with any angle adjustment. These incline dumbbell presses will be covered in a later section of the chapter.

You should wear a lifting belt when doing inclines since there is some strain on your lower back. You will also need a spotter unless your lifting rig has a safety catch.

BIG 6 STANDARDS

Since it's good to know where you stand with regard to strength, the following chart gives high school and college standards. Each of the Big 6 lifts is expressed as a percentage of bodyweight for 1, 5, and 10 repetitions. For example, the high school standards for a "good" squat

Squat

	Good	Excellent
High school	160% × 1 144% × 5 128% × 10	200% × 1 180% × 5 160% × 10
College	200% × 1 180% × 5 160% × 10	240% × 1 216% × 5 192% × 10

Dead Lift

	Good	Excellent
High school	160% × 1 144% × 5 128% × 10	200% × 1 180% × 5 160% × 10
College	200% × 1 180% × 5 160% × 10	240% × 1 216% × 5 192% × 10

Bench Press

	Good	Excellent
High school	120% × 1 108% × 5 96% × 10	150% × 1 135% × 5 120% × 10
College	150% × 1 135% × 5 120% × 10	180% × 1 162% × 5 144% × 10

Incline Press

	Good	Excellent
High school	96% × 1	120% × 1
	86.4% × 5	108% × 5
	76.8% × 10	96% × 10
College	120% × 1	144% × 1
	108% × 5	129.6% × 5
	96% × 10	115.2% × 10

Seated Press

	Good	Excellent
High school	72% × 1	90% × 1
	64.8% × 5	81% × 5
	57.6% × 10	72% × 10
College	90% × 1	108% × 1
	81% × 5	97.2% × 5
	72% × 10	86.4% × 10

High Pull (to collarbone)

	Good	Excellent
High school	72% × 1	90% × 1
	64.8% × 5	81% × 5
	57.6% × 10	72% × 10
College	90% × 1	108% × 1
	81% × 5	97.2% × 5
	72% × 10	86.4% × 10

lift are 160, 144, and 128 percent of body weight for 1, 5, and 10 repetitions, respectively. Thus a high school guy weighing 180 pounds who can squat 288 pounds for 1 rep, 259.2 for 5 reps, or 230.4 for 10 reps is a "good" squatter.

Note that the standards for the incline press are for an angle of 45 degrees with the horizontal. These standards are then adjusted accordingly as this angle decreases. For example, a standard of 120 percent at 45 degrees would increase to 130 percent at 30 degrees, 140 percent at 15 degrees, and equal the associated bench press standard at 0 degrees where, of course, the lift has become a bench press.

SUPPLEMENTARY EXERCISES

The following exercises supplement your Big 6 power movements. They are primarily for people in the intermediate to advanced stages of strength training. Accordingly, you do not need to do them in the beginning stages of your program.

As you advance, you can supplement your Big 6 work with some of these exercises. You can also sometimes work them in place of your Big 6 power work, giving your mind and body a change of pace. Sets of 5 to 12 repetitions generally work well with these movements, depending on the exercise.

Deep Bench Press. This exercise gets its name from the fact that you do it by lowering the bar to a deeper position than with regular bench presses. This positioning is made possible by the use of a special bar that is cambered in the center, and thus when you lower the bar to your chest, this design leaves room for your hands to go down even farther. With regular benches, when the bar is to your chest your hands grip it while they are at chest level since the bar is straight. With deep benches, when the bar is at chest level your hands are several inches lower, and the result is that the muscles you use to bench press are stretched to a greater extent.

The extra muscle stretching provided by the deep bench press results in your working more muscle fibers, and more muscular growth and strength will be the eventual result. This special exercise also forces you to do more work on every rep since you're moving the weight an extra 5 or 6 inches. This has got to help you as far as conditioning your muscles to do more work, something very important for football.

You can also do deep bench presses with a universal gym. All you do is solidly prop the bench up so that there is only a few inches of room between it and the bar. It will take a little maneuvering practice to get under the bar this way, and you might even need a little help in getting the weight started when you go heavy. Be sure to go down as far as you can on each repetition or you'll be defeating the purpose of this exercise. Emphasize sets of 5 to 10 reps with this movement.

Supplementing your regular bench presses with deep benches should help your regular benching. I have added deep benches to my routine fairly recently, and I feel they have helped me to increase my regular bench press. The man who is recognized by many as the greatest bench presser in the world incorporates them into his routine on a regular basis and credits them with much of his success. His usual method is to hit up his deeps after his regular benching, handling about 75 percent as much weight with them. You might want to try the same method, occasionally performing your entire bench press workout with this unique and effective deep bench press exercise method. Yet do so only when in an intermediate or advanced stage of training.

Close Grip Bench Press. This exercise builds primarily triceps and frontal deltoid strength, and it also works the insides of your pectorals a bit. All it amounts to is a bench press with your hands very close together, and some guys like to bring them so close that they touch. It is also felt by some that you should bring the bar down to within only 3 inches or so of your chest when doing close grips, alleviating some of the strain on your elbow joints. You can place some padding on your chest and simply bring the bar down to the padding to monitor this 3-inch clearance, especially if your elbows bother you when doing this lift. I occasionally do close grip bench presses with pads like this.

Ordinarily do your close grips after regular benches, and you can work dumbbell benches in as part of advanced benching routine. If you're getting a little stale on the bench press, you can use close grips and dumbbell benches in place of it periodically to aid you in getting over your mental and/or physical hump. Go with sets of 5 to 10 reps.

Dumbbell Bench Press. This movement develops strength in your frontal deltoids, your triceps, and especially your pectorals. As its name implies, it is simply a bench press performed with dumbbells. Its advantage over regular barbell bench presses is that the dumbbells can be lowered a greater distance than the barbell, strengthening your pectoral muscles, among other muscle groups, more than with regular benches. In this manner, the dumbbell bench press is similar to the deep bench press movement.

To do dumbbell bench presses, grab a pair of dumbbells while seated on bench. Next, very carefully lie down into the bench-pressing position with the dumbbells held at your chest. Then bench press the bells simultaneously, being careful not to get them out of your groove and lose them, particularly when you are still getting used to this lift. When you lower them, do so under control so you don't lose your groove and miss your rep and/or pull a muscle. You want to lower them down about as far as you can while still making your reps, stretching your chest really well in the process. You can twist the bells inward as you lower them and twist them back the other way as you raise them back up.

Dumbbell bench presses are one exercise in which a partner is invaluable. He can help you get the bells into position to begin the movement, and this type of assistance will be a necessity once you get up there in poundage handled. Your partner can also check to see that you bring the bells down far enough, perhaps even very lightly pressing down on them at the bottom of your lift to maximize your stretch if he catches you laming. He can also guide the bells back on track should you lose your groove, enabling you to get more good reps and a better workout this way. This guiding is actually a form of "forced reps" work.

Dumbbell bench presses should ordinarily be done after your regular bench pressing if you are working both lifts the same day. You can also do them as a change up from your regular benching routine, and this is how I use them. Yet remember dumbbell benches are essentially a rather advanced exercise and probably not needed in beginning workouts. You can do sets of 5 to 10 reps with this exercise.

Dumbbell Incline Press. This is just an incline press done with dumbbells instead of barbells, and it builds strength in your frontal deltoids, triceps, and upper pectorals. Like the dumbbell bench press, the dumbbell incline press can really stretch your (upper) pectorals because of the greater stretch permitted with the bells. And like the regular barbell incline press, the pressing angle can vary, with about 30 degrees being a common position.

To perform dumbbell inclines, you have to clean the dumbbells and lean back against the incline support. This move is generally easier than with dumbbell benches since you're usually handling less weight and you only lean back to 30 degrees or so instead of all the way down. It's still a good idea to use a spotter, as he can help keep those bells controlled within your lifting groove, aiding you in more productive work per set, just as with dumbbell bench presses.

A good time to do dumbbell incline presses is right after your barbell inclines, to add a finishing touch to your incline pressing strength

Incline presses done with dumbbells really stretch your upper pectorals. They are an excellent supplement to regular barbell pressing.

development. You can also do your dumbbell inclines in place of your barbell inclines for whatever reason, but remember that the exercise is generally for intermediate and advanced routines. Sets of 5 to 10 reps work well.

Parallel Bar Dips. This exercise strengthens your frontal deltoids, lower pectorals, and triceps. It is done by dipping down between 2 evenly spaced parallel bars that are about 12 to 24 inches apart. You grip the bars with the palms of your hands facing in, and then dip and raise your body between them. For the best results, lower yourself as far as you can on each rep, and this means go down under control. Try not to bob your head up and down when dipping, at least not until you can't make your rep any other way.

Dips are especially effective if done on a V-shaped dipping unit. If you dip at the front of this unit, where the bars are the farthest apart, you'll maximize your pectoral muscle involvement. If you grip the bars back where they are closer together, you'll work your triceps more. I like to do them both ways.

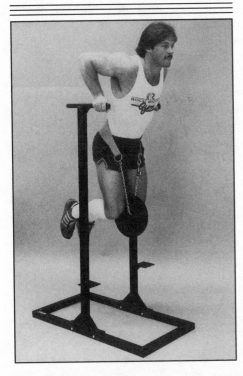

Here is the parallel bar dip done with added resistance. Note the angle of the arms in this "down" position. *Photo courtesy of Rocky Mountain Gym Equipment, Inc.*

You can emphasize sets of 8 to 12 reps with your dips. If you can do 2 or 3 sets of 8 to 12 reps with your body weight, you can add weight by securing a special harness around your waist to which you can attach dumbbells or loose plates.

Triceps Extension. Technically speaking, any isolated triceps movement that you do is a triceps extension. This is because your strict "triceps only" movements involve exercise where the movement is one of extension. The following descriptions will thus cover different types of triceps extensions, referring to them by their popular names. These exercises should be done in sets of 8 to 12 reps.

One type of triceps extension is the *triceps pushdown*, and this is done with the vertical lat pulley unit. You simply grip the lat bar with your hands close together, tuck your elbows in to your body and keep them there, and push the bar down using your triceps. You can use a small V-shaped bar instead of the lat bar, and in this way your palms are turned in, working your triceps at a different angle. This V-bar can often rig right up to the lat unit.

The triceps pushdown should be performed only after any heavy pressing work so that your triceps are not worked prior to pressing. It is an exercise that takes intense concentration since it is so easy to "lose form" with this movement. Concentrate on making your triceps do the work, even at the expense of fewer reps and less weight, at least to begin with. Cheat the weight up only as a last resort, and this means after failing to move it in strict fashion. Use your willpower and restrict all cheating to your final reps.

A very effective way of doing your triceps extension is on one of the special machines made just for this exercise. Nautilus, among others, makes an excellent triceps extension unit that is both safe and effective. You simply sit in the seat, after adjusting it for height, prop your elbows up on the padded support that is in front of you and place each hand in the special hand support pads that are about the only place that they can fit. All you have to do then is keep your elbows locked to the pad as you straighten or extend your arms. The setup is such that your tris do the lion's share of the work. I like doing my triceps extensions this way.

The *lying triceps extension* is a pretty popular movement, and a favorite among bench pressers who want improved triceps strength. The theory here is that if your triceps strength is developed in the lying prone down position, it can be more readily applied to a lying down movement.

The lying triceps extension is done by lying on a bench with your head over the edge, gripping a bar at arm's length with your palms up and your hands close together, and lowering the bar to around your forehead area and then pressing it back up, keeping your elbows as stationary as possible. Many lifters prefer using either a dumbbell, E-Z curl bar, or special triceps bar for this movement.

The *seated triceps extension* is done by sitting on a bench, gripping the bar the same way and then lowering it behind your head and raising it while keeping your elbows up close to your head and as stationary as possible. This movement may also be done with a dumbbell, E-Z curl bar, or special triceps bar. Another name for it is the *French curl*.

As with so many isolation movements, the key to doing lying and seated triceps extensions is to concentrate. These movements are not easy to execute with good form, and you must keep your mind on what you are doing in order to do them correctly.

There are additional triceps movements around, but for the purpose of supplementing your triceps strength for football, those covered should be adequate.

This is a method of doing the triceps extension while seated and utilizing a dumbbell. Be sure to keep your body from swaying, letting your triceps do the work.

Leg Press. The leg press is done by lying on your back under a leg press machine, placing your feet up against the foot support, and pressing the weight straight up with your legs. If you're not already familiar with the leg press machine, all you have to do is look at one and you'll figure out how to use it.

Although leg presses work basically the same muscle groups as squats, they are not quite as tough as squats. Thus you should ordinarily do them as a supplement to the squat movement. If you have lower-back problems or if you have some unnatural pain when doing squats, utilize the leg press movement in place of squats.

Some leg press machines are designed so that you push the weight up at an angle. You can handle more weight with such machines, and this is because you are not raising the entire weight. For example, the 45-degree angle that most of these machines are set at requires only about 70 percent as much force to raise a given weight as it does to raise the same weight on a straight vertical leg press unit. You should remember this to keep from developing a false sense of strength when using these angled leg press devices.

Leg presses are comfortable on the angle leg press machine. Remember that you are using about 70 percent of the loaded weight if the angle of the unit is at 45 degrees.

You can do your leg presses a number of ways, but the method I think is the most effective is to lower the weight until your thighs are about parallel to the floor and then blast it up through the ceiling. You want to use as heavy a weight as possible to get your designated number of reps, and concentrate on trying to "go fast" by straightening your legs out as quickly as possible. (Keep in mind that some medical authorities recommend keeping your knees slightly bent to relieve some of the stress on your knees.) Be sure to always lower the weight under control, and as you gain experience (and strength), you can come down more quickly; this will then aid you in driving the weight back up.

Some guys like to occasionally leg press with a weight that is light enough that it "jumps" off your feet at the end of the upstroke. This is an excellent technique for developing spring in your legs. Another method is to lower the weight only part way down, again exploding back up with it at maximum force. You can use more weight this way since your mechanical advantage is greater as a result of your legs being bent less.

Some people do leg presses with a 2-by-4 or 4-by-4 placed between their feet and the pressing partition. They extend their heels over the edge of the board and this puts the stress on the balls of the feet. The idea here is to develop strength that is more readily applied to actual body movement, and most body movement occurs on the balls of the feet. You cannot handle as much weight when doing leg presses this way, but the concept behind this method is good. I use it myself about every other leg press workout or so.

You should do your leg presses after your squats or in place of them. You also want to do them before your other leg work. You probably want to emphasize sets of 8 to 10 reps or so, done as explosively as possible. Sometimes go for higher reps of 12 to 15 or more and sometimes for lower reps of 5 or 6.

Partial Squats. Although squats done to parallel are the most effective overall, you can work some in where you don't go down this far. The advantage here is that the less you bend your legs, the more weight you can handle. Thus your muscles will get used to handling greater poundages than they do with parallel squats. While partial squats will not stimulate leg growth quite like regular squats, they can aid your regular squats when used in a supplementary manner. They can also serve as a good mental and physical change of pace from regular parallel squatting, and it is for these reasons that I occasionally do them.

You probably want to vary your squatting range from about one-fourth of the way down to a position just a few inches above parallel. You can gauge your depth by placing a box or bench behind you and barely touching it with your buttocks on each rep. You should be absolutely certain that this box is placed in the correct position since you will be backing toward it and "squatting blind" in its direction. You can check this positioning out in light warm-up sets, and then make sure you maintain correct positioning as you go heavier. You can vary the height of the box, and you should refrain from bouncing off it as you work your partial squat reps.

You can do partial squats inside a power rack, setting the pins to regulate your depth. You can wrap towels or some other covering around the pins so that you don't bang the bar off them when squatting.

There are also machines around for performing partial squats. They generally take the form of a device with special pads for your shoulders, and you simply slip right under them and fire away. Since the whole motion is guided, you cannot lose your groove as with free bar squats, and as a result you can do your reps more quickly, aiding your power. You can work sets of 10 to 20 reps performing the motion as quickly as possible, really "stinging" your legs as you build explosive power in them. (Note that you should not do your partial squats in this fast manner if you have back trouble.)

Stiff-Legged Deadlift. This is a version of the deadlift done by keeping your legs stiff so that your back does almost all of the work. You can use the reverse grip of regular deadlifting, but many people prefer a grip with both palms facing toward the body. Some guys like to get up on a 4- or 6-inch platform to do their stiff-legged deadlifting. This method stretches the back and the hamstrings more, and it involves more work since the bar is moved a greater distance.

The stiff-legged deadlift isolates your lower back muscles. Be very careful when you do this exercise; do it slowly and add weight gradually.

This back extension unit doubles as a roman chair for the abdominals.
Photo courtesy of Rocky Mountain Gym Equipment, Inc.

You must take great care when doing your stiff-legged deadlifts this way. The stiff-legged deadlift has its critics, who claim that the possibility of injury negates any of the lift's benefits. It is true that this movement can be dangerous if improperly done. Thus be sure to wear a snugly fit lifting belt, warm up thoroughly, increase poundages very gradually, and raise and lower the weight in a smooth, steady fashion. Do not jerk the weight. Another pointer is to pick a work area where you can drop the weight if you feel the need to.

You can work your stiff-legged deadlift as I do, doing it along with regular deadlifting, and in the long run it should increase your deadlifting power. You can also do it in place of regular deadlifts. Perform sets of 8 to 12 reps with this movement, always lifting under control.

Shoulder Shrug. This is a real heavy-duty exercise that works your trapezius muscles, those slabs of muscle that connect your neck to your shoulders, if you recall. The shoulder shrug is done by grabbing a barbell at about shoulder width with your palms facing in and then locking your elbows and "shrugging" the bar up with your traps. It is perhaps the most effective trap builder around, and it also strengthens your grip. A good time to do your shrugs is on the same day you deadlift and/or high pull. You can follow your deadlifts with shrugs, and you can perhaps precede your high pulls with them; the high pull movement should feel light to you after handling heavy shrug poundages, and this should help you psychologically, if nothing else.

Your shrugs can be done in sets of about 6 to 10 reps for really top results. Do not be afraid to go heavy with this fine, trap-bulking exercise movement.

BODY PART EXERCISES

Here are the exercises that complete the basic football strength package. They are divided into exercises for the neck, knees/hamstrings, abdominals/obliques, abductors/adductors, calves/feet, lats, biceps, and hands/wrists/forearms.

Neck. Of all the muscles that you develop for football, your neck is the most important. Although you don't actually use your neck directly in good football techniques, inevitably you're going to take some punishment in this region. Thus you must have a strong, thick, flexible neck to minimize the risk of injury. Remember that while a knee injury can end a football career, a neck injury can end a human life.

There are some pretty elaborate commercial contraptions around to build your neck, and if your gym has them, go ahead and try them. There is no sense going into detail on them since they are simply various types of neck extension/flexion equipment using different mediums for resistance. If your gym does not have them, don't worry about it because the upcoming harness and plate method will build your neck just as effectively anyway.

For maximum development, you can work your neck 4 or 5 days a week. A good policy is to mix in some neck work whenever you work your traps (high pull, shoulder shrugs) and then also work it 2 or 3 other days. It is possible to work your neck at home if you don't have time at the gym. You can perform the various neck exercises at home using a towel and manual resistance, or using a regular neck harness and manual resistance. I always keep in mind that it is impossible to have too strong a neck for football, and you should have the same attitude.

Neck Extensions. These are best performed with a neck head-strap, a head harness made of webbing with a chain hanging down from it that you can attach plates to. You simply slip the unit over your head with a plate on the chain, place your hands on your knees, and move your head up and down, trying not to cheat too much. This is a high rep exercise, so go for sets of 15 to 20 reps, really concentrating. I do this exercise religiously.

Neck extensions done with the simple neck harness are still as good a way as any to strengthen your neck. You have to really concentrate and make your neck do the work, as I am doing here.

If your gym does not have a neck headstrap, this is one item you should consider purchasing. They are moderately priced, and the benefits derived from them are more than worth the money. Try to buy one over the counter rather than through mail order because the thing has to fit your head well to work.

Neck Flexions. These work opposite to neck extensions, getting the muscles in front of your neck. To do them, lie on a bench with your neck hanging over the edge. Next, fold a towel several times, place it on your face, and put a plate on the towel while holding the plate with your hands. Then, concentrating intensely, slowly stretch your neck down and come back up against the resistance of the plate. Because the tendency here is to raise your trunk up as in the beginning of a situp, you have to discipline yourself to use your neck muscles only. This is another exercise I live by.

Hit 10 to 20 reps with this exercise. If you have a buddy, you can sometimes ditch the plate (but keep the towel) and have him push against your face for resistance.

Side Extensions and Flexions. To get the side of your neck, turn to your side on the bench and again let your neck hang over the edge. Then place the pad and plate on the side of your head and, starting with your neck touching your lower shoulder, slowly lower and raise your neck, trying to touch your head to your uppermost shoulder and getting 10 to 15 reps. Then turn over on your side and work the opposite side of your neck as well. As with regular neck flexions, you can have a buddy resist you in this exercise instead of using a plate. Another possibility is to sit upright and place your hands on the side of your head, using them for resistance as you again try to touch your head to your shoulder. This style takes great concentration, but I have found that it works the side of my neck quite well.

Knees/Hamstrings. Next to your neck, your knees are probably the most important part of your body to strengthen for football. Knee injuries are painful and crippling, and while a good knee-strengthening program cannot grant you immunity from them, it will increase your protection in this area. In other words, the stronger your knees, the less likely you will be to sustain serious knee injury.

Thigh Extension. This exercise is done by sitting on the thigh extension machine, placing your feet under the padded bar and simply straightening your legs all the way out. It works your lower quadricep area, strengthening the muscles around your knee. Consensus has it that consistent performance of this exercise will aid you in preventing knee injury. Also, thigh extensions are done to rehabilitate injured knees.

A lot of guys perform their thigh extensions the wrong way. They'll do their heavy leg work of squats and leg presses, and then do a few sets of thigh extensions almost as if out of duty. They pay no attention to how much weight they use and often don't even count the reps. Instead, they exercise by "feel," going until their legs are "tired."

This is entirely the wrong way to do your thigh extensions. While it's a good policy to do them after primary leg work, you must keep track of your weight, reps, and sets if you want to make progress. The only circumstance under which you should do this exercise by feel or until tired is when you are intentionally working it light. Otherwise, treat it like a major lift, working profusely to go up in both weight and repetitions. Work hard with sets of 8 to 15 reps, and this exercise will aid you in improving overall leg strength and resisting injury. I do it regularly, always keeping track of weight and reps.

In conjunction with strong knees, you need strong hamstrings. If you fail to strengthen your hamstrings when you strengthen your knees, you're more susceptible to muscle pulls in your hamstring area. You should strive for about 5:3 or 3:2 knee-to-hamstring strength ratio.

Leg Curl. To perform this movement, lie belly down on the leg curl machine (sometimes the same unit used for thigh extension), hook your feet under the pads, and bend your legs by bringing your feet up to near your buttocks. Leg curls are an important adjunct to thigh extensions, and the movements should be done together. Remember to strive for about 3:5 to 2:3 as much leg curl strength as thigh extension strength, and do your sets with about 8 to 12 reps, occasionally going

Leg curls are a simple exercise, as you can see. You must do them for a balanced strength development in your legs.

higher. As with thigh extensions, concentrate intensely on bettering yourself in this exercise, constantly trying to increase your weight and repetitions. This exercise has helped me, and it will help you.

Abdominals/Obliques. You probably realize the importance of strong "abs" for football. If you don't, you should get the message the first time an opponent rams his shoulder into your gut. It'll make you wish you'd spent as much time on your abs as you did flirting with the girls.

Your obliques are a muscle group that is just as important as your abdominal muscles. The technical name for them is external obliques, and they're located right around the corner from your abdominals. You can take a hit in this area just as often as in your abs, and a stronger, denser muscle development here will likewise aid you accordingly.

Working abs and obliques is something few guys like to do. It's boring and painful, and progress is tougher to show than with many other muscle groups, possibly because there is a tendency for much of your body fat to accumulate in these areas. Your abs and obliques are also muscle groups that should be worked frequently and with high repetitions. You should hit them 4 to 5 days weekly and with sets of 20 to 30 reps or more.

Situps. The basic abdominal strengthening exercise is the situp. (And the basic oblique strengthening exercise is a variation of the situp.) You're probably already familiar with how to do situps. Lie on your back with your hands clasped behind your neck or head, and, keeping your feet on the floor or at least stationary, simply sit up. You can secure your feet under something, like a barbell, to keep them stationary.

Feet Raised Situp. Here you simply do situps with your feet raised up off the floor, hitting your abs in a little different manner. Concentrate on keeping your feet as stationary as possible to really isolate your abs.

Knee-braced Situp. This type of situp is done with your legs bent and your knees braced very firmly under some object. A good example is a weight-support pin set low in a power rack. By "cementing" your knees against this pin and keeping them there throughout the situp movement, you force yourself to use very strict form. If you can muster the discipline and concentration to do your situps this way, it should

This abdominal strengthening unit offers resistance over a 180-degree range, making situps much tougher.
Photo courtesy of Jubinville Health Equipment, Inc.

take fewer repetitions to "sting" your abs. I like working my abs this way.

Incline Situps. This type of situp is done on a board that is raised to make the movement harder. Many incline situp boards are adjustable, with several different positions up to 45 degrees or more, and they often have straps under which you can secure your feet. Some incline situp units have a triangular hump over which you notch your legs, so that the apex of this hump is then right under the area in back of your knees. The idea is to force you to keep your legs bent when doing incline situps.

Roman Chair Situps. You do these on a special apparatus that has you plant your feet under a bar down near the floor while your buttocks rest on a padded part a couple of feet or so above the floor. You then bend your trunk back and form a sort of semicircle with your buttocks the high point, your head near the ground at one end, and your feet under the bar at the other end. You then come up in a situp movement. This motion works and stretches your abs and stretches your rib cage while hyperextending your lower back. This is definitely a tough, different slant on gut work, and you should give it a try if you

have access to a roman chair unit. I like roman chair situps as a change
of pace.

Twisting Situps. Any of the situp movements covered can be done
with a twisting motion. Simply touch your right elbow to your left
knee or your left elbow to your right knee. You should mix these up
as evenly as possible per set, getting in the same number of reps on
each side. This type of situp works your abdominals a bit differently,
and I include it in my routine.

Resistance Situps. You can do any of the aforementioned situp
movements with extra resistance. There are special gadgets for this,
but you do not need them. Just grab a loose plate and hold it behind
your neck, or even in front of you somewhere, and do any variation
of the situp you prefer. As you get stronger, you can graduate to a
barbell bar for your weighted ab work. Keep careful track of your sets,
reps, and weight used, and you should be able to work up to this. I
use resistance for my situps about every other ab workout or so.

Abdominal Crunches. This exercise is an abbreviation of the situp.
The way to do it is to lie on the floor on your back with your knees
bent fully, your feet firmly on the floor and next to your buttocks, and
your hands behind your head. You then raise up your trunk as far as
you can while working as strictly as possible, holding for a count of 1
or 2 seconds and probably not being able to touch your head to your
knees if you are doing them correctly. This movement is easier on the
back than regular situps, and some people think it isolates your abs in
a manner different than situps.

Leg Raises. These exercises work your lower abs, and you can
do them several ways. You can lie on the floor and raise your legs up,
bending them some at the knees in the process but keeping your head
flush to the floor. You can also lie on the situp board with your head
up and your feet down, and then grip the board while bending your
knees and bringing them up toward you. Another way is to grab on to
a chinning bar or a special leg raise device, doing your leg raises by
bringing your knees up as high as you can. Eventually you can wear
iron boots or other weighted device when doing any version of this
exercise.

Sidewinders. These work your obliques; essentially what they amount to are situps done sideways. You hook your feet under something solid, turn over on your side, and perform the same situp motion. Be sure to work both sides of your obliques with this exercise.

Oblique Extensions. These are really just a tougher and more complete sideways situp. You need a large bench or table to do them, and it has to have a strap or else you need someone to hold you down. You then lie on one side with your hip at the edge of the unit and your trunk extending over with your legs secured under a strap, or with someone holding you down. You bend down slowly toward the floor as far as you can, stretching your obliques for all they're worth. You then come back up, and you have done 1 rep.

A good way to do your oblique extensions is with a buddy holding you down for one side and then you immediately hold him down. You then each do the same for your other sides, and you work through your sets this way. I have found this to be very effective.

Abductors/Adductors. To understand what muscles we are talking about here, lie down on your back with your legs straight. Now spread your legs while keeping them straight; you are using your abductors, a muscle group on the upper outside of the thigh. Next, bring your legs back together while keeping them straight; you are using your adductors.

Your abductors/adductors are essentially an ignored muscle group; many athletes fail to work them at all. In part, this is because there are not a lot of exercises for them. Yet strong abductors/adductors can aid your ability to move laterally and can prevent injury to these muscle groups. It is for this reason that I work them.

Abductor Extension. You can do this exercise by fastening a piece of rubber shock cord around each ankle, and then spreading your legs as far as you can while keeping your legs straight. You should perform 10 or more reps, really concentrating on getting your legs as far apart as you can. Work on flexibility exercises for this area of your body in conjunction with this abductor extension exercise.

Adductor Flexion. This exercise is a bit more complicated since you must fasten one end of the shock cord to an immovable object and fasten the other end around your ankle. You then have to lock your

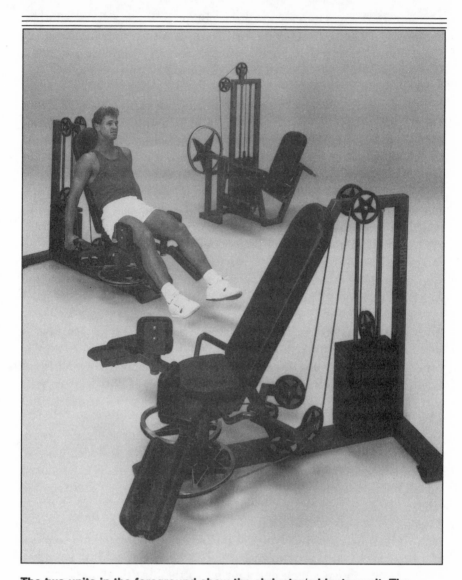

The two units in the foreground show the abductor/adductor unit. The resistance is against the outside of the legs as you "abduct," and the opposite is true of the adductor motion.
Photo courtesy of Iron Company/Polaris.

opposite ankle around another immovable object for support, and you pull the leg with the shock cord on it toward you, keeping it straight while bringing your two legs together. Perform 10 or more reps.

Calves/Feet. You definitely need strong calves and feet for football. When you have a stronger and more stable base from which to launch each stride, your overall movement can improve. You also want to develop these muscles to prevent injury.

A lot of football-related activity (sprinting, driving the blocking sled, etc.) builds your calves and feet. Yet there are specialized exercises that are necessary if you want maximum strength and development. These are generally high-rep, high-set exercises, as your calf and foot muscles are stubborn and require a lot of work. You can go with 15 to 20 reps or more, and upward of several sets, depending on your time. A good calf/foot workout can be achieved in 5 or 10 minutes.

Calf Raise. To perform the calf raise—or toe raise or heel raise, as it is also called—you simply raise up and down on the balls of your feet with a weight on your shoulders. Most gyms have a special ap-

A calve unit like the one shown isolates your calves for specialized work. Note the pin selection process for choosing weight. *Photo courtesy of Rocky Mountain Gym Equipment, Inc.*

paratus for this exercise, and you simply fit your shoulders under its padded "shoulder pads," step up onto a raised partition, and drape your heels over the edge. When you lower yourself, you can stretch your calf muscles considerably as your heels can extend below the edge of the partition.

If your gym does not have a calf machine, you can make do with a power rack or any other device against which you can brace the bar as you move up and down. Take a 4-by-4 and use it as your partition to stand on to get that good heel-lowering extension. Hammer a 2-by-4 placed on its edge onto each end of the 4-by-4 to keep it from tipping, making a big H out of it.

There are a few minor points to consider when doing your calf raises. You should always lock your knees in order to place all of the stress directly on your calves. This takes great concentration, particularly on those final reps when the natural tendency is to move at the knees a little. I have been doing calf raises for years and years and still must concentrate to lock my knees and let my calves do the work.

Yet there is a place for slight cheating in the calf raise, especially if you want to handle heavy weights. The thing to do is to perform as many strict reps as possible and then move your knees for assistance only when you cannot extend up fully in a strict manner. As a beginner, you don't need to be concerned with such cheating techniques. You should use a weight light enough that your technique is pure, getting into the habit of strict movements, because cheating is always a last resort anyway.

You should probably vary your range of motion with your calf raises. One extreme is a slightly less than full motion where you go up and down quickly in order to "burn" your calves. The idea here is to keep a maximum of constant pressure on them in order to get a good burn. The other extreme is a slower motion where you carefully "bottom out" with each rep by lowering your heels as far as possible. You can then hold this position for a second or two to guarantee that you have reached it; after going back up, hold your position at the top of the movement also. This full-range method probably hits more muscle fibers, as well as deeper ones. You may not feel it "burn" you as much as the faster method when actually doing the exercise, but there can be a delayed effect that you really feel after the set.

You might want to vary the position of your feet when you do your calf raises. You want them fairly close together, and you can keep them straight, point your heels out, or point your heels in. Each position hits different parts of your calf muscles, so get them all.

Seated Calf Raise. The seated calf raise works a different part of your calves than the standing, and it's a good supplementary exercise for sprinting. When you sprint, note that your leg is bent when your feet hit the ground. Thus your calves must be strong in this bent-leg position that the seated calf raise emphasizes. There are special devices for performing calf raises in this manner.

Leg Press Calf Raise. Here all you do is get under a leg press machine and do calf raises. A disadvantage is that most leg press machines do not have a raised partition to extend your heels over, although with some of them you can extend over the edge of the platform if you are careful. You can also place a 2-by-4 under the pressing portion.

An advantage of leg press calf raises is that you can put more pressure on your calves since your being bent at the waist naturally stretches them. In other words, figure that your back is on the ground, your legs are straight up at a 90 degree angle to it, and your calves are stretched and under more pressure.

You can vary your leg press calf raises the same as you can with your other calf work.

Donkey Calf Raise. This exercise is done by stepping up onto a raised partition from which you can extend your heels over, grab on to something to brace yourself, and then bend over and have somebody climb onto your back for resistance. It is an extremely effective way to work your calves since the bending over stretches and puts stress on them. Additionally, you can lower your heels as much as you wish using the raised partition.

One problem with donkey calf raises is finding someone to ride you for resistance, and this is probably the main reason that this fine exercise is not done more often. You can theoretically circumvent this by placing a bag of something heavy onto your back in place of a person. Here the difficulty is that the bag is awkward and probably will not weigh as much or stay on you as well as a person; also, it is not the kind of thing found lying around the gym. You can try a barbell if you pad it and get someone to hold it.

Foot Flexor/Extensor. This simple exercise is done by just curling and straightening your toes. You must concentrate on getting full extension each way, thus bending them down as if you are trying to firmly grip something with them and then straightening them back up as high as you can while simultaneously spreading them.

As a more challenging form of this movement, place your hand under your foot and resist the downward curling motion. Then put your hand on top of your foot and resist the straightening motion. Ultimately, you might try doing both at once, using both of your hands. You can also rig up a rubber cable for resistance, something that I do when I work this exercise.

Vertical Foot Extensor. Just move your foot up and down at the ankle with this movement, which lends itself well to added weight on the upstroke. You are working the "opposing" muscles of a calf raise, loading your muscles as you stretch your Achilles tendon rather than as you shorten it.

Foot/Ankle Rotator. This is another really simple exercise that takes just a few minutes. All you do is raise one foot up and rotate it clockwise in a circle from your ankle, in effect trying to draw as large a circle as possible with your big toe. Then do the same thing going in the other direction; 15 to 20 reps each way are good.

For extra resistance, you can wear a heavy boot when doing this exercise, at least if you have enough flexibility at your ankle. A better way might be to strap on an iron boot. These are solid, cast-iron "shoes" that strap onto your foot, and while not as popular as in bygone days, they are still available, often with holes for bars to be inserted to hold more weight.

Horizontal Foot Pointer. Here you lock your ankle and move your toes from side to side as if trying to draw a horizontal line with them in this position. If you add pure weight, you will probably have to lie on your side with your foot's flat surfaces perpendicular to the ground. This is the only position in which any extra resistance can work the movement you are trying to effect. You can also add resistance in the form of a rubber cable, perhaps an old bicycle inner tube secured to something, and try to maintain the horizontal movement. I like to do this exercise against such a resistance.

Foot Flapper. Place your heel lightly on the ground and raise the rest of your foot. Using your heel as the pivot point, move your foot from side to side, and when you move it inward, flex your toes and simultaneously curve up on the side of your foot. This exercise is like trying to knock an object across the floor with the bottom of your foot while keeping your heel in one spot.

Lats. Your latissimus dorsi muscles are worked in any pulling motion done with your arms. Thus any pulling motion you do on the football field uses these muscles. You also need lat development to counter the pressing (pushing) strength you develop. You are less likely to sustain injuries in either direction with such a balanced development.

A good time to work your lats is after your pressing exercises. You can follow each pressing movement with a lat exercise that is its exact opposite. This will assure the balanced development that is so desirable. Emphasize sets of 8 to 12 reps.

One good thing about lat work is that there are a wide variety of exercises available. Thus you can build your lat strength from different angles and also remain mentally fresh by being able to switch exercises.

Vertical Lat Movement. This lat exercise is done by pulling down on a bar in order to pull the weight up, utilizing a cable that passes through a pulley. It works your lats in a manner very similar to chinups

This basic lat machine can be used for several types of pulling movements, including the vertical movement shown. Note the pulley at the bottom right, which can be used to make the motion a horizontal one.
Photo courtesy of Rocky Mountain Gym Equipment, Inc.

and is done in a manner exactly opposite to the seated press. It's one of the most popular lat movements, and practically every weight room has some type of equipment for performing it.

To do this exercise, you grip the bar with your hands spaced somewhat wider than shoulder width and your palms facing either away or in, depending upon the bar. You then sit down on the floor —looping your legs or feet under a dumbbell to hold yourself down, if necessary—and pull the bar down. You can either pull the bar in front of you or behind you. If you pull the bar in front of you, pull it anywhere from directly under your chin to directly against your chest, leaning back a bit for the latter movement. If you pull the bar behind you, touch it to the area where your neck meets your shoulders. Pulling it down in front might get a little more "pure lat" development, and pulling it down behind you ties in a little more anterior deltoid. You can do both for best results, and I like to alternate them in the same set.

Horizontal Lat Movement. For this exercise, you merely grip the bar and pull the weight toward you, a movement whose opposite is the bench press. Often the bar is more of a handle that you hold with your hands facing in and maybe 6 or 8 inches apart. This style hits the lower portion of your latissimus dorsi muscles. You can also do your horizontal lat work with a regular wide lat bar or with a wide bar on which your hands face in; with both bars, you grip in that wider-than-shoulder width position. This wider grip style hits your upper lats a little more.

Angle Lat Movement. The guy who thought of this exercise was probably pretty serious about building solid lats. Actually, all it amounts to is doing your lat pulley work halfway between horizontal and vertical, or at a 45-degree angle with the floor. This positioning is to lat pulling movements what the incline bench is to pressing movements. You can do your angle lat work with a wide bar and with your hands down or in or with the aforementioned handle.

Chinups. This exercise—sometimes called pullups or chins—was the one used to build lats when lat machines were not yet around. It is done by finding a horizontal bar that will support your weight, grabbing it with both palms facing away or toward you, and pulling yourself up until your chin—or the whiskers thereof—are over the bar. You can also chin by bringing yourself up so that the bar is behind your neck; this is done with your palms facing away from you and the bar gripped with your hands spaced to at least shoulder width. I like chinups as part of my lat routine.

After you can chin 8 to 10 times, you might want to add some weight. There are special harnesses for this (comparable to the harnesses for dipping). You slip them around your waist with plates or dumbbells attached to them.

Bent-over Row. This movement—also called bent-forward row—is probably the best "bulker" of your lat exercises. It can be done less strictly than the others, and you can handle more weight with it. You can emphasize fewer reps with this exercise than with the rest of your lat movements, with sets of 6 to 10 reps working well.

Bent-over rows are done by bending down and grabbing a barbell, your palms down and somewhat more than shoulder width apart. You then pull the barbell straight up as you remain bent over, trying to touch it to your chest. The more you raise up when doing this exercise, the more you bring your deltoids into it. Some guys like to remain bent over with their back nearly parallel to the ground; others prefer about a 45-degree bend, tying in their lats and deltoids.

There is a special gadget available for bent-over rowing called a T-bar. With this you bend over and grab a T-shaped handle at the end of the bar, which has plates loaded onto it. You then simply pull up, with the other end of the bar secured so that it can pivot. A rough version of the same thing is a barbell loaded at one end with the other end stuck into a corner. Here you have to grip hand over hand unless this bar also has a T-handle.

Bent-arm Pullovers. Bent-arm pullovers work some muscle groups in addition to your lats probably a little more than the aforementioned lat movements. Among other muscles, they get your pecs a bit, hit your frontal delts, work a muscle group called the serratus (which is located under your armpits between your lats and pecs), and they stretch your rib cage and abdominal muscles.

Bent-arm pullovers are done by lying flat on a bench while gripping a barbell at about shoulder width, and then lowering the bar behind you in a circular motion all the way to the floor, stretching the involved muscle groups as much as possible. You then bring the bar back up in the same fashion; your deltoids form, as it were, the center of the circle during the movement.

You have to go slowly when you begin this exercise because the bar can be fairly hard to control at first. You're using your muscles in a combination that you're not used to, so your coordination will need some time. Thus it's a good idea to use spotters and go up slowly, taking care not to lose control of the weight and pull a muscle.

The new way of doing bent-arm pullovers is on a machine made specifically for this exercise, and I prefer doing them this way. Nautilus makes a fine unit, and there are also reasonable facsimiles on the market that get the job done. With these machine units, you set the weight, adjust the seat to your arm length (usually), strap yourself in, and perhaps press the weight up a bit with your legs through a special platform, just to get it started. Your advantages are safety and economy of motion; you're not balancing the weight and can thus use your muscles to lift it. You also eliminate the need for spotters with these finely specialized machines.

Biceps. There are some football strength programs that virtually exclude biceps work, reasoning that it is not an important muscle group for playing football. Yet the development of biceps strength is necessary. You need to be strong in the biceps to balance your triceps development. You also need strength in this area because you definitely use your biceps during football activity.

Strong biceps are also necessary to aid you in keeping this part of your body injury free. If you ever take a direct shot to your biceps muscle groups, you'll be glad you took the time and made the effort to strengthen and toughen this area.

All of your biceps development revolves around the biceps curl exercise, or curl, as it is commonly referred to. This exercise is done by first grabbing the bar at roughly shoulder width, with your palms up. You then brace your elbows against your body (lower ribs), and use your biceps to raise the bar in an arc to just under your chin. Your braced elbows serve as the pivot point; therefore you should concentrate on keeping them solidly against your body as you curl the bar. There is a unit called the biceps blaster that you can use for securing your arms, thereby minimizing cheating and making your biceps do the work. I have used it and found it effective.

There are many variations of the biceps curl, various movements that work this muscle group in different ways and from different angles. The following descriptions cover the more basic ways of doing curls and are entirely adequate for biceps strength development as applied to football.

Curls are a medium rep exercise with sets of 8 to 10 reps working well. You can also mix in sets of 5 or 6 reps with this exercise.

Barbell Curls. These are simply curls done with a regular barbell, and you usually do them standing up. To keep from cheating, you can place your head and buttocks against some solid object and hold them there as you curl. If you want to go really strict, stay glued to the object when you lower the bar. This will keep you from lowering it as quickly, thus working your biceps more during the negative stroke. The slower lowering will also prevent you from bouncing the bar to gain momentum on the bottom of your curling stroke, and the result is that you're curling back up with more dead weight, working your biceps that much more.

Dumbbell Curls. A lot of guys prefer curls done with dumbbells instead of a barbell. The thinking is that the exercise motion is less restricted and its range greater.

You can do your dumbbell curls while sitting on a bench since this keeps your legs from aiding you in getting the weight up; this ordinarily stricter form will then isolate your biceps more. You can also vary your curling style similar to the way you can for your seated dumbbell presses. Thus you can curl both bells at once, curl one bell at a time with the rep fully completed before starting to curl the other bell, or curl see-saw style by starting one dumbbell up while lowering the other one. You might combine all three methods at various times for best results.

E-Z Bar Curls. The E-Z curl bar is a barbell with ordinarily 4 bends of 45 degrees each, and the idea is to grip it at these bends and hit your biceps at a different angle. Some people thing that E-Z bar curling places less stress on your elbows and forearms. You can use either the 2 inside or 2 outside bends, the inside hitting more the peak of your bicep and the outside hitting more the lower area where it ties into your forearm. Your E-Z bar curls can be done using the same guidelines as those for regular barbell curls.

Cheating Curls. With cheating curls, you deliberately sway your body to get the weight up. Such cheating allows you to use more weight and is regarded as a good way to add size to your biceps area. You can basically do your cheating curls standing up with a barbell, dumbbells, or an E-Z curl bar; you can also do them seated with dumbbells or even with some of the various curling machines, swaying from the waist up.

A good way to incorporate cheating into your curling workout is to do as many strict reps as you can and then to cheat just enough for 2 or 3 extra reps. It is the performance of these extras that will aid you in building even more size and strength in your biceps.

The E-Z curl bar is a popular curling instrument. You may also use a closer grip with this bar for your curls.

Curling Machine Curls. This category includes any curls done on one of the many curling machines around. Some of the various features of such units are Nautilus-type cams for variable resistance, pin selector set plate stacks for quick weight changes, E-Z curl bars for the gripping portion, individual curl movements so each arm can be worked separately, and other features. Probably one thing almost all curling machines have in common is that they guide the bar movement so that your curling motion is even and strict; for this reason, they are a great biceps isolator. Generally, I like to do curls on curling

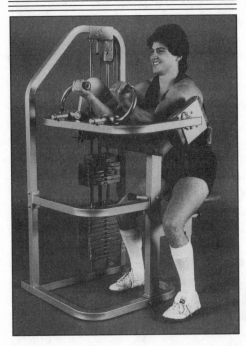

An example of an arm curl machine that really isolates the biceps. *Photo courtesy of Rocky Mountain Gym Equipment, Inc.*

machines but they must fit me correctly and actually isolate my biceps to be effective.

Preacher Bench Curls. The preacher bench is really a curling machine in its own right. Physically, it's a padded podium set at about a 45-degree angle. You place your armpits over its top edge and your elbows then lodge against it near the bottom. All you do then is grab a barbell, dumbbells, or an E-Z curl bar and curl away. If you keep your elbows flush to the padding and don't let your body rock, you can get some strict curling motion with the preacher bench. It's probably as good a substitute as any for the more elaborate curling machines.

Hands/Wrists/Forearms. I include these muscle groups in my strength workout because it is important to strengthen them for football. Strong hands are important for anyone who handles the ball and for use on opponents during contact. Strong forearms are important since they are also used in contact, and strong wrists are the link between strong hands and strong forearms. You should strengthen each of these muscle groups to help prevent their being injured, if for no other reason.

Actually these three muscle groups are worked to some extent with any good all-around strength program. Yet to get optimal strength in each one you must isolate them with special exercises. Since this is something that a lot of guys don't do, just an extra 5 or 10 minutes a day spent on such exercises will give you an edge.

You can work your hands/wrists/forearms several times weekly, emphasizing sets in the 15- to 20-rep range. If you have the equipment, you can work them at home during odd moments, thus cutting down on the time you spend in the weight room.

Four-Finger Squeeze. This is probably the most popular of the hand-strengthening exercises. It involves using your four fingers and, to a minor extent, your thumb in a closing motion against a resistance. You can do this drill on a variety of gadgets, among them those V-shaped grippers you can pick up in most any sporting goods section for just a few bucks. These units use a spring type of resistance which is nonadjustable, so you might want to try them out before purchase. Another device offers straight extension springs as the resistance; you simply wrap your palm and thumb over one handle and your four fingers over the other before closing your hand against the springs. This device is adjustable as to the number of springs, but costs a bit more than the V-shaped grippers.

This grip-developing unit is very effective. You simply slide a plate over the extending bar and squeeze the top two pieces together. *Photo courtesy of Jubinville Health Equipment.*

A common V-shaped furniture clamp can be used to work your four fingers, giving you a tougher workout than the V-grippers. If you cannot get it closed with just one hand, use your other hand to help until you build up your strength. You can also work your thumbs in with a furniture clamp, as will be seen.

One of the best hand-grip devices around is the Super Gripper, and this uses two adjustable extension springs for resistance. You both move the springs up and down, and grip the unit at different distances from its pivot point to change leverage, and thus resistance. The Super Gripper, built to last, is available by mail order from ads in the various muscle magazines.

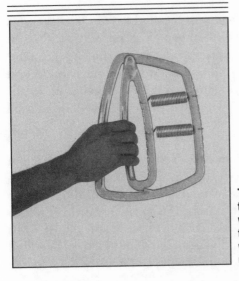

This adjustable gadget is called the Super Gripper, and the way it works is self-evident. Just move the springs to the tension you want and squeeze and release it until you run out of gas.

Another hand-grip unit that uses regular barbell plates for resistance is advertised in the muscle mags. Essentially all this amounts to is two bars that you squeeze together with your hand, raising up a small plate-loaded platform in the process. These units work your hands out quite well, and you can load them up and use both hands at once. Another plus is that you know just how much weight you are using, which is not the case with spring-loaded units.

To improve your deadlifting grip, one drill you can do with this unit is to load it up heavy, grip it with both hands and then squeeze the bar together as hard as you can for as long as you can. This will add staying power to your deadlifting grip.

Full-Hand Squeeze. There are a few items available that permit you to get the old thumb in there when working your hand, and you really should include some type of full-hand technique in your hand-strengthening curriculum. One of the simplest of such units is a soft rubber ball. You just wrap your whole hand around it and squeeze it over and over, like it was money. Because these balls are not expensive, you can go with two or three different sizes and/or strengths. Try to make sure that the ball is big enough to give your thumb some duty, though.

You have probably seen those smallish footballs made of a soft sponge rubber. They are great for "whole hand" exercises since you can grab them and turn them every way but loose as your fingers and thumb get some good work.

One very excellent whole-hand unit is called the Eagle Claw. This contraption features stirrups for each of your fingers and your thumb. These stirrups are connected to springs, and the springs then mount on the circular base of the unit. All you do is stick your hand in and open and close it as if you are trying to recover from pegging snowballs without gloves on. The Eagle Claw is advertised in newsstand martial arts magazines, among others.

Fingers/Thumb Squeeze (Pinching). You probably know what I'm talking about here. It is hand work that involves bringing your thumb and fingers together against resistance, giving old mother thumb some needed exercise. About the best unit for this kind of "pinching" hand movement is the furniture clamp. All you do is grip it with your thumbs at the top of the V on one side and your fingers on the other side, and then squeeze and squeeze. Your thumbs will pay the price but become much stronger.

The sponge rubber football is good for pinching, as is a soft, smallish rubber ball. You can't have a lot of resistance because it's your thumb against four fingers and your thumb alone just cannot handle that much resistance.

Reverse Finger Spread. This exercise, close to being just the opposite of the Eagle Claw exercise, is done with rubberbands. Simply touch the tips of your four fingers and your thumb together and then snug one or more rubberbands around them. Then try to spread your fingers and thumb back out against the resistance of the rubberband(s). This exercise is great for the joints of your fingers.

Mirror Fingertip Pushups. Here is another unusual finger strengthening exercise that you can do in odd moments. Place the tips of your thumbs and fingers together and then put pressure on them as you open and close your hands over and over. The residual muscle tension of each hand gives you your resistance here, and you must really concentrate to get any benefit.

Wrist Curls. This exercise catches the underside of your forearms. You merely sit on a bench while holding a light barbell palms up. You can space your hands any distance apart that suits you, or you can use a dumbbell instead of a barbell. You then just curl that barbell or dumbbell up and down with your wrists and forearms. You should go very slowly and quite strictly so you do not get your biceps into the act. There is also a portable spring-operated gadget that gives you the same basic wrist curl motion, which is handy to have around the house for wrist and forearm work.

Wrist curls, *the* exercise for the underside of your forearms, are a painstaking movement that requires a lot of patience to do correctly. Again, the important thing is to go as slow as you have to in order not to cheat. If you do them with a dumbbell, work only one wrist at a time to assure proper concentration. Use 15 to 20 reps.

Reverse Wrist Curls. These are done the same as regular wrist curls, except that your palms face down. You can use either a barbell, a dumbbell, or the same portable gadget for top results. Again, do them rather slowly and as strictly as possible, concentrating 100 percent on working your wrists and forearms. Use 15 to 20 reps.

Wrist Roller. Along with wrist curls, the use of the wrist roller is a top forearm exercise. The wrist roller device is just any bar or piece of round stock (a dumbbell bar, for example) with a rope or chain fastened to it; the other end of the rope or chain fastens to your barbell plates. Grab the wrist roller bar and roll it right up with your wrists. If you roll the bar in a motion up toward you, the action is quite similar to reverse wrist curls. Roll the bar up away from you and your motion is like regular wrist curls. With either motion you can roll the bar all the way up a time or two, or you can simply perform the wrist action on it for 15 to 20 reps.

This wrist roller device features the convenience of changing weights merely by pulling a pin out and putting it into another hole.
Photo courtesy of Jubinville Health Equipment.

Reverse Curls. This exercise is an effective forearm strengthener, particularly working the area where the upper forearm ties into the lower biceps. You simply grip a barbell with your palms down and perform a strict curling movement with it. You can use an E-Z curl bar and do this exercise with your palms at a 45-degree angle to the ground, and there are also special bars with which your palms are turned straight in. This exercise works my forearms about as well as any.

You can do your reverse curls at the end of your regular biceps curling session, performing a couple of sets of them to top things off. You don't need a lot of weight with this exercise. Instead, concentrate on strict form.

ADVANCED METHODS OF STRENGTH DEVELOPMENT

Although conventional weight-training methods will take you a long way in your strength development, sooner or later you will reach a point where your progress slows down considerably, or perhaps even stops altogether. In effect, your muscles have become immune to the workout you are giving them, and they no longer respond by becoming stronger. When this happens, it is time to work some advanced methods of strength development into your routine. As such, these methods are part of at least intermediate and, more likely, advanced workout routines.

These methods are effective when used properly. Yet the tendency is to overtrain with them, which not only decreases their effectiveness but is actually counterproductive. When using any of these methods, you should guard against overtraining by adjusting your workout properly. Generally, count sets utilizing power pause, variable resistance (with noted exceptions), or isokinetics the same as sets of regular isotonics, adding them against the principle of 3 sets to failure, excluding warm-up sets. For example, if you do 2 sets of seated presses using regular isotonics, you can do 1 set of power pause, variable resistance, or isokinetics for your 3 sets total. If you do 1 set of regular isotonic seated presses, you can do 2 sets using power pause, variable resistance, or isokinetics as long as you restrict yourself to 3 sets total using any combination.

For sets using isometrics, count each 3 to 4 positions of an isometric contraction as 1 set of isotonics. Thus if you do 2 sets to failure of isotonics for one exercise, you can do 3 or 4 positions of isometric contraction for the same exercise, resulting in the equivalent of 3 sets to failure total.

The methods of isometronics, forced reps, resisted reps, descending sets, rest pause, and eccentrics must be counted differently since they are more stressful. First, you can count any set using any of these methods as 1.5 sets of regular isotonics. Thus your limit here is 2 sets to failure per workout per exercise since this is the equivalent of 3 sets to failure of regular isotonics. Second, you should limit yourself to a total of 2 sets per exercise per week featuring any combination of these 6 methods. Thus, if you do 2 sets of incline presses featuring resisted reps on Tuesday, do no more incline presses featuring resisted reps, or any of the other 5 advanced methods, until the following Tuesday.

POWER PAUSE

This is a simple yet effective supplementary method, one that has aided me in getting over sticking points. It amounts to pausing completely on the bottom stroke of any lift before going back up with the weight. The idea is to eliminate the rhythmical bounce of the weight at the bottom of the lift. The complete pause causes you to lift dead weight, and thus your muscles alone have to overcome the complete load without any assistance from momentum.

One exercise that lends itself very well to the power pause method is the squat. Here, you employ a power rack and set the pins so that the bar will rest on them in your bottom-out position (your thighs parallel to the floor). You then get under the loaded bar while within the rack, clear it off its supports, and squat down and pause for a second with the bar weight completely on the pins. Next, you explode back up with the weight for 1 rep, and you do all the reps of your set this way.

A good way to do your power pause routine is to lower the bar and then drive it back up on the verbal command of someone else. Have a buddy shout "hit" or "up" or "explode" at you; by concentrating on this audio signal, you can improve your initial lifting speed. If you really want to get scientific, have your partner time each complete positive rep with a stopwatch, and then have a third party write down each time as it is called out. Try to pause about the same time between each rep, and constantly strive to improve your rep times in an effort to improve your power. Do not attempt this time improvement method with the deadlift.

You can top off your power pause set with regular touch-and-go work (ordinary lifting). When doing squats, for example, you will probably reach a point where you barely get a rep with the power pause method and know that you cannot get another. Instead of racking the bar, finish your set with as many touch-and-go reps as you can. Instead of cheating the weight up by altering your form or bouncing the bar off the pin, have someone assist you in forcing your final few touch-and-go reps. (This again is the process known as forced reps, which will be covered in detail shortly.)

The power pause method works very well on major power lifts (yet be sure not to jerk the weight with the deadlift), and you can also use it on a number of supplementary lifts. It is probably no more stressful than regular touch-and-go lifting; some people think it is easier, at least with certain lifts, because of the slight rest you get between reps. There are some guys around who can actually handle more weight and get more reps doing certain lifts power pause style. Accordingly, count your power pause sets the same as regular isotonics.

VARIABLE RESISTANCE

This supplementary method involves isotonic lifting in which the resistance increases throughout the motion of the lift. For example, the effective resistance might be 160 pounds at the beginning of the lifting motion and increase uniformly to 215 pounds at the end of the lifting motion, abbreviated as 160/215. This uniform increase in resistance is achieved as the lifter loses mechanical advantage as the weight is raised.

As mentioned earlier, the Nautilus machines feature this type of resistance with their cam, and yet their devices mainly offer accessory type exercises. The universal machines offer variable resistance on major power units such as bench press, seated press, leg press, and squat. On these units, they print two different numbers at each key setting: The number at the left is the beginning resistance, and the number at the right is the ending resistance. It should be noted that these resistances are only approximate, mainly because individuals with longer limbs will move the weights up a greater distance. Since the effective resistance keeps on increasing as the weights go up, guys with longer arms and legs will utilize a greater "top in" resistance. As well, the previously referred to deep bench presses move the weight up a greater distance by design, and so their top in poundage is greater when done on variable resistance units. A 160/215 on a deep bench press might be 160/230 or so because of the extra bar distance.

A valuable advantage of some variable resistance devices is that you can alter your beginning and ending resistances on them. You simply add extra plates at the lifting point and this weight adds equally to both beginning and ending resistances. For example, if the unit reads 125/160, a couple of 25-pound plates at the lifting point increases this to 175/210. Compared to 160/215, this improvised resistance is 15 pounds heavier at the beginning of the lift and 5 pounds lighter at the end. The different way this altered resistance works your muscles is excellent, giving them the change they need to work through sticking points, among other things. You can use your imagination to think up a wide variety of different beginning and ending weights.

Variable resistance is an excellent supplement to free bar power movements. It is a kinesiological fact that your pushing muscles have a greater mechanical advantage as they straighten; to correspondingly decrease the machine's mechanical advantage loads them with the extra weight they can handle. Those who do not advocate variable resistance machines feel that free bar movements are superior for football strength development; yet this point of view overlooks the issue that a supplementary program of variable resistance can actually help to improve free bar strength.

A particular kind of dynamically variable resistance (d.v.r.) uses springs or rubber shock cords. These devices give a sharper increase in resistance as the bar moves up than does ordinary mechanical d.v.r. Their basic formula is the resistance equal to a constant (varying with the spring or cord used) times the distance squared. If the constant for a particular spring or cord is 10, for example, and the bar with it attached is moved 2 feet, the resistance varies from 0 pounds at the beginning of the movement to 40 pounds at the end of the movement. Halfway through the movement, at 1 foot, the resistance would be 10 pounds.

If you utilize the spring or cord with a weight of 200 pounds lifted through the same 2-foot distance, you will be moving 200 pounds at the start of the lift and 240 pounds at the end of the lift. If you add a second spring or cord of the same composition, your lift will vary from 200 to 280; a third spring or cord will cause it to vary from 200 to 320; and so forth.

This type of variable resistance work is more stressful than that done using the variable resistance machines, namely because the tension that is on your muscles is not diluted by acceleration. For this reason, count each set as 1.5 sets of regular isotonic work, and do no more than 2 sets per week per exercise.

You can check your local hardware store for springs or rubber shock cords. If you're on a tight budget, check your bike shop for shot bicycle inner tubes, then cut those tubes of the same strength to equal length, fastening them on either side. Regardless of what you use for your resistance, keep each resistance unit a constant distance from the end of the bar to maintain balance, and have the floor fastening points straight down from the bar fastening points.

ISOKINETICS

This is a form of exercise in which the speed of movement is covered, if you recall. Thus with isokinetics, the bar will move at a set speed regardless of how hard you push or pull on it. With regular isotonics, the bar will accelerate as you push or pull on it with more force.

One manufacturer of isokinetic equipment used to demonstrate isokinetics in a way that explained the concept better than the best of written words. He turned his isokinetic device upside down and attached a 5-pound plate at the same place that force was applied when the unit was used normally. He would then take a stopwatch and time the plate's descent to the floor. Next, he substituted a load of a couple hundred pounds or so in place of the 5-pounder, and when he repeated the timing of the descent he would come up with equal times.

With isokinetics, you actually have to generate your own resistance since the bar is going to move at the same speed whether you're loafing or really humping it. In a sense, this makes isokinetics a mind-over-matter concept since you can force that bar just as hard as you are capable of on each and every rep. If you let up, it's not because you aren't capable of overcoming a resistance; it's because you choose not to push as hard as you can because it hurts too much.

Isokinetics have a lot of advantages as an exercise method. They are very safe, because there are no weights to drop and because, with their governed speed of movement, it is difficult to pull a muscle when doing them. They are quick, with little warm-up needed and no weights to change. They do not produce the muscle soreness of isotonics, probably because there is no back pressure, or negative resistance.

Another distinct advantage of isokinetics is that you cannot cheat with them as you can with isotonics. Regardless of what you do, you cannot get that bar moving any faster. The advantage here is that the muscles you utilize in a particular lift have to do all of the work since any arching, swaying, bouncing, etc., will not help them. Since these muscles do the work, they gain the benefits. Additionally, this strict lifting form that isokinetics "force" on you can carry over to your regular isotonic lifting.

When you compare isokinetics to regular isotonic weights, you can actually do more work per rep and per set with the former. If you max press a 150-pound barbell overhead isotonically, this really means that you can handle 150 pounds at the weakest point of your lift. You might have been able to handle 200 pounds at the strongest point of your lift, and yet you are limited to working with the 150-pound weight.

If you use an isokinetic device for the same maximum-effort pressing motion, you can push with a 150-pound effort at your weakest point and a 200-pound effort at your strongest point. You can also push with forces greater than 150 pounds but less than 200 pounds when you are between your weakest and strongest points over this same one repetition. As your muscles fatigue over the succeeding repetitions, the forces you push with will vary automatically between your strongest and weakest points over each repetition, regardless of what these points are.

Isokinetics are excellent for developing outstanding muscular endurance as well as strength, because theoretically you can do unlimited reps with them, each rep performed at your maximum ability to apply force. This is very effective for the purpose of conditioning your muscles for football work. You train your muscles not only to apply more peak force, but also to maintain a higher average force application over more repetitions.

This device combines isotonic and isokinetic resistance simultaneously. Note both the plates and the hydraulic cylinder. *Photo courtesy of Rocky Mountain Gym Equipment, Inc.*

Two major types of isokinetic devices are utilized, along with a third sort of hybrid isokinetic unit. The first is a gadget utilizing a friction brake for resistance. The concept is that the harder you push or pull, the greater is the friction of the brake, because of an automatic adjustment. These devices also feature a manual adjustment that sets the so-called exercise speed limit; you can set this from a point so low that you cannot move the bar (isometric) to a speed that feels like moving a stripped-down barbell bar.

The other major isokinetic unit incorporates hydraulic cylinders for the speed-governing unit. When you apply force, you move hydraulic fluid through a hole; the hole size is adjustable to vary the time it takes to move the fluid under a wide force variation. In other words, if you can push with 200 pounds of force, the fluid will take about as long as if you push with 300 pounds of force.

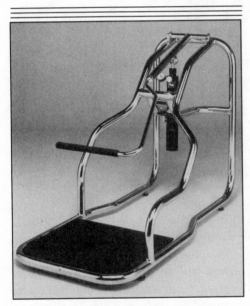

This upright row/triceps extension device uses hydraulic fluid as its isokinetic resistance. The cylinder is double action, enabling a pushing and then a pulling motion within the same exercise set. *Photo courtesy of Hydro-Fitness, Inc.*

The hybrid isokinetic device uses compressed air as the resistance, and it features a means where the amount of air let into its cylinder is controlled by the user. Since the volume of the cylinder is constant, the more air that is let in to be further compressed by the pressure of exercise movement, the greater the exercise resistance. This unit is not purely isokinetic since the resistance is a direct function of the amount of air in the cylinder rather than automatically variable to what is needed. Also, the compressed air generates a tremendous back pressure against you as you work the unit; this contrasts with the friction brake and hydraulic cylinder units, which have no back pressure. Yet the unit is isokinetic in the sense that you cannot accelerate the air as you can a barbell or dumbbell. This prevents cheating and forces stricter lifting, with all of its benefits.

The Leaper is perhaps the most popular of the isokinetic units. It aids in developing vertical explosiveness.
Photo courtesy of Fitness Systems, Inc.

The manufacturers of isokinetic equipment suggest exercising with the machines set at fast speeds. This practice has been successful in improving power by use of the speed end of the power spectrum. If you remember, power is work done over time, and fast-speed isokinetic work seems to reduce the time required to perform work, particularly in events such as running and jumping. One isokinetic device called the Leaper has been associated with significant increases in vertical jumping ability, and the manufacturers claim it will improve dash times as well. Users set the machine at a very high speed, then get under it and simulate the jumping motion, working as quickly as possible with sets of 10 to 20 reps.

While performing isokinetics at fast speeds has been successful and should be incorporated into any isokinetic program, one great benefit of isokinetics that is largely overlooked is the development of strength. Raw, brute strength. In regular isotonic training, you never quite reach a level where you apply all of the force you are capable of, even in a maximum-effort lift. The reason is that it takes more time for maximum muscular fiber recruitment than you have available in a maximum-effort lift. If you took the time for maximum muscle fiber recruitment in an isotonic lift, you would not be able to complete the lift.

You've probably seen a guy working a heavy power movement struggle with a rep, and then told yourself he's not going to be getting any more reps. This "struggle" was actually the very slow speed at which he moved the iron. Yet to recruit the maximum number of muscle fibers, he must move the iron at an even slower speed (while exerting maximum force, of course). He finds it impossible to achieve this speed level with isotonics since the amount of weight needed to slow his muscles to this "maximum recruitment" speed is such that he cannot lift it. Likewise, the level of fatigue needed to slow his muscles to this maximum recruitment speed is such that he cannot do any more reps.

You can overcome this problem with isokinetics, setting the machine at as slow a speed as you wish and then doing as many reps as you can stand. Remember that with isokinetics there is no set resistance as such to overcome since you create your own by how hard you push. Thus without the super-high isotonic resistance that limits your upward movement, you can force out more of these slow reps that are so effective for pure strength building. They will get your muscles used to "going slow" while straining to "go fast," and with more reps and at a slower speed than isotonics can afford you. This "muscle learning" should then carry over to your regular isotonics, enabling your muscles to function more effectively at the slow speeds that heavy isotonic loads place on them.

One way to work in isokinetics is to simply do as many repetitions as you can within a given time period, say a minute. If the unit has a speed adjustment, have it adjusted accordingly as you fatigue. You should be sure to generate all of the force you are capable of over each repetition.

An excellent time to do isokinetics is right after your heavy isotonics. There is nothing like topping off a tough isotonic workout with an all-out set or two of isokinetics. This practice is most effective if you go from isotonics to isokinetics immediately, while your muscles are still fatigued from isotonics. Yet don't plan on doing any more isotonic sets under these circumstances. Your muscles are going to feel enough fire that you will not even want to think about any more sets for a while. I have experienced this myself, reaching a state where all I could do was sit and cry real tears as I waited for the pain to go away.

Isokinetics are tough, but they do not seem to stress your system overall as much as some of the advanced isotonic methods. You can generally treat your isokinetic sets the same as your isotonic sets, thus working up to 3 sets to failure for any combination of the two.

ISOMETRICS

The technical name for isometrics is isometric contraction, a term that was touched upon earlier in this chapter's section on strength measurement. Isometric contraction is a form of muscle strengthening exercise that involves no movement. Instead, you contract your muscles against an immovable object as hard as you can for a period of about 6 to 8 seconds.

Isometrics are not complicated to execute. You brace against the immovable object that is your resistance and slowly build up to a maximum contraction. You then hold this maximum contraction for about 6 seconds and exhale through its duration instead of holding your breath. Hyperventilation can occur from holding your breath, and this can cause you to pass out.

Unless your gym has a special apparatus for isometrics, your best bet is a power rack. Just set the pins at the position you desire and apply force against them with a stripped-down barbell bar. You can perform isometric contractions with all of the major lifts this way.

Isometrics are ignored by many lifters, perhaps mainly because they view regular isotonics as so superior to them. The reasoning is that isotonics develop more muscular size, flexibility, stamina, explosive power, and full-range stength. By contrast, isometrics develop mainly just strength, and mostly at the position the contraction is held. Yet when properly done, isometrics are an excellent supplement to an isotonic program. They will help you get more out of your isotonics. They are also excellent for in-season work since they take relatively little time.

Isometrics have traditionally been done right after isotonic work. Yet recently the Soviets, among others, have suggested doing them intermittently during the workout. They indicate that performing an isometric contraction for a certain exercise while between isotonic sets of that exercise can slightly improve performance for the next isotonic set.

A good way to use isometrics is to apply them at the positions in your lifts where you are weakest. For example, if you tend to fail on your bench press about halfway up, place the bar there and perform isometrics. If your problem is in the lockout area—inches from completion of the lift—place the bar there and go to work. This strategy can help you improve upon the weak spots of your lifts.

If done properly—that is, with maximum force—isometrics are quite strenuous. Therefore, you should reduce your number of isotonics sets when incorporating isometrics into your program. Cut out 1 isotonic set for each 3 or 4 positions of isometric contraction done per exercise.

ISOMETRONICS

This method utilizes both isotonic and isometric techniques; the term is a combination of the other two. Isometronics are performed by utilizing a regular isotonic movement and incorporating an isometric contraction at some point in the isotonic lift. Isometronics are very stressful, and you can easily overdo them. You should restrict your isometronic work to 2 sets per exercise weekly, and utilize only one of the four mentioned isometronic methods when doing so. You can do both sets on the same day, or do one set on one day and another set 3 or 4 days later.

A very effective way of doing isometrics is to combine the isometric portion with full-range isotonic movements. This integrates the "pure strength" benefits of isometrics with the muscle-stretching and neuromuscular facilitation of isotonics. Following are some ways in which isometrics and full-range isotonics may be combined into effective isometronic movements.

Hold and Explode. This method will aid you in developing outstanding "blast off" power to aid you in getting your lift going, and I have found it to be of great assistance in helping me to overcome sticking points in my strength development. Choose a weight that you can handle for about 10 reps. At the bottom of your lift, have your partner hold the bar just enough that you cannot move it and perform an isometric contraction for several seconds. Then your partner suddenly releases his pressure, and you send the bar to the moon. You can do 2 or 3 reps like this, and finish your set with as many regular reps as you can get, working to failure. You can have your partner aid you with a forced rep as you finish up your set.

When using the hold-and-explode method, you are introducing more variables into your lifting procedure. You can not only vary the weight you use and the number of reps that you do, but also the time you hold the isometric contraction (although you should not go beyond 6 seconds). You can also vary your reps by changing the number of reps over which you utilize the isometric contraction, and you can vary the number of set-ending reps in which you do regular isotonics. You should keep close track of these variables, going so far as to utilize a stopwatch to time the isometric phase.

Stop and Go. Choose a weight that you can handle for a good 10 reps. On the first rep, have your partner stop the bar at three different positions for about 2 or 3 seconds at each position; perform an isometric contraction at these positions. Then finish your set with as many regular reps as you can get, working to failure. You can have your partner aid you with a forced rep as you finish your set.

You can add weight and regular reps to your stop-and-go set, but do so gradually. You can also add more isometric positions and increase the time of the isometric contraction at each position, but if you still want to get some isotonic reps after your sole stop-and-go rep, you might have to use less weight to do this.

Keep close track of all variables when employing the stop-and-go method, even using a stopwatch to time the isometric portions of your set. This method is very stressful, and you should not do more than the mentioned 2 sets weekly.

Variable Position Isometrics. This method is very similar to the stop-and-go method, and you again go with a weight you can lift for a good 10 reps. Have your partner stop the bar at a particular position on the first rep, perform an isometric contraction for 2 or 3 seconds, and then complete the rep. Then continue this sequence for another 2 or 3 reps, utilizing a different position with each rep. Finish your set with regular isotonic reps to failure, perhaps working in a forced rep.

You can begin with your isometric position at the bottom of the lift and then move it up on each successive rep. Or you can begin with your isometric position at the top of the lift and move it down on each successive rep. You can vary weight, isometric reps, the time of each isometric contraction, and the number of regular isotonic reps. Remember to keep close track of all of your variables, and do not overtrain with this method.

Sticking-Point Isometronics. Most people have one point in their lifting motion where they are relatively weak. This is the spot where the bar slows down a little bit as it moves upward. It's also the spot where the bar most often stops on the reps that you do not get.

Sticking-point isometronics are used to strengthen the weak point of any lift. To do them, use a weight you can handle for about 10 reps and move it up against your partner's hands, which are held at your sticking point. You then perform an isometric contraction against his hands; after several seconds of this, he releases the bar and you move it up the rest of the way. You can perform 2 or 3 reps in this manner and then finish your set with regular touch-and-go reps, including 1 or 2 forced reps at the end.

Sticking-point isometronics are very similar to the hold-and-explode method, the difference being the location where the isometric is done. You might want to consider periodically raising or lowering this isometric holding point a few inches each way to be sure you cover the entire range of your sticking point. Another option is to have your partner greatly slow, but not stop, the bar over the entire range of your sticking point. He can force you to take a few seconds to move the bar the several inches or so of your entire sticking-point range.

You can increase the intensity of your sticking-point isometronics by performing more such reps per set, by increasing the time of the isometric contraction per rep, or by having your partner offer more resistance if you are having the bar slowed instead of stopped. As with the other isometronic methods, sticking-point isometronics are very stressful, and 1 or 2 sets per exercise weekly are enough.

FORCED REPS

If you have any experience, you have probably experienced occasions when you were unable to get a weight back up and had your spotter grab the bar and help you. In effect, you were utilizing a method called forced reps, in which you are aided in getting one or more reps with a weight you cannot handle on your own. The true forced reps method is purposefully used as part of your set rather than randomly occurring when you miss a rep. This method can be used at the end of any exercise set.

Forced reps are an extremely effective strength builder since they increase the intensity and efficiency of each workout set. Assume you can handle 200 pounds for 5 reps in a particular exercise movement, working to failure. Thus even though you are unable to get a sixth rep with this 200 pounds, you still have some strength left that you are not putting to use. Using the forced reps method, your spotter will assist you in moving that 200-pound weight, in effect making it 195 pounds or 190 pounds or whatever weight you can handle in your sixth rep. He then repeats this assisting process over each succeeding forced rep that you do, naturally having to assist you more on each rep since your fatigued muscles continue to lose strength.

Although there are really several ways you can do your forced reps, the best way is probably something close to the method just described. Use a weight with which you can get at least several unaided reps, and then do all the unaided reps you can before having your spotter assist you.

If you want to survive to get more than one forced rep, have your spotter pull the bar up with just enough force to keep it moving steadily. Naturally, the bar is going to be moving more slowly on any forced rep than on your first fresh reps of the set. Yet too many spotters will pull with such little force that the bar barely moves or stops moving altogether. This is isometric type of work; although it is beneficial, it is really not the purpose of forced reps. Additionally, your muscles will be shot for any additional forced reps when your spotter "pulls too slow" like this. You should communicate with him ahead of time and tell him not to kill you so dead on the first forced rep that you aren't alive to get the one or two more that you want.

Of course, you can go ahead and die on that first forced rep if it's the only one you're going to be doing. Under this setup, your spotter might—at a certain point, anyway—loop his fingers around the bar without grabbing it, and he will invariably have a big grin on his face as he watches you take half an hour to lock the weight out.

One problem with the forced rep method is failing to perform as many unaided reps as you can. You might let up because you know that your spotter is going to "rescue" you, helping you with any rep you can't get. You might also let up to "save" yourself for the forced rep action. And of course you can always let up on the forced reps themselves. The entire forced rep process is quite painful when done correctly, and it's understandable for you to stop pulling or pushing as hard when the fire shoots through your muscles.

A possible way of circumventing this is by closing your eyes as you do your forced rep sets, a method that I use. This can help you concentrate by blocking out your immediate visual environment, and it keeps you from knowing if and when your spotter is aiding you. Instead, you can concentrate on moving the bar up as many times as possible with as much power as you can muster, ignoring the pain and oblivious to everything around you. (Make sure that your spotter is there to guide the weight as needed, and it is not recommended that you use this closed eyes method with free bar squats.)

Forced reps are exceptionally strenuous, and a couple of sets each week is enough for any single exercise movement. Since their efficiency and intensity is greater than that of regular, unaided reps, less work is needed.

RESISTED REPS

These are just the opposite of forced reps, as resistance is added to the bar instead of taken off. Use a weight that you can handle for about 10 reps and have your partner resist the bar for the first 2 or 3 reps. You then do as many regular (unresisted) reps as you can, and you might finish your set with 1 or 2 forced reps.

The key to working resisted reps is for your partner not to resist you too hard, especially when you are first starting out with this method. You want about 10 or 15 pounds of extra pressure; the way to tell what is right is by how you get the bar up. The lift should be intense but still smooth with no jerky spurts or pauses. Communicate with your partner to make sure that this happens, telling him "a little less" or "a little more," depending upon how your resisted reps feel.

With resisted reps, you can have your partner add more resistance as you get stronger. A good way to gauge this is to time your lifting motion with a stopwatch; as you gain strength, have your partner offer more resistance so that it takes you longer to lift the same weight. Keep track of your times as well as your weights and your resisted as well as your regular reps.

The combination of resisted reps and forced reps lends great efficiency to your lifting motion. You have extra resistance over your beginning reps where your fresh muscles can handle it; this extra resistance is eliminated over your middle reps as your muscles tire, and the resistance is reduced even further, with forced reps, over the last few reps of the set where muscular fatigue is maximum. Since this method is so efficient, as well as very taxing, you need only 1 or 2 sets per exercise weekly when employing it. I do it about this often, and find it extremely effective.

DESCENDING RESISTANCE SETS

This very effective supplementary technique amounts to reducing the weight over the duration of your set so that you can continue to get reps. What you do is work to failure with one weight, and then, instead of stopping, have your spotters remove some plates from the bar so that you can keep going. You then work to failure with the lighter weight, finishing with a forced rep, if you can.

The amount of weight to use when doing descending resistance sets might take a little experimenting. A pretty good rule of thumb for a starting point is to use weight you can get around 5 reps with, and after working it to failure, have your spotters remove somewhere around 20 or 25 percent of the total. If possible, you want to load your bar up in such a way that removing just one plate from each end will reduce it by about this amount.

One advantage that the descending resistance method has over manual assistance/resistance methods is that since you know exacly what you're working with, you can more accurately gauge your progress. If you bench press 255 pounds for 5 reps and then get 4 more with 205, you know just what you did; this is not the case with some of the other methods.

You can increase your intensity with descending resistance sets by increasing your primary weight, primary reps, secondary weight, or secondary reps. Keep your increases gradual but steady, and always keep close track of them.

Like many of the other advanced methods, descending resistance sets offer increased workout economy over regular sets. They not only develop strength and power; they also develop more muscular endurance than regular sets and are tougher on your system. For these reasons, you need only a couple of descending resistance sets per exercise movement each week. If you go all-out with them, you should benefit from this grueling method. I have made gains with it, using it as a change up with forced and resisted reps.

REST PAUSE

This method employs the principle of resting for a specific time during your set, and results in more repetitions per set. Ordinarily, the only rest you get between reps is a brief pause to catch some air before getting after it again. With the rest pause method, you actually rack the bar and time your rest.

One way to use the rest method is to choose a weight that you can get about 5 reps with, and then pause for a given time between reps while going for as many reps as you can, forcing a rep at the end of the set. You might begin with 10 seconds between each rep and try to reduce this time by 1 second every few workouts while maintaining the same number of reps.

Another method is to pause for a given time between a given number of reps. You could go with a weight you can handle for 10 reps, perform 5 reps with it, rest 15 to 20 seconds, perform another 5 reps, rest another 15 to 20 seconds, and continue on like this for as long as you can get sets of 5 reps, doing as many reps as possible on your last set, including a forced rep. You would then try to gradually cut down on the amount of rest between sets as you progressed, or perhaps increase the number of reps per set, or the weight used, always keeping close track of the variables to chart your progress.

A third way is to again choose a weight you can regularly lift for about 5 reps, and see how many reps you can do in a given time, say a minute, resting between reps as you see fit. You then gradually decrease the time or increase the weight for the same number of reps, or increase the number of reps themselves. An offshoot of this method is to use the same weight you can get for 5 reps and time how long it takes you to get 10 reps, pausing as you see fit. You then try to decrease this time for the same 10 reps, or increase the weight used.

Regardless of which rest pause method you use, you should keep close track of the variables involved (weight, reps, and time). You will also need a spotter to help you rack and unrack the bar and to time your sets. Have your spotter wear a wristwatch with a seconds function so that he has both hands free to assist you.

The rest pause method is strenuous since you are doing a considerable amount of work during each set. Accordingly, limit yourself to just a couple of sets per week per exercise when employing it.

NEGATIVES

The technical name for this method is eccentric contraction, and the common term used to describe it is negative resistance, or simply negatives. To do negatives, you resist the bar on the way down. To a certain extent all regular lifting involves this method; the reason is that after each successful repetition you must lower the bar somewhat slowly if you want to keep from injuring yourself. Pure negatives, though, emphasize only the lowering portion of the lift.

Negatives benefit you by enabling your muscles to handle more weight. The fact that you cannot lift the weight in a positive fashion is secondary as long as you are *trying* to lift it positively. Your muscles are lengthening (bending) under an unusually heavy load while they are trying to shorten (straighten). Since the lifting motion is the same, only "in reverse," most of the neuromuscular benefits of the positive stroke are retained while handling extra weight. The weight then handled for regular lifting will not only *seem* lighter to your muscles, it will *be* lighter.

In a sense, eccentrics can be compared to overspeed sprint training. Just as you are ordinarily limited in how fast you can run by your present rate of speed, you are limited in how much you can lift by your present strength level. Yet just as running faster develops more speed, lifting heavier develops more strength. Negatives "cheat" you into a new strength level by helping you go heavier artificially just as overspeed cheats you into a new speed level by helping you go faster artificially.

Since with eccentrics you have to use more weight than you can lift in a regular positive motion, you need some means of getting this excess weight into a position where you can resist it coming down. Very few gyms have contraptions for doing this, so you're probably going to need some assistance. Have a guy stand at either end of the bar and pull it up during the positive stroke, lettting you handle it during the negative stroke. You might need to let up slightly the first few inches to get out of the lockout position, especially on your initial reps when you're still fresh. After that, you should have enough weight on the bar—about 20 or 25 percent more than your maximum—that you can try to move it up with all the power you have and it still goes down.

You want to work your negatives to failure, or until you cannot effectively resist the weight any longer. For this reason, have your spotters ready to slow the bar's descent once your muscles have lost their "braking" ability, as you can be injured if the bar gets away from you. You can top off your set of negatives with a forced rep, although you will need lots of assistance to get the weight back up if you have worked to failure.

Negatives are very effective, but they supplement rather than replace regular positive lifting. They are also extremely taxing, and a couple of sets per major lifts done once or twice weekly is plenty. I have found that they help me to get stronger, but only if I do not overtrain with them.

COMBINED METHODS

It is possible to combine advanced forms of strength development if you do so properly. Remember to restrict any method using isometronics, forced reps, resisted reps, descending sets, rest pause, or eccentrics to 2 sets per week per exercise, however combined. Combinations not using any of these 6 methods may generally be treated as regular isotonic sets.

STRENGTH TRAINING WITH LIMITED EQUIPMENT

Thus far the talk has centered around strength training with conventional equipment. Yet even if you do not have access to such equipment, you still don't have to be the guy who gets sand kicked in his face, for you can develop strength with a limited supply of hardware. It might take you longer and you might not have the "lifting" strength of guys who use barbells and dumbbells, but the strength you develop will definitely help you in football.

Some of the previously mentioned exercises take very little equipment, with chinups, neckwork using manual resistance, most of the abdominal/oblique, and many of the hands/wrists/forearms exercises coming to mind. Other exercises that require very little in the way of equipment are explained on the following pages.

PUSHUPS

Just about everybody knows how to do pushups, and they're a good basic upper-body strengthener that develops about the same muscles that the bench press does. If you want more of a challenge with your pushups, you can always place extra weight onto your back when doing them. You can also bring your hands in so that you touch your thumbs and forefingers together, forming a triangle. Then do your pushups by touching your front face area down to your hands on each rep. For an even greater challenge, place one hand over the other and interlock your fingers, again touching down to your hands on each rep. You can always do your pushups one arm at a time; this takes discipline and concentration since the tendency is to cheat. Try to work these strictly and touch your chin to the floor on each rep.

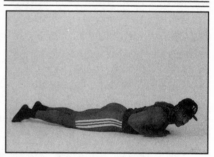

Pushups done this way are tougher than regular pushups. Placing your hands next to each other places more stress on your triceps.

HANDSTAND PUSHUPS

You have to be a pretty stout fellow to do this type of pushup. Get yourself a couple of solid supports the same height, about 2 feet or so off the ground. Make sure they will hold your weight, and then move them about shoulder width apart and place the palm of your hand on each of them. With a partner spotting you, rise up and do a handstand on the supports, and a good place to do this is against a wall so you won't tip over. Once you're up, simply dip down between the supports and then push yourself back up.

You're actually pressing almost all of your bodyweight with handstand pushups. This might take some working up to, and you can have your partner assist you a bit in pulling your body up until you're strong enough to handle the movement on your own.

CHINUPS

The earlier section on lat development covered the way to do chinups, and this is undoubtedly a good strength-building exercise to do when your equipment is limited. It's a lot easier to find a bar from which to chin yourself than it is a lat pulley machine, and you can get very similar results with a little adaptability. Just have someone boost you a bit if you can't yet chin satisfactorily, and have them boost you in any event as part of a forced rep regimen. For added resistance, have your partner resist you and/or add some extra weight by strapping on a barbell plate or wearing a weighted belt or vest.

HAND-OVER-HAND

Here is a unique little exercise method that works your biceps and triceps together. Just take one hand and place it palm-to-palm over the other, interlocking your fingers if you wish. Then with your elbows tucked against your body, simply curl up with the underneath arm, working your biceps positively, and resist with the top arm, working your triceps negatively. Once you're up, press back down with your top arm, working your triceps positively, and resist with your underneath arm, working your biceps negatively.

This exercise takes tremendous concentration, especially at the top part of the movement where your triceps leverage is not good. If you really concentrate, you can substantially improve your biceps and triceps strength with this method. I do this exercise on the rare occasions that I cannot get access to regular equipment.

ONE-LEGGED SQUATS

To do these, simply stand on one leg and bend the other so that your foot is just behind your rump. Then drop down and lightly touch the knee of your bent leg to the ground and then come back up. You might have to grab hold of something solid for assistance when you start these; if so, you should work toward doing them unaided. As you gain proficiency, you can do them more quickly, perhaps eventually getting to the point where you can spring back up after touching the ground.

LOAD SPRINTING

There are a number of home-brewed ways to sprint against resistance, all of which strengthen and add power to your legs. They'll be covered in detail in the next chapter.

PLYOMETRICS

Chapter 4 covered plyometrics as applied to improving your sprinting speed. Yet since their general benefit is that of improving your strength/ speed tie-in, plyometrics can also be beneficial in improving your strength.

Wall Push-Off. A good beginning upper-body plyometric drill is the wall push-off. Stand a few feet from a wall and free fall toward it, keeping your body straight and catching yourself with your hands. You then snap yourself back out with maximum force as soon as your hands touch. You can gradually increase your distance from the wall as you improve.

Hand Clap Pushups. Pushups in which you clap your hands between reps are a good plyometric drill. You should try to spring up as explosively as possible on each rep, and you might even find a way to gauge how far upward you are able to propel your body. You can vary your hand spacing when doing plyometric pushups.

One-Armed Pushups. Another good technique is to do a one-armed pushup with one hand behind your back, and then switch hands as you push yourself up. Place your original hand behind your back and extend your other hand to land on and then to push back up with. This was the type of pushup done by Sylvester Stallone in the movie *Rocky*.

Upper-Body Depth Jump. Another good plyometric drill is the upper-body depth jump. Get yourself a couple of very sturdy, flat-surfaced objects maybe a foot or so high (a couple of solid stools would be good). Place yourself in the pushup position with your hands placed on each of these objects at about shoulder width apart; you might place a mat between the objects. Next, free fall toward the floor and catch yourself with your hands; then spring back up with maximum force and catch your hands back on the props. As you get better, you can gradually raise the height of the props.

GADGET EXERCISES

There are a few effective but inexpensive items around which you can use to build strength.

Cable-Spring Stretcher. You're probably familiar with spring-stretching devices, the ones that contain from one to five springs. They're also available with rubber instead of the springs. They work your deltoids and triceps pretty well, and you can also hit your lats

This spring stretcher apparatus works your deltoids and triceps when used as shown. You can perform the same basic movement behind your neck for variety.

and biceps a little if you use your imagination. I sometimes use them to hit my triceps and deltoids after a weight training session.

If you want to save some money, check out your local bike shop for some shot bicycle inner tubes. You can use them to rig up a home-made version of the same thing.

Power Twister. You may also have seen a gizmo called a power twister, a large, tough spring with gripping handles extending from either end of it. You simply grap the handles and twist the spring from various angles, primarily working your pectorals and deltoids. These power twisters cost about the same as the spring or rubber-stretching devices.

Here is a simple movement done with the power twister. Use your imagination and make up your own movements with this device.

Crusher. Another gadget is called the adjustable crusher, and it consists of two long handles in a V-shape, the ends of which you grip and push together against one to five extensions springs. You then perform different exercises by varying the positions by which you hold the device.

The foregoing gives a good foundation for developing strength with limited equipment. You can use your imagination to discover other methods.

YOUR STRENGTH TRAINING ROUTINE

Since there are about as many strength training routines as there are people lifting weights, it would be impossible to list all of them here. Thus the upcoming routines are kept fairly basic; you can vary them as you see fit, provided you adhere to the strength training workout principles discussed earlier in the chapter. The routines are categorized as beginning, intermediate, advanced, and in-season. Essentially, they list which exercises and body parts to work on which days and the approximate sequence in which to do them. They do not list the number of sets and reps to do since this information has been covered. Nor do they list the amount of weight to handle since this will vary so much from person to person. On those routines listed as 3 days per week, do not work them on 2 consecutive days.

With some very basic exceptions, the listed routines do not feature supplementary exercises and methods. Reason that if you ask ten different "experts" which ones are tops, you'll get ten different answers. Just mention that you want to up your bench press and one guy will suggest adding close-grip bench presses and dips, another will swear by negatives and isometrics, and a third guy will tell you that you don't need any workout "extras" at all as long as you "go heavy" (which you were trying to do in the first place) and take the food supplement that he recommends.

The fact is that there are no universally best "extras"; and the best ones for you as an individual are those with which you gain the most strength. Finding them will take some trial and error, so you want to keep good records and see what happens when adding any "extra" movements.

If you're pressed for time, you can use what are termed staggered sets. These are simply sets where you do an exercise working one body part while resting from sets working another body part. For example, you might work your calves in between sets of high pulls, or work your neck in between sets of lat work, and so forth.

BEGINNING ROUTINES

The term "beginning routine" can be a little misleading since people who are not beginning lifters can make strength gains with these routines. Yet these routines are particularly solid for those just starting out. They emphasize 3 workouts a week with two or three Big 6 movements and all other body part exercises done each workout. A good example is to bench press and squat at least twice a week (since both of these exercises are so basic to good strength development), deadlift once a week, and then fill in with other Big 6 exercises as well as your necessary body part work.

For these 3-days-per-week routines you can work a little harder on your first and last days each week; you will have had 2 days of rest before the first day and 2 days of rest after the last day for recuperation. For example, if you are training on Monday, Wednesday, and Friday, you can work relatively hard on Monday, a little easier on Wednesday, and then relatively hard again on Friday.

SAMPLE BEGINNING ROUTINE

Day 1	Day 2	Day 3
Bench press	Incline	Same as day 1
Squat	Deadlift (optional)	
High pull	Seated press	

At least 2 days

Neck (4-way)
Knees/hamstrings (do both)
Abdominals/obliques (do both)
Abductors/adductors (do both)
Lats
Calves
Biceps
Hands/wrists/forearms (do all)

This sample beginning routine hits all of the Big 6 exercises each week. It can be done exactly as listed each week with the lifts performed on days 1 and 3, and thus emphasized since they are done more often. Or the pattern can be altered week to week, as the sequence listed above alternates with a following-week sequence of incline/deadlift/seated press on days 1 and 3 and bench press/squat/high pull on day 2.

Another sample beginning routine is as follows, with the same body part work to be done afterward.

Day 1	Day 2	Day 3
Bench press	Same	Same
Squat		
High pull		

This routine concentrates on 3 excellent football lifts, and you can supplement the bench press with the incline press. Another method is to once weekly substitute the incline press for the bench press and the seated press for the high pull.

INTERMEDIATE ROUTINES

Although it is difficult to tell just where beginning routines leave off and intermediate routines begin, it can generally be said that the latter utilize some type of "split" system. This type of system splits your body up into parts that are worked each session. In its most basic form, a split system works your upper body on certain days and your lower body on other days.

Intermediate routines usually work your upper body or lower body only twice a week. Therefore, you might utilize more supplementary strength exercises and perhaps some supplementary forms of strength development.

When should you advance from a beginning routine to an intermediate one? A good time is as soon as you stop making gains from your 3-day routines. If you are stuck with no strength gains for two or three weeks on a beginning routine, your body is probably stale and needs a change. You can, of course, try another beginning routine. Yet if you have been working out for several months, you can try an intermediate routine.

Following are some examples of intermediate routines.

SAMPLE INTERMEDIATE ROUTINE

Days 1 and 4	Days 2 and 5
Bench press	Squat
High pull	Deadlift
Incline or seated press	Leg press
Triceps	Leg curl
Biceps	Leg extension
Lats	Abductors/adductors

All 4 days

Neck
Abdominals/obliques
Calves/feet
Hands/wrists/forearms

This is the basic pattern for an intermediate routine featuring 4 workouts weekly in a split sequence. You can do a little more each workout since you are doing the lifts on only 2 days weekly. With the deadlift, in one session you can go for low (4–5) reps and in another you can do high (8–10) reps.

Do not be afraid to try some of the advanced methods of strength development if you reach sticking points. Yet be sure to use them as has been outlined in the section that featured them. You may wish to review this section before incorporating these advanced methods.

ADVANCED ROUTINES

As a general rule, you should try advanced routines only after a year or so of steady lifting and then only when not making progress with your present routine. Since they incorporate 5 or 6 lifting sessions per week, you do not have a lot of time left for your other training. Resultingly, you should not utilize such routines for extended time periods since you need your other training.

SAMPLE ADVANCED ROUTINE

Day 1 and 5	Day 2 and 6	Day 3
Bench press	Squat	High pull
Incline press	Deadlift (optional)	Seated press
Lats	Leg press	Shoulder shrug
Biceps	Leg curl	
Triceps	Leg extension	
	Abductors/adductors	

At least 4 days

Neck
Abdominals/obliques
Calves/feet
Hands/wrists/forearms

This is the basic pattern for an advanced routine featuring 5 workouts weekly. You can work fairly hard each session and give Day 3 a little extra since you are doing these movements only once weekly. You can change your lifts around some, perhaps switching the incline press with the high pull, or even adding high pulls to Day 1 or Day 5, if you can handle it.

If you are not making progress with this routine, try some of the advanced forms of strength development. You may wish to review the section "Advanced Methods of Strength Development" prior to incorporating them into your workout. Be sure to follow the outlined procedures when employing these methods, being careful not to overtrain with them.

IN-SEASON ROUTINES

In-season strength training can be termed the second major breakthrough in strength training application for football. The first breakthrough, of course, was when football players initially took up weight training, and for many years this was done on an off-season basis only. Only fairly recently has in-season strength training been recognized as just as important as off-season work since it aids in maintaining the strength developed in the off season and helps to cut down on in-season injuries.

Your in-season routine should primarily concentrate on strength maintenance work, and this is true because you have less time to lift during the season. You are also sore from playing and have less physical and mental energy to devote to serious strength training. However, there have been cases of players gaining strength during the season.

Since time is of the essence for in-season strength training, your workout must be very efficient, involving a lot of work for the time allowed. You should utilize staggered sets under these conditions. You can also utilize some of the advanced forms of strength development since they are so efficient. One good method is to do a set to failure featuring an advanced method that utilizes isotonics and follow this with some isokinetics or some isometrics if you do not have access to isokinetic equipment.

SAMPLE IN-SEASON ROUTINE

Day after game	3 to 4 days later
Bench press	Incline press
Squat	Deadlift
High pull	Leg press
Biceps	Seated press
Lats	Leg extension
	Leg curl

Both days

Neck
Abdominals/obliques
Abductors/adductors
Calves/feet
Hands/wrists/forearms

You can alter your in-season routine to meet your needs, but try to work each of the Big 6 exercises at least once a week and the listed body parts twice a week.

A FINAL WORD ON STRENGTH TRAINING

So much material has been covered in this chapter on strength training that it's just about impossible to summarize all of it here. Yet if things had to be summed up in just a few words, the following three principles would apply: (1) always stick to the ideas discussed in the section "Strength Training Workout Principles," (2) have a plan for reaching realistic goals, and (3) have the right attitude.

The strength training workout principles don't really change regardless of what training level you are on. As long as you utilize them, you can't go wrong in your basic approach.

A plan to reach some realistic strength goals is very important. It gives you something to shoot for as you push the iron month after month. Yet your goals must always, but always, be realistic. If you can bench press 200 pounds at present, it is not realistic to expect to bench press 350 pounds a year from now. A gain up to 250 pounds is more like it. Then, with regard to the goal of a 50-pound increase within a year, concentrate on gaining 10 pounds on this lift over the next 6 weeks. Then concentrate further on gaining 2½ pounds over the next week. Remember that a substantial increase on any lift consists of many very small increases.

With regard to having the right attitude about your strength training, this concept can be very simply summed up with a theme that remains applicable to anything you do: Always do your best. Never mind that some guys are stronger than you right now or that others seem to gain strength at a greater rate. Concentrating on these things is not going to help you reach your realistic strength training goals. Rather, doing your best through a firm commitment to a thorough, rigorous strength workout program—giving it all you've got on every set, exclusive of warm-ups—is the only thing that's going to work for you. And if you stick to this approach, you just might surpass those guys who are presently stronger and those who presently gain strength faster.

Yet whether you surpass these people or not, the bottom line is that if you do your best as you train the right way, you've done everything you possibly can to develop your strength. And this is all anyone can ask of you.

6

Conditioning Wins Games: A Program for Football Stamina

"Fatigue makes cowards of us all."
The late Vince Lombardi, former head football coach, Green Bay Packers

AN OVERVIEW OF CONDITIONING

CONDITIONING DEFINED

Conditioning means the ability to sustain a given level of performance, and stamina may be thought of as the same thing. Actually, the term "football condition" involves more than simply stamina, but for the purposes of this chapter conditioning and stamina are used more or less interchangeably.

Although there is such a thing as general stamina, you largely build stamina specific to the exact event that you train in. Thus running exactly 12 miles per hour will develop stamina for this event, and doing pushups will develop stamina for that event. Accordingly, stamina is not necessarily transferable from one event to another. Experiments showed trained cross-country runners to possess relatively poor stamina when wrestling, and, conversely, trained wrestlers to lack stamina for cross country. Though both groups were in shape for their events, such conditioning was sport specific and not very transferable.

IMPORTANCE OF CONDITIONING

Next to fundamentals, conditioning is probably the most important part of football. While you undoubtedly need size, speed, strength, and quickness/agility, etc., without stamina you're not going to be able to maintain these traits as effectively. The lack of proper conditioning has wilted many a 4.5 sprinter or 400-pound bench presser in the heat of football combat. The late Vince Lombardi was telling it like it is when he said that fatigue makes cowards of us all.

Your conditioning needs are directly related to sustaining football activity. This means that you want to sustain the effectiveness with which you sprint, block, tackle, etc., over the duration of the game. The end result of improved football conditioning is not improvement in these skills, but a reduction in the degree to which they are lost due to fatigue.

When you do any football activity, your body reacts with a higher lactic acid content in your muscles (a performance hindering by-product of anaerobic work) and a higher pulse, among other things. Both of these factors detract from your ability to perform football skills. Yet the better your "football condition," the less your lactic acid content and pulse increase when the same amount of football activity is done, and the greater the rate at which your body will move back toward its normal state.

It is obvious that football condition can be an equalizer when two players differ in physical ability. It is this difference in conditioning level relative to the difference in physical ability that determines the extent to which conditioning can help even things out.

Good conditioning reduces your chances of being injured. When you're in shape, you're going to maintain more of the physical as well as mental faculties that you use to protect yourself on the field. You're not as susceptible to the "fog" of fatigue that can so adversely affect your physical reactions and cause injury. Indeed, my having remained injury free throughout my career is to a good extent due to my conditioning level.

Being a well-conditioned football player will help you psychologically. In getting yourself into top shape, you stood up to everything your hard-core conditioning program dished out to you. You're now both mentally and physically ready to go all-out on the football field, and you don't have to worry about running out of gas because you know your stamina will leave you plenty in reserve.

DEGREE OF CONDITIONING IMPROVEMENT

It's more difficult to measure improvements in conditioning than it is improvements in, say, strength or speed. This is because there are many more possible variables: distance, time, repetitions, the interval, and the actual event. Yet it is a widely held opinion that conditioning can be improved substantially by anyone in good health, for conditioning is largely a function of how much hard work you're willing to do.

TYPES OF CONDITIONING

In any discussion of conditioning work, you're talking about aerobic and anaerobic exercise. Aerobic exercise consists of any activity where the oxygen system can furnish adequate amounts of energy to the muscles. By contrast, anaerobic exercise takes place when the oxygen system cannot furnish adequate levels of energy to the muscles, and the result is oxygen debt. A prime example of aerobics is slow jogging, and an example of anaerobic work is sprinting. Certain exercises contain both aerobic and anaerobic characteristics, some examples being boxing, wrestling, basketball, and speed play. These exercises consist of sustained sub-maximum work efforts interspersed with brief periods of maximum work.

CONDITIONING WORKOUT PRINCIPLES

EMPHASIZE ANAEROBIC EXERCISE

Since it involves brief (several seconds or so) periods of all-out exercise, football is a highly anaerobic game. It follows that your football conditioning program should be of a highly anaerobic nature. However, some coaches test their players with aerobic drills such as the 1-mile, 2-mile, or 12-minute run, which have little to do with football condition. If the times for such runs were related to football performance, coaches would continue their players on them throughout the season. Yet few if any coaches stress distance running once the season is underway.

UTILIZE INTERVAL TRAINING

The majority of your conditioning work should emphasize interval training, which is a series of exercise periods alternated with controlled periods of relief. Some experts maintain that interval training has developed more well-conditioned athletes than any other system of training.

With interval work, you can strictly control your training intensity by varying the speed at which you run (although it should generally be full speed), the distance you run, the number of repetitions, and the time between each repetition. By keeping accurate track of these variables, you can plan and adjust your interval training program accordingly.

Probably the best time interval to utilize between exercise bouts is 25 to 30 seconds, since this is the average time between plays in a football game. The various conditioning drills given later will make mention of this time interval.

INCREASE YOUR INTENSITY STEADILY

This is one of the most important principles of conditioning work. Its practice will not only assure you a good level of conditioning, but will reduce your chance of injury from doing too much too soon.

A good method of steadily increasing your conditioning intensity is to begin with 2 reps of a given drill and systematically work to reach a set goal by the start of pre-season practice. As an example, say it is your goal to sprint 6 × 100 yards at an average time within 10 percent of your best, maintaining the 25- to 30-second recovery interval between each rep. If you start working out 8 months before practice begins, you can reach this goal of 4 additional 100-yard sprints by adding 1 rep every 2 months. With 8 to 10 such workouts a month, this amounts to 1 added rep every 16 to 20 workouts, something your body can handle.

You can utilize this same general method of gradual progression for any conditioning drill. You simply set your goal, and then divide the time you have to reach it (8 months, in the example given) by the number of additional reps you need to reach it (4 reps, in the example given); this will give you the time you have to add each additional rep (2 months for each additional rep, in the example).

CYCLE YOUR CONDITIONING

Depending on how often you do conditioning work, you might have to follow a tough conditioning workout with a more moderate one. Your body just can't take high-powered conditioning work day after day without bringing on energy-robbing fatigue that decreases training effectiveness and increases your chance of injury.

As a general rule, you do not want to condition vigorously for more than 2 days in a row. Thus, if you work on conditioning 3 or 4 days a week, you can probably work fairly hard each time, provided you build up to this level gradually and do not feel yourself getting stale. Any conditioning workouts in excess of 3 or 4 per week should perhaps be relatively moderate ones.

VARY YOUR CONDITIONING DRILLS

Varying your conditioning drills has some definite advantages. It alleviates the monotony of doing just one drill, keeping you from going stale mentally. Practicing a variety of drills can also result in more overall stamina development, in the same way that a variety of strength training exercises will aid in more overall strength development. Your body can also tolerate more overall conditioning work this way since different conditioning drills stress you in diffferent ways.

Although there are a number of different anaerobic conditioning drills, they can basically be separated into exercises that incorporate regular sprinting and those that incorporate load sprinting, which will be defined later. A good basic way to vary your workouts is to alternate these two modes of football stamina development from workout to workout. Obviously, you can do various conditioning exercises within each mode.

END YOUR WORKOUT WITH CONDITIONING

Stamina work takes a lot out of you, so it's best to do it at the end of your overall workout. In fact, there is nothing like topping off a good quickness/agility and sprinting speed workout with some vigorous conditioning, a practice that my own body is very familiar with.

Your schedule might be such that you have to do your strength work shortly after heavy conditioning. Your lifting might suffer a little at first, but you should eventually build up enough tolerance that this effect is minimized. I have entered the weight room immediately after heavy anaerobic conditioning and proceeded to handle my customary reps and poundages.

TIME YOUR CONDITIONING DRILLS

It is important to get some times down for various conditioning drills because improved times are indicators of progress. You might think you are progressing by adding more distance and repetitions, and/or by decreasing your rest interval. Yet these apparent improvements are nullified to the extent that your overall times are slower. Often a guy will let up a little, even subconsciously, when he adds an extra rep or an extra 10 yards. By timing your drills, you can keep track of this tendency and work to minimize it.

A good procedure is to take time on the first and last workouts of the same conditioning routine. For example, time all of your reps of the first session, where you sprint, say, 3 × 100 yards with 25- to 30-second recovery. After doing this one workout for a given time period—be it 4 weeks or 10 workouts or whatever—again time all of your reps over 3 × 100 yards/25- to 30-second recovery, and note any improvement all over.

The ultimate goal in conditioning is to add reps and improve times. Thus if you can sprint 4 × 100 yards/25- to 30-second recovery with an average time per rep that is lower than 3 × 100 yards/25- to 30-second recovery, you are on your way to developing superior condition.

KEEP RECORDS OF CONDITIONING WORKOUTS.

In order to gauge improvement and plan your conditioning workouts, you must know what you did on previous workouts. This requires accurate record-keeping. Your record book should list the date and then exactly what you did. Following is an example:

Date	Exercise	Distance	Reps	Recovery
6–5	Hill sprints	150 yards	5	Jog back
6–7	Sprints	100 yards	4	30 seconds

You should also include the area where you worked out, if you utilize more than one, and you should record any times that you take.

CONDITIONING WORKOUT DRILLS

LOAD SPRINTING

Load sprinting is any sprinting that is done against resistance. It develops both power and acceleration, and is perhaps the most effective anaerobic conditioner there is since it puts you into oxygen debt more quickly than a like amount of regular sprinting. Load sprinting is also very football specific because it conditions your anaerobic system for these repeated applications of power, and football is an anaerobic sport requiring power.

The most effective way to do your load sprinting is through the mentioned interval training approach of keeping track of all the variables (distance, reps, recovery interval, and the resistance used). You should also periodically time your load sprint drills to note any improvement. Make sure any resistance you use is the same when comparing the times of any drill over a given number of reps at the same distance and with the same recovery interval.

Following are some load sprint conditioning drills. Unless you are fully warmed up from other sprinting work, you should warm up thoroughly by jogging, stretching, and running at gradually increased speeds before performing any of these drills. You also might do a little stretching of your leg muscles after load sprinting, and finish off with a couple of easy, loose striding runs of 100 yards or so.

Hill Sprinting

Objectives:

To develop anaerobic condition, to develop explosive power, and to improve sprinting acceleration

Procedure:

 (1) After warming up thoroughly, sprint up a hill as far as you can.
 (2) Jog back down the hill and repeat.

Comments: Hill sprinting is one of the finest football conditioning exercises available. It can be done on anything from as steep a hill as possible to one with an incline of a few degrees. The steeper the incline, the more you are working on the strength aspect of your power development: the less steep the incline, the more you are working on the speed aspect. Accordingly, the steeper the incline, the earlier the phase of your 40-yard dash you develop, and as the incline lessens, the later the phase of your 40. For best results, you should sprint hills of various inclines, something that I make sure I do.

Training Tips: If you are limited in your selection of hills, you can add a weighted belt or vest when you sprint. This extra weight works somewhat like increasing the hill incline, and is effective if you have reached a sticking point on your hill sprinting. You can sprint the hill with the extra weight until you are nearly "out of gas," and then decrease or remove the weight over the final few reps. I have sprinted hills in this fashion and found it to be extremely effective.

Step Sprinting

Objectives:

Same as for hill sprinting

Procedure:

 (1) After warming up thoroughly, sprint up a flight of steps to the top, or as far as you can.
 (2) Jog back down and repeat.

Comments: Step sprinting is similar to hill sprinting, one difference being that steps do not vary as much as hills in their slope. You cannot wear football cleats on steps, and your sprinting stride length is regulated. Step sprinting might also be a little harder on your knees and feet since steps are often made of concrete; for this reason, you should be very cautious when adding extra weight, adding it very gradually and removing it at the first symptom of problems.

Sprinting steps has the advantage of a constant distance each time you run to the top, and a constant recovery distance between each rep. So if you sprint to the top each time, all you need to keep track of is the number of reps that you do.

When sprinting steps, your stride should cover the maximum number of steps (usually 2 or 3). This will result in a more acute angle between your thigh and calf, as well as a faster pace up the steps, which means more power. For a change of pace, you can occasionally take your steps at less than full speed, emphasizing more trips to the top while still maintaining your full stride length.

Training Tips: After you have been sprinting the steps for a few months, sprint to the top as many times as you can and then continue on with a few more reps in which you do not make it to the top. This requires a fairly large flight of steps. If your flight of steps is small (the typical high school stadium steps), you should consider adding extra weight, taking care as mentioned earlier.

Caution: A stair-climbing machine can be used as an alternative, since it is less stressful to the knees.

Soft Surface Sprinting
Objective:
Same as for hill sprinting, with a little more speed maintenance development
Procedure:

(1) After warming up thoroughly, sprint on a soft surface (sand, snow, or soft dirt) for as far as you can.
(2) Jog 25 to 30 seconds and repeat.

Comments: This is another excellent football conditioning exercise, one that is a major part of my conditioning program. Like hill and step sprinting, it overloads your sprinting muscles, yet in a slightly different way since it involves sprinting on a flatter surface. The deeper and softer the surface you sprint on, the more the overload. You should thus work on surfaces of varying depth and texture, if they are available.

A soft surface is the best for sprinting with a weighted vest or belt, because your feet, ankles, and calves take less of a pounding from the increased weight due to the shock-absorbing effect of the surface. As with hill and step sprinting, you can run a number of soft surface sprints while wearing a given weight, and then decrease or remove the weight over the final few reps. I do most of my soft surface sprinting this way.

Training Tips: I like to sprint at least 100 yards when doing this drill, and work up to a given number of reps while maintaining the 25- to 30-second interval. If you can master this method, your regular sprinting will be easy by comparison.

Load-pull Sprinting
Objectives:
Same as for hill sprinting
Procedure:

(1) After warming up thoroughly, sprint as far as you can while pulling a load.
(2) Rest 25 to 30 seconds and repeat.

Comments: Load-pull sprinting is similar to hill sprinting in that a heavier load affects you the same way as a steeper hill. Thus you should vary your load for top results, keeping track of exactly what you use for it.

Your load can be any durable object of ample weight that will pull fairly smoothly, such as tires or a chain. You can attach your load to a steel cable or nylon cord, and attach the other end of the cable or cord to anything that will fit comfortably around your waist and leave your arms free. A commercially available unit that includes a harness and a resistance sled can be ordered from Speed City, Inc., P.O. Box 1059, Portland, OR 97207. They may be reached at 1-800-255-9930. Another commercially available unit is the earlier mentioned Speed Chute, available from All-Star Athletic Systems, Inc., P.O. Box 751622, Memphis, TN, 38175-1622, and they may be reached at 1-800-828-5047.

An alternative method of load-pull sprinting is to use a partner for resistance. Just have him grab the rope or cable that extends from your harness (making sure he wears some tough work gloves) and then resist you as you sprint forward. You can adjust this resistance by simply calling "more" or "less" to him while you are sprinting.

Training Tips: Monitor your stride length when load pull sprinting (covered in chapter 4) and try to gradually increase it for a given load. Add slightly to the load when you reach a sticking point, and try to equal your old times. Perform your load sprints uphill or on a soft surface for a change of pace, lightening your load to compensate.

Load-push Sprinting
Objective:
Same as for hill sprinting, with more emphasis on the strength factor of power development
Procedure:

    (1) After warming up thoroughly, brace yourself behind a solid, movable object, and push it as fast and as far as you can.
    (2) Rest 25 to 30 seconds and repeat.

Comments: Load-push sprinting works just the opposite of load-pull sprinting. Brace yourself behind a solid, movable object and push it as fast and as far as possible. You can use a vehicle, putting it in neutral gear and having someone else steer it. If you can't find anyone to steer, get something to secure the steering wheel and do it solo, making sure you are in an area where you can't run into anything, and preferably where you can also wear your football shoes. A large empty field is ideal.

Another way of doing push sprinting is by using a partner for your resistance. Simple square off against him and have him place his hands on your shoulders and resist you as you sprint forward. He will have to rather adroitly move backward while at the same time resisting you, and thus it might take a few trial runs to synchronize this drill. Be sure to do your work in an area where your partner cannot bump into anything as he moves backward.

Training Tips: Push sprinting is an excellent way to finish off a weight session in which you have worked your legs. Your warm-up does not have to be as extensive as usual since you are already warmed up from your strength session.

When I do load pull or load push sprints, I make a game out of it by equating each repetition to one ball-carrying effort from scrimmage, with the extra resistance simulating the resistance of the defenders. I sprint as fast and as far as I can just like in a game, and then rest 25 to 30 seconds before sprinting again, the same as the time between plays in a game. I do this drill at least twice a week in the off season, varying the resistance some and working up to as many "carries" as possible by the time training camp opens.

Real Runner

Objectives:

Same as for hill sprinting

Procedure:

(1) Set the Real Runner to a specific resistance.

(2) After warming up thoroughly, sprint using the Real Runner for a designated time or a designated number of repetitions.

(3) Rest for 25 to 30 seconds and repeat.

Comments: The Real Runner is a very effective power building and anaerobic conditioning device put out by the company that makes Universal Gyms. It is a machine that basically simulates the act of sprinting, and against adjustable resistance. After deciding on the resistance you want with a simple dial, you mount the machine by placing each foot in a sort of stirrup that extends down from the unit's legs. You grab the handlebars for support and sprint in place, moving the legs of the machine, which in turn move against the resistance you have set.

Since the Real Runner is an inside device, you cannot always warm up for it with regular running. For your warm-up, you can run in place, stretch, and then gradually increase the pace at which you use the unit. You can top off a heavy leg strength session with Real Runner work; in such a case, be sure to stretch your legs before using it.

Training Tips: Once you have been steadily using the Real Runner for a month or two, you can sprint a given number of strides and then have someone decrease the resistance and immediately continue sprinting. You can continue this until you run completely out of gas, and you'll have to take more than a 25- to 30-second rest if you want to do more Real Runner work.

REGULAR SPRINTING

Regular unhindered sprinting is also a large part of any good football conditioning program. While it does not put you into oxygen debt quite as quickly as load sprinting, it is nonetheless very football-specific conditioning. It also works on speed a little more than load sprinting does. Additionally, since you will be doing a lot of unhindered sprinting once practice starts, you should prepare for it as well as you can. This is why unhindered sprinting forms the core of my conditioning program.

Following are some regular sprinting conditioning drills. Before performing any of them, be sure you are thoroughly warmed up with jogging, stretching, and running at gradually increased speeds.

Interval Sprints

Objective:
To develop anaerobic condition
Procedure:

(1) After warming up thoroughly run a sprint for a set distance.
(2) Jog for 25 to 30 seconds and repeat.

Comments: This drill is actually the basis of all unhindered conditioning sprints; the rest of the drills are basically extensions of it. You can begin this drill many months before the season starts, and steadily add repetitions and distance while maintaining the same 25- to 30-second interval.

If you are doing 100-yard interval sprints on a football field, you can readily monitor your 25- to 30-second recovery interval. Sprint 100 yards down one sideline, jog across the field, and sprint 100 yards down the other sideline, continuing this sequence for your reps. Each 100-yard sprint should carry you about 15 to 20 extra yards before you slow enough to turn, the jog across the field is 53⅓ yards, and then you have the same 15 to 20 yards before you reach the beginning point of your next 100. This comes out to about 85 or 90 yards between each sprint, and it should take you 25 to 30 seconds to cover this distance. You can time it with a stopwatch and adjust your jogging pace accordingly.

Training Tips: Make your last rep a "sell out" sprint by running it as fast and as far as you can; then, without stopping, jog for several minutes to warm down. Training yourself to give such an all-out effort when already fatigued will result in superior condition.

40-yard Interval Sprint Drill

Objective:
To develop anaerobic condition
Procedure:

(1) After warming up thoroughly, sprint 40 yards.
(2) Rest 15 seconds and sprint another 40 yards.

Comments: Add one 40-yard dash every 2 weeks to a month until you have reached 10 of them, all the while maintaining the same 10-second interval. Once you are able to sprint 10 × 40 yards with 15 seconds between them, you are ready to be timed for each one as a test of your anaerobic condition. This is the topic of the next drill.

Training Tips: Plan your long-range workout schedule so that you reach your 10 × 40 goal a good 4 to 6 weeks before the start of practice. Then spend these 4 to 6 weeks improving your average times for the entire 10.

Interval Sprint Test, 10 × 40 Yards
Objective:
To test anaerobic condition
Procedure:

   (1) After warming up thoroughly, sprint 10 × 40 yards with 15 seconds rest between each.
   (2) Time each sprint and record the time.

Comments: This drill is used to test your anaerobic condition. Add up each 40 that you sprint and divide by 10 to get your average time. You then take your best-ever 40 time and divide it by your average time to get a percentage. For example, suppose your best 40 time is 4.8, and you run 10 of them with 15 seconds between each in: 4.8, 4.9, 4.95, 5.0, 5.2, 5.25, 5.4, 5.5, 5.5, and 5.7. These average out to 5.22 seconds for each 40, and when your best time, 4.8, is divided by this 5.22, your percentage is 92 percent, which is considered reporting condition.

Training Tips: Rather than add to the 10 forties that you sprint, first work on improving your times for the 10. Anything above the 92 percent figure is a bonus.

Maximum Distance Sprints
Objective:
To improve anaerobic condition
Procedure:

   (1) After warming up thoroughly, sprint for as long as you can.
   (2) Jog to recover and repeat.

Comments: This drill was covered in chapter 4, the chapter on sprinting speed development. It is one of the toughest conditioning drills there is, and I include it as a major part of my conditioning work. As noted there, a good way to do it is to run alongside a car at a given pace. If your top sprinting speed is 21 miles per hour, have the driver go at 19 or 20 miles per hour and keep up with him for as long as you can. Jog for about a minute to recover and repeat. Have the driver keep track of how long you sprint at the given rate each time. Make sure he does not start his stopwatch until you are sprinting at the designated speed.

Training Tips: Use the same car, course, and driver each time, if you can. Begin with 2 repetitions and add 1 for longer distances. Keep your jog recovery interval at a constant 60 seconds.

Buddy Sprints
Objective:
To develop anaerobic condition
Procedure:

   (1) After warming up and while jogging side by side with his partner, the first man takes off and sprints while the second man continues jogging.
   (2) As soon as the first man is finished sprinting he resumes jogging, and the second man takes off sprinting and catches up with the first.
   (3) The first man takes off sprinting again as soon as the second man catches up to him, as this process is repeated.

Comments: This drill adds a little variety, and working with a partner like this seems to help you get through your conditioning. Whenever I can coax a friend to work out with me, I offer this drill as a "present." A good thing about this drill is that each guy covers very close to the same distance. Since this drill is done for a change of pace, it is not crucial to keep track of distances and times. Instead, you can count the number of sprinting steps you take and the number of reps you do.

Training Tips: You can run 2 or 3 of these buddy sprints, jog together for a minute, and run 2 or 3 more. If you count your sprinting steps, try 50, 40, and 30 for each of the 3 sprints, respectively. Increase the intensity of your buddy sprints gradually.

Speed Play
Objective:
Development of anaerobic and aerobic condition
Procedure:

    (1) After warming up, mix jogging, running, and sprinting at will.
    (2) Continue this for 20 minutes or so.

Comments: This drill is a refreshing but effective alternative to heavy conditioning, and I like to do it on a light conditioning day. The idea is to more or less work as the spirit moves you. Move gradually from a jog to a loose run to a very relaxed sprint, and gradually slow back down to a jog, all the time not forcing the issue. Continue jogging for as long as you wish, breaking into a run or sprint when you feel like it. Take a good run for 50 steps, sprint easily for 50 steps, and run for another 50 before jogging again. Continue this for up to 20 minutes, never allowing yourself to become more than moderately fatigued. At the end of your speed play session, you should feel pleasantly tired.

Training Tips: You can vary the terrain on which you do speed play, using grass, hills, or soft surfaces.

DISTANCE RUNNING

If your coach is going to test your reporting condition with a distance run, you should do some training for it. You can also do some distance running as a change of pace from sprinting. Do some of your distance running while wearing heavy boots and/or while running on a soft surface (the latter as long as you do not need precise measurement of the distance covered). Although such procedures will throw off your running "form," the benefits they deliver by making you work harder more than make up for this. Remember that you are distance running to build stamina for football rather than to become a distance runner.

Timed Distance Run
Objective:
To test aerobic condition

Procedure:

(1) Time yourself over the distance your coach is going to check you on.

(2) Record the time and use it as a reference for improvement.

Comments: If your aerobic condition is checked, it will usually be with a 1-mile, 2-mile, or 12-minute run. Once you find out which one it is and get a time over it, you will know how much work you need on this event. You can then plan a systematic training program in an attempt to meet your goals.

Constant Pace Distance Run

Objectives:

To develop aerobic condition and to reach distance run time goals

Procedure:

(1) Calculate the pace required to meet your distance run goal.

(2) Run at this pace for a lesser, measured distance.

(3) Gradually increase this distance until you reach your complete distance.

Comments: Your pace can be calculated to the nearest quarter mile for this drill. Let's say you run 2 miles in 15 minutes, and your goal is 13 minutes 30 seconds. This latter figure comes out to 1 minute and 41.25 seconds for every quarter mile, or just a fraction over 100 seconds for each lap around the track. You can then run at this 100-second/lap pace for a calculated distance to start, and add 110 yards (a quarter of a lap) every 2 weeks or so. Note that 100 yards is the distance between the 50-yard line and the middle of the goal post on a quarter-mile track.

Training Tips: The initial distance you run your "racing pace" (in this example 100 second/lap) will, of course, depend upon your present aerobic condition. Yet if you have the training time available before reporting, your starting distance need not be such that you run yourself to exhaustion. You can cut it back a little to allow your body to gradually adapt to your training. If you add 100 yards of "racing pace" distance every 2 weeks, you will have added 1 mile after 8 months of training.

A good way to check your pace is by carrying a stopwatch with you and checking your time every 110 yards or quarter lap. Some watches can be set to give off a beep every so many seconds.

Variable Pace Distance Run

Objectives: To develop aerobic condition and to reach distance run time goals

Procedure:

(1) Run at a pace slightly greater than that required to meet your distance run goal.

(2) Mix this faster pace in with recovery intervals of slower running.

Comments: Using the same goal of 13.30 for 2 miles, you might go with a pace of 90 seconds per quarter mile, or down about 10 seconds per lap from your 13:30 pace. You can run the entire 2 miles, mixing this 90-second/lap pace in with slower-paced recovery runs, and gradually increase the percentage of the 2-mile distance that is done at the 90-second/lap pace. For example, you might start with 4 × 90-second laps alternated with 4 × 160-second laps for recovery. You might add 110 yards to one of your 90-second laps every 2 weeks, and thus at the end of 2 months, you would be doing 4 × 1¼ laps at 90 second/lap pace alternated with 4 × ¾ lap at 160 second/lap recovery. You would then continue to add to your intensity in this manner.

Training Tips: There are many other ways you can perform variable-pace distance running. By juggling the variables of pace, distance, and recovery interval, you can come up with some very effective ways of improving your distance running this way. However, for top results you must keep very close tabs on all of these variables and manipulate them for gradual improvement.

Lapping Drill

Objective:
To improve aerobic condition

Procedure:

(1) As partners jog on a quarter-mile track, the first man picks up the pace and runs until he laps the second man, who has merely continued jogging.

(2) The second man then laps the first man in the same manner.

Comments: This is a drill that will alleviate some of the boredom of distance running. If the jogger is running at a 10-minute/mile pace and the runner at a 6-minute/mile pace, it will take about ⅜ths of a mile, or a lap and a half, for the runner to lap the jogger.

Training Tips: For variety, perform this drill at different places.

CONDITIONING WORKOUT SCHEDULE

A well-balanced conditioning schedule is one featuring load sprinting 2 days a week and regular sprinting 2 days a week, with some distance running done perhaps once weekly. Your conditioning goals should be to do as well as you can on what your coach is going to test you in; therefore, you should find out from your coach the distance, the repetitions, the recovery interval, and any expected times, and work toward these ends. Although few coaches find it practical to test their players in load sprinting conditioning drills, it is still a good idea to work on them since they are so valuable for football. If you start your conditioning program early enough and work on it consistently, you can work on load sprinting and still meet any testing standards set by your coach.

On the days that you feature load sprinting, try to do two different types of load sprinting exercises. It does not matter which two you do as long as you follow the principles discussed above. Obviously, the facilities available to you (hills, steps, vehicle, a soft surface) are going to dictate which drills you do. Before excluding a particular load sprint drill, be sure to scout around for the facilities that are available.

On the days when you do your unhindered conditioning sprints, you can do any of the listed drills, gearing them toward what your coach is going to emphasize. If you cannot find out what your coach has in mind, emphasize maximum performance on the interval sprint drill, and work on any of the other drills as a change of pace. Generally, one unhindered sprint drill per workout is enough if you are doing other "pure" speed work, as in chapter 4. If you are doing no other pure speed work (which might be the case over the last 6 weeks or so of your summer training), you can add another sprint drill to your conditioning workout.

A good way to arrange your conditioning schedule is to do your load sprint conditioning on days you do weight training for your legs. Your regular sprint conditioning can be done on days that you work your upper body, or else on days you do no weight training at all, and any aerobics can be done on an off day. The next chapter will go into greater detail on how to integrate your conditioning with all of your other work.

Following are some examples of conditioning workout schedules:

2 Days per Week

Day 1: Regular sprinting
Day 2: Load sprinting

or

Day 1: Load sprinting
Day 2: Regular sprinting

or

Days 1 and 2: Regular sprinting, load sprinting

3 Days per Week

Day 1: Regular sprinting
Day 2: Load sprinting
Day 3: Regular sprinting

or

Day 1: Load sprinting
Day 2: Regular sprinting
Day 3: Load sprinting

4 Days per Week

Days 1 and 3: Regular sprinting
Days 2 and 4: Load sprinting

or

Days 1 and 3: Load sprinting
Days 2 and 4: Regular sprinting

5 Days per week

Days 1 and 3: Regular sprinting
Days 2, 4, and 6: Load sprinting

or

Days 1 and 3: Load sprinting
Days 2, 4, and 6: Regular sprinting

or

Days 1 and 3: Load sprinting
Days 2, 4, and 6: Regular sprinting

6 Days per Week

Days 1, 3, and 5: Regular sprinting
Days 2, 4, and 6: Load sprinting

or

Days 1, 3, and 5: Load sprinting
Days 2, 4, and 6: Regular sprinting

Following are lists of the conditioning drills covered in this chapter.

Load Sprinting Drills

Hill Sprinting
Step Sprinting
Soft Surface Sprinting
Load-pull Sprinting
Load-push Sprinting
Real Runner

Regular Sprinting Drills

Interval Sprints
40-yard Interval Sprints
Interval Sprint Test, 10 × 40 Yards
Maximum Distance Sprints
Buddy Sprints
Speed Play

Distance Running Drills

Timed Distance Run
Constant Pace Distance Run
Variable Pace Distance Run
Lapping Drill

FINAL WORD ON CONDITIONING

You now have enough information to implement a good conditioning program. Yet before I let you go, I would like to talk a little bit more on what football conditioning is really all about. I remember an All-Pro running back whose coach was legendary for his brutal training camps. While other players were dropping like flies during the conditioning drills, it was said this guy was not even winded. He would even admonish his veteran teammates for visibly showing their fatigue during the final killer sprints of practice, maintaining that they had to set a good example for the rookies and should not "breathe so hard."

The great thing about conditioning is that if you are willing to pay the price, you can be the guy who isn't even breathing hard. Yet it will hurt to attain this level of conditioning. It will hurt real bad, and then hurt real bad some more.

Remember that you have your ace in the hole, which is starting your conditioning early and sticking with it consistently, month after month after month. This way you will increase your pain tolerance gradually. You'll also be hurtin' a lot less than everybody else once practice starts, and you'll be able to concentrate on your game without even worrying about the conditioning work your coach gives you.

The bottom line on conditioning is that the choice is yours. You can begin training like a champion now, and then "show off" your conditioning when you report. Or you can come up with excuses for why you can't begin training, in which case you're just another chump who didn't work hard enough.

My advice to you is to take the route of the champion. With this in mind, let's go on to the next chapter.

7

Consistency
Is the Key:
Establishing a
Workout Schedule

"The body thrives on regularity."

Arnold Schwarzenegger,
seven-time Mr. Olympia

AN OVERVIEW OF ORGANIZING
AND PLANNING

ORGANIZATION DEFINED

The term organization is sort of like another equally common but more controversial term in that it's hard to define but you know it when you see it. Actually, organization can be thought of as a process that involves the pre-arrangement of affairs and activities in such a way as to promote maximum efficiency. It is a "preventive medicine" concept in that, when you are organized, you have anticipated all (or at least most) of the things that could go wrong and have developed a plan to meet them that involves a minimum amount of time and effort. As an example, when you are getting ready for an event—any event—you make a list of everything you need and simply check it off. If the list is complete, it serves as your plan because if you had to sum up what organization means in two words, they would be "complete planning."

When you organize your workout schedule you are developing a complete plan for it.

Yet as an athlete in training, there is another side to your overall concept of organization. You must not only be organized in the technical sense, but you must do the applicable training drills in the correct proportion and sequence. This is to say that you have to organize your training in a manner that integrates the development of strength, speed, stamina, quickness/agility, and flexibility, putting everything together for balanced development.

THE IMPORTANCE OF SCHEDULE ORGANIZATION

Good schedule organization is always important to you as an athlete, and particularly important when you are an athlete as well as a student. You must find time for studying, class attendance, and home and social life, as well as training and/or practicing. In order to effectively work all of these things into your available time, you simply must be well organized.

All else being equal, the better organized you are, the more effective your workouts will be. You'll get more work done per unit of time and more productive work at that. While it remains an understatement to say that you must work hard to succeed in your training, mere hard work by itself is not enough. For you must also work smart, getting everything you can from your available time and energy. The importance of a thorough, well-planned workout schedule cannot be overemphasized.

WORKOUT SCHEDULE PRINCIPLES

EMPHASIZE DETAILS

You are probably familiar with Murphy's Law, which states that if something can go wrong, it will go wrong. There seems to be a lot of truth to this axiom, and while you may not be able to prevent all mishaps from taking place, you can minimize their damage to your training with thorough attention to details. How is this done? By analyzing every aspect of your training needs and planning for every variation thereof you can think of.

Basically, you're going to be working out in a gym for your strength training. Thus you want to know everything about the place that is of possible pertinence to your training. Find out the hours, the membership arrangement (if applicable), the names and hours of the instructors (also if applicable), who to see when a piece of equipment goes bad, when the light and busy times of the day are, what, if any, are the upcoming days the gym will be closed, and so on. Then write all of this information down in a notebook where you have ready access to it. (The inside covers of your strength training notebook are good places.)

While you're at it, check out another gym and note the same data along with what equipment it has. Then write down what they charge for a one-time workout since you might have to use this alternate gym if your regular place is temporarily closed for remodeling or repairs. You might as well get some membership information about this gym while you're at it, in case your current gym goes out of business. (Obviously, this does not apply to school gyms.) This procedure could save you from missing strength training workouts.

You want to follow the same general procedure regarding the field or fields where you work on your speed, stamina, and quickness/agility. Get information on any use restrictions, when the field is crowded, when it is scheduled for use, when the sprinklers go on, when grounds maintenance is scheduled, etc., and log it in your book. Then do the same for an alternative field, again potentially saving yourself from having your training interrupted. It is admittedly easier to find another place to run than it is to find another weight room, but you still could lose valuable training time in looking.

If you're also running on an auxiliary spot—say a soft dirt surface or a hill—you should get some preliminary information. First find out who owns it and get permission to run there; then find out if and when it is scheduled for any work that would prohibit your using it. Get the same information if it is publicly owned.

One more thing involving training details is your dress equipment. It is easy to take your jocks, shorts, sweats, shoes, and socks for granted, at least right up to the time that something goes wrong with them. So you might want to have spares of these things if possible, and even if your finances are not good, you can probably afford some extra socks, jocks, and shoelaces. You can also note the locations and hours of stores that sell the rest of what you might need, possibly including any second-hand places that will be easy on your budget. Once again, this kind of meticulous preparation can keep you from missing future workout opportunities.

WORK ALL PHYSICAL TRAITS

Your training schedule must revolve around all of the mentioned factors, and yet flexibility work is automatically part of each. It's been mentioned that you must stretch out before any work on quickness/ agility, speed, or stamina (which usually involves sprinting), and after strength work. So in planning workouts that include these factors, flexibility does not have to be scheduled for separately.

WORK EACH TRAIT TWO TO FIVE TIMES WEEKLY

As a general rule, you want to hit each trait from 2 to 5 times a week. Fewer than 2 weekly sessions is ordinarily not enough to effect improvement, and more than 5 is usually too much. During the season, you may only have the time for 1 session a week with certain traits, concentrating on whatever practice work your coach gives you.

In order to work all of the physical traits in, you might assign a given number of weekly workouts per trait. For example, you could go with 3 strength workouts, 3 speed, 2 stamina, and 2 quickness/ agility. Such a schedule does not necessarily mean that you undertake 10 separate training sessions. You can work more than 1 trait per session, and specific examples on how to do this will be forthcoming.

WORK NO MORE THAN THREE TRAITS PER SESSION

Ordinarily you want to work only 2 traits per training session, and certainly no more than 3. If you do have to work 3 traits at one session, try not to include a heavy strength training workout since this usually takes a substantial amount of time. I always try to schedule my training with this in mind.

WORK YOUR TRAITS IN PROPER SEQUENCE

The rule of thumb here is that for any single training session you should do your strength work last, and thus try not to do any sprinting following strength work (heavy load sprinting being the exception). If you are not including strength work during a particular session, do your stamina work last. This puts your quickness/agility and speed work first during multiple trait sessions, and in the order you prefer. The given schedule examples will refer to this.

VARY YOUR TRAINING EMPHASIS

In order to add variety to your schedule and to keep from going stale, you should vary the emphasis you place on the development of certain physical traits. Your particular emphasis should depend upon which of the traits you need the most work on, how close it is to the start of the season, and, at times, upon the weather. The position that you play can also influence your emphasis somewhat, the exception being stamina development, which must be emphasized by all, regardless of position. Personally, I emphasize strength and speed work a little more in the early off season and quickness/agility and stamina more as training camp approaches. Yet I never neglect any of them at any time in the year.

KEEP ACCURATE RECORDS

This chapter on schedule planning and organization emphasizes a "big picture" approach to records. In the upcoming section featuring sample workouts, the traits that are worked are listed as to morning and afternoon/evening sessions; all that needs to be added is the exact date.

Suggested layouts for record-keeping for the individual physical traits have already been covered. Accordingly, you should go not only with the "big picture" workout schedule record but with the detailed exercise-by-exercise system for each trait, thus marking down virtually your every workout movement. Only through this method can you get an accurate overall assessment of where your workouts are going.

PLANNING YOUR YEAR-ROUND SCHEDULE

PRELIMINARY PROCEDURE

In planning your year-round training schedule, a good place to start training is right at the end of the season, which is usually sometime in November (but carries up to the first of the year, in the extreme).

You probably don't want to rush right into heavy training at this time. Give your body a chance to recover from the bumps and bruises of contact, and give your legs a rest from all the sprinting of games and practices. Of course if you have been injured, you will have to get medical clearance to resume training.

After taking a few days or even a couple of weeks off, gradually ease back into training. Take a few fairly light weight workouts and do a little jogging and stretching. This will get you to the start of the winter phase of your training.

WINTER

Although your winter workouts might be influenced by local weather conditions, this is a good time to emphasize strength training and speed training, and to at least maintain the conditioning level with which you ended the season. You can ease off quickness/agility for a little while, particularly if you have no place to do it.

If you live in a part of the country with snow, try to find a cleared space for your speed work. Be sure to use shoes that give you good traction. Sprinting in the snow, although a power builder and great conditioner, throws your sprinting form off a bit and should be used as part of your load-sprinting conditioning program.

If your school has spring football practice, you should do a little more conditioning work and quickness/agility work over the winter to get ready for it. Of course if your school has spring practice, you may well be involved in a planned off-season program anyway.

Following is an example of a winter training schedule that gives you 5 strength, 2 speed, 2 stamina, and 2 quickness/agility workouts weekly.

DAY	Morning	Afternoon/Evening
1	Speed	Strength (upper body)
2	Stamina (load sprint)	Strength (lower body)
3	Quickness/agility	Off
4	Speed	Strength (upper body)
5	Stamina (load sprint)	Strength (lower body)
6	Quickness/agility	Strength (upper body)

SPRING

This is a good time to do a lot of pure speed work. Having sprinted somewhat throughout the winter, you can move right into quality sprint workouts as the spring brings warmer weather. You can also continue with some strength and stamina work, and perhaps add a bit of quickness/agility, if weather conditions permit.

If your school has spring football practice, your own supplementary training should be similar to the in-season training that you do in the fall.

Following is an example of a spring workout schedule featuring 3 strength, 5 speed, 2 stamina, and 2 quickness/agility workouts weekly.

DAY	Morning	Afternoon/Evening
1	Speed	Strength
2	Quickness/agility	Speed, stamina*
3	Off	Strength
4	Quickness/agility	Speed, stamina*
5	Speed	Strength
6	Quickness/agility	Speed (light)

*Note that your stamina work can include free sprinting, load sprinting, or a mixture of the two. If you include load sprinting, you might do it with a fairly light load (less weight or less of an incline).

SUMMER

Over the summer, you want to work very hard on stamina development; as you near the date that pre-season practice begins, you should work more and more on quickness/agility. You do not want to de-emphasize strength and speed work during the summer; you simply want to make sure that you get in plenty of stamina work and increasing amounts of quickness/agility work.

Following is an example of a summer workout.

DAY	Morning	Afternoon/Evening
1	Stamina (load sprint)	Strength
2	Speed, stamina (free sprint)	Quickness/agility
3	Off	Strength
4	Speed, stamina (free sprint)	Quickness/agility
5	Stamina (load sprint)	Strength
6	Speed, quickness/agility	Stamina (distance run)

FALL

During the fall, your training emphasis is on quickness/agility and conditioning work, both largely done at practice with specific football drills and wind sprints. Unless your coach has set aside some practice time for pure speed work, you should get in 1 or 2 speed workout sessions weekly if you can. The same holds true for strength work.

Here is an in-season schedule for the fall (or spring, if you have spring practice). You basically work on maintaining strength and speed, and perform 2 strength, 1 speed, 1 stamina (load sprinting, which is not usually part of formal in-season practice), and no quickness/agility workouts weekly, since you will be getting this work at practice.

DAY	Morning	Afternoon/Evening
Day after game	Strength	Off
2 days later	Speed, stamina (load sprint)	Practice
4 days later	Strength	Practice

MASTER SCHEDULE

If you were limited to one workout schedule, it would include a balanced mixture of work on all of the traits. The following schedule includes 4 workouts per week on each trait, with easy speed play thrown in once a week for fun.

DAY	Morning	Afternoon/Evening
1	Speed, stamina (free sprint)	Quickness/agility Strength (upper body)
2	Speed,* stamina (load sprint)	Strength (lower body)
3	Quickness/agility	Off
4	Speed, stamina (free sprint)	Quickness/agility Strength (upper body)
5	Speed,* stamina (load sprint)	Strength (lower body)
6	Quickness/agility	Easy speed play

*Note that since you are working on leg strength on these days, your speed workout should include 40-yard dash drills and perhaps plyometrics. Please refer to chapter 4 under the section "Sprint Training Workout Schedules" and look at the listings that feature this combination.

It should not be any problem at all to engineer your own training schedule. You probably saw the possibilities for doing so by changing some things in the schedules given. Feel free to do this, and then try the schedule out to see how your body responds to it.

A FINAL WORD ON PLANNING YOUR SCHEDULE

Once more, the importance of thoroughly planning your workout schedule cannot be overemphasized. You simply must make the most of every training moment if you want to maximize your results. You cannot afford a haphazard approach in which you "think" or "feel" you have gotten the all-around workouts that you need. So sit yourself down and plan your overall workout program as though you were getting ready for World War III. I like to plan my workout schedule for weeks in advance, as I feel that only through such a systematic approach will I obtain the maximum benefits. I recommend that you do the same.

You have now covered a lot of information on football training. You've been schooled in diet, flexibility, quickness/agility, speed, strength, and stamina, and you've also been given ways of putting them all together. This information, as valuable as it is, remains incomplete without one more ingredient: motivation. Accordingly, the next chapter, the last one of the book, deals with this most important trait.

8

You Must Be Motivated: Having a Champion's Attitude

"I got up to run at 5:30 instead of 6."

Rocky Bleier,
Fighting Back

AN OVERVIEW OF MOTIVATION

MOTIVATION DEFINED

Motivation may be defined as the willingness not to simply do something, but to do it with all of the energy and effort you can muster. It is related to desire, enthusiasm, pride, discipline, and guts, among other traits, since the common denominator is the same. A person who is motivated has these and similar qualities, and he gets right after things like a champion and gives it all he has, regardless of ability.

All champion football players are extremely motivated, but this does not mean that every All-American or All-Pro player is motivated. This is because All-American or All-Pro football players are not always champion football players. For being a champion is more than receiving all-star recognition.

THE IMPORTANCE OF MOTIVATION

It is an understatement to say that motivation is important for football training and playing. It is probably the single most important trait that a player can possess. Natural strength, speed, stamina, size, quickness/agility, and athletic ability are all important, but a player can be born with an abundance of these traits and, if he lacks real motivation, he has nothing. All of the natural ability in the world is of little help to the unmotivated football player.

At the other extreme, a player fairly ordinary in natural physical traits and athletic ability can go a long way with great motivation. Such a player will be motivated to improve both his physical traits and football skills to try to reach his maximum potential. This person is likely to realize considerable improvement in strength, speed, and stamina, and to overcome relative physical shortcomings en route to becoming a champion player. There are a number of individuals in the NFL today who have done just this, and in this chapter you will meet some of them through their stories.

THE MYSTERY OF MOTIVATION

Why are some football players a lot more motivated than others? Anyone with the answers to this question is not residing on the planet Earth. Coaches everywhere have been forever trying to discover the key to motivating their athletes. And the jury is out as to whether any more is known now about motivating people than was known centuries ago. Some coaches do seem to light a higher fire under their players, but they probably couldn't tell you why they're able to achieve this. Then when other coaches emulate them by copying their motivation techniques to use on their own people, they often fall flat on their faces. Motivation remains something of a mystery.

MOTIVATION PRINCIPLES

The basic principles of motivation are really very simple: You train hard, practice hard, and play hard.

TRAIN HARD

If you are a truly motivated individual, you will train as hard as you can on your own. This means that you will keep every training session that you schedule yourself for, missing workouts only for illness, injury, or other circumstances beyond your control. You will complete every exercise and drill that your workout consists of, never shortening your scheduled work load unless absolutely necessary. You will also do every exercise and drill in the proper manner and for the correct times, distances, numbers of repetitions, and so forth. In short, you will make the most of every single workout session that you undertake, giving your training everything you have, like a true champion.

PRACTICE HARD

As a motivated athlete, you will practice like a champion. You will work as hard as you can, going all-out on every drill, exercise, and play, as if there is no tomorrow. You will follow your coach's instructions to the T, carrying out every assignment as if you're in the fourth quarter of a title game with the score tied. If you are motivated, you will undoubtedly carry out the axiom that you play like you practice.

PLAY HARD

As a motivated athlete, you will play as hard as you can. You will give it everything you have on each and every snap of the football, playing with the same level of intensity whether your team is three touchdowns behind or three touchdowns ahead. You will rely on your hard training and hard practicing to put every ounce of effort you can muster into every move you make on the field, and the only way you will know how to play the game is like a man possessed.

EXAMPLES OF GREAT MOTIVATION

Though nobody has unlocked the secrets of motivation, it's pretty easy to tell motivated football players when you see them. By their inspirational achievements in physical improvement and by their application of the same to outstanding play, they stand out. Such motivated players are not always the best players, for natural ability plays a part. But they come the closest to being the best players that they can be.

Following are some stories on intensely motivated football players who improved themselves with rigorous training. They are living examples of the results that can occur when one is really motivated to train.

RANDY WHITE

Football fans take a look at Randy White and figure "no problem." Here is just a big, strong guy who has been knocking around offensive linemen for years and is going into his fourteenth year in the NFL as of this writing. At 6-4 and 260 pounds, with strength, speed, and quickness to boot, no wonder the guy has been a perennial All-Pro. I mean they didn't give this guy the name "manster"—half man and half monster—just because he *looks* tough and aggressive.

But there is more to the Randy White story than that. Coming out of high school in Delaware in 1971, he was regarded as a good, but not great, college prospect. As a freshman at the University of Maryland, he was 6-4 and 212, motored a 4.9 forty and bench pressed 260, adequate but not overwhelming numbers. Then at Maryland, his coach, Jerry Clairborne, took him aside and asked him if he wanted to be an All-American football player. Randy said sure, who wouldn't. Yet Coach Clairborne was able to get through to him that to be an All-American he had to work and train like an All-American, and the message stuck.

Randy White went to work like few football players have ever gone to work. He ran and he lifted weights, he stretched and he worked on quickness/agility. He sacrificed and punished himself, becoming well acquainted with discipline and making friends with pain. He worked so hard that going into his senior year three years later he had improved himself physically to a most remarkable degree. He was the same 6-4, but now packed 250 pounds of rock-hard muscle on his body. He improved his bench press up to 450 pounds (and then went on to top 500 in the pros), and I can already hear what the skeptics are thinking. So what if the guy was bigger and stronger; football is a quickness game too, and all that extra weight probably slowed him down and hurt his game, right?

Wrong. Because Randy White improved his 40 from the 4.9 he did as a freshman to 4.65 as a senior. Amazingly enough, he had gained 38 pounds, improved his bench press by 190 pounds, and improved his 40 time by .25 of a second, and all in three years. He then used his new-found strength, speed, and size along with his finely honed football skills to win both the Outland Trophy and the Vince Lombardi Trophy as the nation's top lineman his senior year, was the number one draft choice of the Dallas Cowboys, and went on to become one of the top defensive linemen in football history. He played in nine Pro Bowls and is a sure bet for pro football's Hall of Fame. And he could not have accomplished this without the tough, dedicated training that helped him reach his peak as a player. For Randy White is a very, very motivated person who trains—and then plays—like the champion he has become.

WALTER PAYTON

Walter Payton needs no introduction. He is simply the most productive—and some say the greatest—running back to ever put on a pair of shoulder pads. He carried the ball more times and for more yards than anyone in history and also owns the NFL single-game record for rushing yardage. They call him Sweetness because he's a nice guy, but they would have been just as accurate to call him Greatness.

So how did Walter Payton do it? Speed? Sure, Walter was fast, but there were faster backs around as far as outright, high-gear, overdrive speed. Quickness? You bet he had it, but so did a lot of other backs in the league and backs who were as big or bigger. Size? You've got to be kidding. Not only did his 202 pounds look small compared to those oversized NFL beasts who lick their chops at the sight of a guy his size, but he was on the smallish side for an NFL running back as well. No, Walter Payton never achieved any greatness because of his size. Then how about strength, stamina, and toughness? Did Walter Payton possess these traits to the point that he rose far above other athletes who had natural physical gifts equal to his?

Yup. Walter Payton possessed strength, stamina, and toughness to the point that he rose far above other athletes who had natural gifts equal to his. In fact, he did this possibly as much or more than any athlete in the history of sport.

Walter Payton was a very strong football player. He could bench press 400 pounds, right at twice his body weight, and leg press more than 600 pounds. His philosophy regarding strength training was for short, intense sessions, getting in and out of the weight room in a minimum period of time, and it worked for him.

Yet it had to work because Walter needed to save time for his legendary training on stamina. His program went beyond toughness and into another dimension, a dimension that few athletes in any sport dared to enter.

During his training, Walter ran his share of regular sprints on regular flat surfaces, of course, but his favorite touch was sprinting in the sand and up hills. Rumor has it that his friends tried to avoid driving by hills and sandy surfaces because he would have them stop the car and get out and run. He looked for new, challenging places to run like the average guy looked for new girls to date. His training partners would drop like flies, but Walter kept going and kept going and kept going with the same All-Pro determination that earned him all of his records. He would simply sprint and sprint and sprint with a motivation that should have been declared illegal.

Walter Payton worked so hard and became so tough in the process that he was able to take anything the gridiron dished out and come back for more. Of the yards he gained in his career, he probably "stole" a good percentage of them by simply being stronger, less fatigued, and less susceptible to injury than his opposition. And all of this was the result of a training program that was as rigorous and thorough as any ever undertaken by any athlete in any sport. For Walter Payton was arguably the best-conditioned football player of all time. He indeed was a champion's champion.

ROCKY BLEIER

On paper, Rocky Bleier never should have played pro football. Coming out of Notre Dame about ten thousand years ago (actually it was 1968), he was drafted by the Steelers in the sixteenth round and considered too small and too slow to make it as an NFL running back. Yet this lack of size and speed turned out to be the least of Rocky's problems. For, after making the Steeler team with the hard work that was always his trademark, toward the end of the season he was drafted again, this time by the U.S. Army. He was sent to Vietnam and injured so badly in combat that it was questionable if he would ever walk normally. It was viewed as medically impossible for him to ever play football again.

Most of us would have quit right there, losing ourselves in self-pity and daydreaming about the glory that could have been. Not Rocky Bleier. He went to work and he went to work hard, injured or not. Although it was extremely painful for him to run because of shrapnel lodgings in his right foot and toes, run he did, at least if you refer to the pathetic way he hobbled along as running. He also stretched and lifted weights and ran stadium steps, torturing his still-injured body beyond belief.

Despite his hard work, he reported to the Steeler training camp in 1970 just a shell of the marginal player he had been two years before. He was pitifully slow, his injuries having cost him what little speed he had. He was rusty on techniques, his time away from the game having detracted from his basic football skills. And with every step he took, excruciating pain shot through his body, pain that would have halted a lesser man in his tracks.

Yet Rocky was not the only one in pain at that 1970 training camp. His coaches and teammates also felt pain as they watched him work out. Not a one of them felt he had a chance in his comeback attempt, and they couldn't stand to see Rocky put himself through such misery when his possibilities were so poor. Many of them advised Rocky to quit, and under the circumstances most people would have.

Not Rocky Bleier. He stuck it out at that 1970 camp and was finally placed on injured reserve. He then had another operation on the toes of his right foot and was activated for the last game of the year. Afterward he immediately went back to his off-season program of getting his body in better shape to play football. He rose at 6 A.M. to run in the bone-chilling cold, and he ran until he fell down. Then he got up and he ran some more. He pushed heavy iron in weight rooms, piling larger and larger loads on his already overworked muscles. He stretched and he sprinted, he ate right and he went to bed early. He felt he was making progress when, just a week before the 1971 training camp was to open, he pulled a hamstring in the leg he had hurt in battle. He was then again advised to retire, by the team physician among others, and most people would indeed have then hung up the cleats.

Not Rocky Bleier. He hung in there and barely made the 1971 Steeler team. He was then injured early in the year and not activated until December when he got into three games in spot duty. By this time, his comeback had been going on for 2 seasons, and he had yet to carry the ball from scrimmage.

Rocky spent the next off season working out harder than ever, dedicating himself to this Spartan program with an intensity that bordered on fanaticism. He got up at 5:30 instead of 6, and he slipped in an extra afternoon running workout for a total of 3 each day, one of them always the Steelers' own program. He lifted more weights. He ran more stairs. He stretched his aching muscles faithfully and fed them carefully.

When Rocky reported to camp in 1972, all of his hard work began to pay off. Four years earlier, as a 205-pound rookie, he had run 40 yards in 5 seconds flat. Yet at the 1972 training camp, he ripped off a time of 4.6, and while weighing 210 pounds, no less. He had done the impossible: Improved his sprinting speed over what it had been prior to receiving those crippling war injuries.

For all of his improvement, you would think Rocky would have been back on the field as a player for the 1972 season. Instead, he languished on the Steeler bench. Here was a guy who had literally tortured himself into superb physical condition, and he earned only one carry from scrimmage. Most of us would have quit right then.

Not Rocky Bleier. Instead he undertook an even heavier workout schedule, training 6 days a week instead of 5, improving his diet, and working doubly hard on flexibility. He consulted black belts and body builders, weight lifters and exercise physiologists, garnering all the information he could in order to improve his physical condition even more. He upped his bench press to 440 pounds to become the third strongest man on the Steeler team, not bad for a 210-pound back competing against 275-pound linemen. And when the 1973 training camp came around, he recorded the third fastest 40 time on the squad.

This combination of strength and speed helped Rocky lead the team in rushing during the 1973 pre-season. Then during the year he earned a reputation as one of the league's top specialty team players. Yet in regular season duty, he returned only 2 kickoffs and carried only 3 times from scrimmage. Thus over the 4 years of his comeback attempt, he had run the ball a total of 4 times from scrimmage. All the sweat, pain, and discipline he had put himself through had not been enough to play regularly. Most people would have quit.

Not Rocky Bleier. It was back to yet another off season of lifting and running, running and lifting, and then more lifting followed by more running. He played paddleball, he ran up the ramps at Three Rivers Stadium, and when he wasn't doing these things, he was haunting weight rooms for extra workouts or sneaking in additional wind sprints (all the while still finding time to be involved in charitable activity). And when training camp opened in 1974, he was as physically ready as ever to play football.

The beginning of the 1974 season looked like a repeat of the previous years for Rocky: He sat on the bench and watched. Then several games into the year, the team floundered, and Rocky got his chance. He played the second half of a game against Houston, and the following week he made his first professional start against Kansas City and scored his first professional touchdown. Finally, at the age of 28 and after years of grueling work, he had made the team.

An injury temporarily forced Rocky out of the lineup, but by the end of the season he had worked his way back in and he stayed there. He stayed there through that year's playoffs, which culminated in a Steeler Super Bowl victory. He stayed there through the 1975 season and playoffs that resulted in another Super Bowl championship. He stayed there through the "off" seasons of 1976 (when he rushed for more than one thousand yards) and 1977 as the Steelers had winning years and made the playoffs but not the Super Bowl. He stayed there through the 1978 and 1979 seasons, both resulting in Super Bowl championships for the Steelers. And he stayed there through the 1980 season, his last one, ending his incredible career with a winning team.

Through all of those years, Rocky played and played well for a team that was the best in professional football. He was widely regarded as a strong, solid, dependable player who gave it all he had on every snap. While not a spectacular runner, he got the job done effectively, and there were those who regarded him as the best blocking back in the game.

They say that Rocky lacked great speed. Yet he was clocked as low as 4.55 seconds over 40 yards. They say he had no real size. Yet he played at a rock-hard 210 pounds. They say he lacked outstanding athletic ability. Yet he was a first team running back on 4 Super Bowl champion teams, and it's tough to accomplish that without being an outstanding athlete.

But the greatest asset Rock had was his strength. He was steel strong. He could bench press 460 pounds and squat with more than 600. He could incline press 350 and straight press 275. And if there is another running back anywhere able to match these lifts, he is unknown to me. In fact, Rocky was probably the strongest back of his time, if not one of the all-around strongest backs in the history of the game.

But maybe such awesome physical strength was not Rocky's greatest asset, after all. Because there was probably never a performer in any sport who had more of the so-called intangibles than Rocky Bleier. Call it intestinal fortitude, mental toughness, desire, pride, courage, or just plain guts, and Rocky had it and he had it in abundance. Because through pain and injury and surgery, through disappointment after disappointment and setback after setback, through blood and sweat and tears and outright agony, there was one thing Rocky Bleier would not do: *He would not quit!*

In short, there has never been a truer champion than Rocky Bleier in the long history of football. And perhaps there never will be.

A FINAL WORD ON MOTIVATION

Earlier I used the word "champion," and I stated that it takes more than being a good football player—more than being an All-American or an All-Pro, even—to be a champion. This should be evident by those naturally talented individuals who don't work as hard as they can and yet are All-NFL types. Are such players champions, really champions, in the true sense of the word? Not on your life.

A champion is not necessarily the guy who wins all the time. A champion is the guy who prepares and strives to win all the time. He is concerned about the thrill of victory and suffers the agony of defeat. Yet more importantly, the true creed of a champion is the thrill of all-out effort brought about through the agony of preparation.

No football player who gives less than his best—either when playing the game or when training in preparation to play it—has the right to call himself a champion. In fact, any player who gives less than his best in either regard is a cheater. He is cheating his coach, his team, and himself, and such a cheater can never be called a champion.

A champion rises at 5 A.M. to train, facing the numbing cold of a dark winter's morning instead of cheating by lying in bed. A champion sprints right through the pain barrier, instead of cheating by slowing down or quitting. A champion forces "one more rep" and then "just one more" out of a savage set of squats or deadlifts, instead of cheating by letting up in effort. A champion sticks to good natural foods, instead of cheating by eating garbage food and drinking alcohol. A champion uses his lack of great natural ability to train harder, instead of cheating by using it as an excuse not to improve. And on the field, a champion reacts to getting hit by hitting back with everything he's got, instead of cheating by shying away from contact.

As a final word, remember that you are the one who decides whether or not to be a champion. For you and you alone are the one who decides if you're going to work as hard as you can. Not your coach. Not your doctor or trainer. Not your teammates. But you.

So let's get one thing straight. If you want to be a champion, get it in your mind right now that you're gonna train and play as hard as you can, and ain't nothing or nobody gonna stop you. For you're on your way to becoming a champion, and God help whoever gets in your way.

Index